Praise for *The Rules of Programming*

The Rules of Programming combines great guidance for beginners with subtle lessons that may teach even the experts. Zimmerman keeps it fun, too—proving that it's possible to be both entertaining and instructive.

—*Mark Cerny, Lead System Architect, PlayStation 4 and 5*

The Rules of Programming provides great insights for both new and experienced coders. Zimmerman's style makes it an entertaining read, and the 21 rules are an important contribution to better software at a time when technology is pervasive in every part of business and society.

—*Paul Daugherty, Group Chief Executive of Technology and CTO, Accenture*

The Rules of Programming is full of pragmatic rules of thumb any software engineer can use to level up their skills. I was fortunate to learn these lessons directly from Chris early in my career, and have successfully applied them across a wide variety of software disciplines. With this book, you have the opportunity to do the same.

—*Chris Bentzel, Director of Software, Boston Dynamics*

The Rules of Programming

How to Write Better Code

Chris Zimmerman

Beijing · Boston · Farnham · Sebastopol · Tokyo

The Rules of Programming

by Chris Zimmerman

Published by O'Reilly Media, Inc., 1005 Gravenstein Highway North, Sebastopol, CA 95472.

O'Reilly books may be purchased for educational, business, or sales promotional use. Online editions are also available for most titles (*http://oreilly.com*). For more information, contact our corporate/institutional sales department: 800-998-9938 or *corporate@oreilly.com*.

Acquisitions Editor: Mary Treseler	**Proofreader:** Kim Cofer
Development Editor: Sarah Grey	**Indexer:** Potomac Indexing, LLC
Production Editor: Gregory Hyman	**Interior Designer:** Monica Kamsvaag
Copyeditor: Charles Roumeliotis	**Cover Designer:** Susan Thompson

December 2022:   First Edition

Revision History for the First Edition

2022-12-09:   First Release

See *http://oreilly.com/catalog/errata.csp?isbn=9781098133115* for release details.

978-1-098-13311-5

[LSI]

Contents

Preface

Welcome to *The Rules of Programming*, a set of easy-to-remember and easy-to-apply Rules that will help you write better code. Programming is hard, but following the Rules makes it a little bit easier.

Here are some tips on reading the book:

- All of the Rules stand on their own. If you see an interesting-looking Rule in the table of contents and want to jump straight into the middle of the book, feel free. That reading pattern is fully supported.

- That said, I'd suggest starting off with Rule 1, "As Simple as Possible, but No Simpler". It's a good setup for the rest of the Rules.

- The examples in the book are all written in C++. If you're a Python or JavaScript programmer, you'll be happier if you read Appendix A, "Reading C++ for Python Programmers", or Appendix B, "Reading C++ for JavaScript Programmers", before getting too far into the Rules. The two appendices act as Rosetta Stones to translate that C++ into the concepts you're used to. If your experience is with some other language and you find the C++ examples hard to follow, then I suggest the phenomenal website Rosetta Code (*https://oreil.ly/Rr2BL*).

- If you're a C++ programmer, note that I've simplified a few things in the code examples to make them easier to read for non-C++ programmers. For example, the examples use signed integers in a few places where unsigned integers would be more typical for a C++ program, and I disabled warnings about implicit conversion between signed and unsigned values. I also compiled the examples with an implicit "using std" to avoid a boatload of distracting "std::" references.

- And finally, I'm capitalizing *Rule* when I refer to an actual Rule in the book. If you see *rule*, it's just a regular old rule, not an officially sanctioned one. The distinction between the two senses of the word was confusing without the capitalization; I hope that excuses me.

I hope you enjoy what follows! I think you'll discover a few useful thoughts that help you sharpen your programming skills.

Girls Who Code

All royalties from this book go to Girls Who Code (*https://oreil.ly/QyCTX*), an organization working hard to help young women discover just how rewarding programming can be. When I graduated from college, over a third of computer science graduates were women; these days, it's more like a fifth. I think we'd all be better off with a more representative gender balance. You probably do, too. And supporting Girls Who Code through donations or volunteering is a step toward making that hope a reality.

Conventions Used in This Book

The following typographical conventions are used in this book:

Italic

Indicates new terms, URLs, email addresses, filenames, and file extensions.

`Constant width`

Used for program listings, as well as within paragraphs to refer to program elements such as variable or function names, databases, data types, environment variables, statements, and keywords.

Using Code Examples

Supplemental material (code examples, exercises, etc.) is available for download at *https://oreil.ly/rules-of-programming-code*.

If you have a technical question or a problem using the code examples, please send email to *bookquestions@oreilly.com*.

This book is here to help you get your job done. In general, if example code is offered with this book, you may use it in your programs and documentation. You do not need to contact us for permission unless you're reproducing a significant portion of the code. For example, writing a program that uses several chunks of code from this book does not require permission. Selling or distributing examples from O'Reilly books does require permission. Answering a question by citing this book and quoting example code does not require permission. Incorporating a significant amount of example code from this book into your product's documentation does require permission.

We appreciate, but generally do not require, attribution. An attribution usually includes the title, author, publisher, and ISBN. For example: *"The Rules of Programming* by Chris Zimmerman (O'Reilly). Copyright 2023 Chris Zimmerman, 978-1-098-13311-5."

If you feel your use of code examples falls outside fair use or the permission given above, feel free to contact us at *permissions@oreilly.com.*

O'Reilly Online Learning

O'REILLY® For more than 40 years, *O'Reilly Media* has provided technology and business training, knowledge, and insight to help companies succeed.

Our unique network of experts and innovators share their knowledge and expertise through books, articles, and our online learning platform. O'Reilly's online learning platform gives you on-demand access to live training courses, in-depth learning paths, interactive coding environments, and a vast collection of text and video from O'Reilly and 200+ other publishers. For more information, visit *https://oreilly.com.*

How to Contact Us

Please address comments and questions concerning this book to the publisher:

O'Reilly Media, Inc.

1005 Gravenstein Highway North

Sebastopol, CA 95472

800-998-9938 (in the United States or Canada)

707-829-0515 (international or local)

707-829-0104 (fax)

We have a web page for this book, where we list errata, examples, and any additional information. You can access this page at *https://oreil.ly/rules-of-programming.*

If you have reactions, comments, or questions you'd like to share with the author, see *The Rules of Programming* website (*https://oreil.ly/jTEGo*) for pointers. You can also email *bookquestions@oreilly.com* to comment or ask technical questions about this book.

For news and information about our books and courses, visit *https://oreilly.com*.

Find us on LinkedIn: *https://linkedin.com/company/oreilly-media*

Follow us on Twitter: *https://twitter.com/oreillymedia*

Watch us on YouTube: *https://youtube.com/oreillymedia*

Acknowledgments

First off, thanks to my lovely and talented wife Laura, who encouraged me to spend time writing this book instead of doing all the other useful things I could have been doing.

A big round of thanks to all of the people who helped develop the Rules in this book. That includes all Sucker Punch coders past and present, since you all contributed whether you intended to or not, but especially Apoorva Bansal, Chris Heidorn, David Meyer, Eric Black, Evan Christensen, James McNeill, Jasmin Patry, Nate Slottow, Matt Durasoff, Mike Gaffney, Ranjith Rajagopalan, Rob McDaniel, Sam Holley, Sean Smith, Wes Grandmont, and William Rossiter.

And thanks to the non–Sucker Punchers who provided a view from outside the forest: Adam Barr, Andreas Fredriksson, Colin Bryar, David Oliver, Max Schubert, Mike Gutmann, and Seth Fine.

Extra special thanks to the intrepid readers who made it through every single one of the Rules: Adrian Bentley, Bill Rockenbeck, Jan Miksovsky, and Julien Merceron. I officially owe you all a favor.

And finally, thanks to everyone on Team O'Reilly who patiently coached me through my fumbling attempts to write this book: Charles Roumeliotis, Gregory Hyman, Libby James, Mary Treseler, Sara Hunter, Suzanne Huston, and very especially Sarah Grey, who did the rest of you a massive favor by filtering out the least funny of the jokes I kept insisting on adding.

The Story of the Rules

The Rules of Programming were born of exasperation.

I'd spent about a decade running programming teams at Microsoft, then cofounded the video game company Sucker Punch in 1997. Both companies have been successful—in large part because of their ability to recruit and develop top-notch programming teams. At Sucker Punch, that's led to a 25-year run of successful games. There were the three *Sly Cooper* games, which let kids of all ages experience the thrilling life of the master raccoon thief Sly Cooper and his pals. There were the five *inFamous* games, which gave gamers superpowers and the choice to use them for good or evil. And then there's what is to this point our magnum opus, *Ghost of Tsushima*, where gamers play a lone samurai fighting back against the 1274 invasion of Japan.[1]

A big part of the recruiting strategy at both Microsoft and Sucker Punch has been hiring smart young programmers, then training them in the ways of professional developers. This practice has been undeniably successful, but it also leads to a particular flavor of frustration.

I kept running into one problem over and over again. We'd bring a new programmer onto the team, often someone fresh out of college. I'd review some new feature they planned to introduce into the code, usually to solve a very simple problem—only to discover that they'd written code that attempted to solve a much bigger problem, one that included the very simple and concrete problem as a small subcase.

Aargh! We didn't need that bigger problem solved, certainly not right now! Invariably, the solution to the bigger problem was a mediocre solution to the simple problem we did have—more complicated to use, more complicated to

---

1 The eagle-eyed among you may have noticed I left out *Rocket: Robot on Wheels*, the first Sucker Punch game. That's because very few of you have played it; if you're one of the few, you have my gratitude.

understand, and capable of hiding a lot more bugs. But just saying that in the code review[2]—that we didn't need the bigger problem solved, that they should only try to solve problems they understand—was ineffective. They kept doing it.

Out of frustration, I put my foot down. "OK," I said. "Here's the new rule. Until you have three examples of a problem, you're not allowed to write a general solution."

To my surprise and delight, this actually worked! Turning the general philosophy into a specific rule with specific criteria was an effective way of getting the message across. Sure, most of our new programmers made the premature generalization mistake once, but the rule helped them avoid making it again. It also helped them recognize when it *was* time to generalize. Fewer than three examples? Don't generalize. Three or more? Start looking for opportunities.

The rule worked because it was easy to remember, and the situations where it applied were easy to recognize. When coders could see that they had started moving past the bounds of the well-defined problem at hand, they could take a step back, count the number of concrete examples of that sort of problem they'd run into, and make a better decision about whether to generalize or not. They wrote better code.

Over time, we found other important bits of Sucker Punch philosophy that could be distilled into easy-to-remember phrases—aphorisms, to be precise. There's a long history of aphorisms—those short, pithy statements that capture some essential truth. I bet you can rattle off quite a few from memory. Shoot, I could limit you to *bird-related* aphorisms, and you'd still be able to come up with at least two! I'll offer a few:

- Don't count your chickens before they're hatched.[3]

- A bird in the hand is worth two in the bush.

- The early bird catches the worm.

- Don't put all your eggs in one basket.

Aphorisms stick around because they work. They're viral, in the modern sense—aphorisms have been "infecting" people with bits of wisdom for

---

2 All code committed to the Sucker Punch project gets code reviewed. See Rule 6 for more details.

3 In its original form, from Thomas Howell's *New Sonnets and Pretty Pamphlets* (1570): "Count not thy chickens that unhatched be...." A small demonstration of the staying power of a good aphorism.

thousands of years.[4] It's not surprising that they're an effective way of infecting new team members with the Sucker Punch coding philosophy.

So, bit by bit, what was once a single rule grew into a list of rules: the Rules of Programming described in this book. They represent many of the most important aspects of Sucker Punch engineering culture: the things that we believe have led to our success, the ideas that new coders on the team need to absorb to be effective. The things that even senior coders like me need reminding of at least once in a while!

Each of the chapters that follows describes a Rule, with plenty of examples to illustrate the thought behind it. After reading a chapter, you should have a clear idea of the coding practice the Rule encourages and the situations where it applies.

Are the Rules equally contagious in book form? Let's find out.

---

4 The word *aphorism* itself was coined by Hippocrates around 400 BCE. Well, strictly speaking, the word he coined was Ἀφορισμός. That was the title of his book of rules for medical diagnosis and treatment, some of which are still spot on millennia later, like aphorism 13 from section 6—"a sneezing attack will cure a case of hiccups." So true.

How to Disagree with the Rules

I hope that you don't sail smoothly through all 21 Rules.

If you find yourself politely nodding along with each of the Rules and the examples I use—"Oh yes, that makes sense, this example is familiar, I've had this thought before, I just used different language to describe it"—well, that's a failure.

I hope I'll give you things to think about. A new insight or two, ideally. Maybe I'll be able to put a name to a vague feeling you've had, or give you a crisp example of something you've been unable to nail down. Maybe I'll even give you something entirely new to consider.

But it's also likely that you'll run into one or two ideas that you disagree with. You might think I'm entirely wrong about something—that one of the Rules is bad advice.

That's great! Finding a Rule you strongly disagree with is an opportunity. Rejecting it immediately and reflexively would be a mistake.

I promise that the Rule in question isn't entirely wrong—but it may be right for *us* while simultaneously being wrong for *you*. Understanding why this is will help you understand and strengthen your own programming philosophy. It means understanding the differences between Sucker Punch and your own team, because those differences are what make a Rule an important part of our culture but a poor match for yours. The Rules use examples from the video games we've built at Sucker Punch, which should illuminate some of the things that make video game programming different. Many of the rest are addressed in the last chapter, "Conclusion: Making the Rules Your Own".

Here's the reconciliation process I've found helpful when I've run into some statement of coding philosophy discordant with my experience:

1. Find the truth in the statement, not just the flaws. I may disagree with the statement, but that's likely because of my own assumptions. What are the circumstances under which the statement would be true?

2. Work the problem from the other side, too. What are the circumstances under which my own contrary view on the statement would be false? What's the difference in circumstances that changes the truthfulness of the statement?

3. Be mindful that circumstances change. The statement might be wrong for you now, but right for you on your next project. You've identified a situation where your philosophy would need to change; be alert to the possibility that you've wandered into exactly that situation.

I've gone through this process many times. Here's an example: test-driven development (TDD). It's discordant with our experience at Sucker Punch; still, the truth in it is obvious to us. You'll see references in the Rules to the ways in which our circumstances make TDD an awkward fit, but we know that those circumstances might change. We're watchful; if things change, so will our philosophy.

So I hope that you find value in the Rules you find most objectionable...but I understand if you choose to follow a different course of action, one credited to Dorothy Parker:

This is not a novel to be tossed aside lightly. It should be thrown with great force.

If so, I suggest aiming for something soft.

As Simple as Possible, but No Simpler

Programming is hard.

I'm guessing you've already figured this out. Anyone who picks up and reads a book titled *The Rules of Programming* is likely to both:

- Be able to program, at least a little

- Be frustrated that it's not easier than it is

There are lots of reasons why programming is hard, and lots of strategies to try to make it easier. This book looks at a carefully selected subset of common ways to screw things up and Rules to avoid those mistakes, all drawn from my many years of making mistakes of my own and coping with the mistakes of others.

There's an overall pattern to the Rules, a common theme that most of them share. It's best summarized with a quote from Albert Einstein describing the goals of a physical theorist: "As simple as possible, but no simpler."[1] By that, Einstein meant that the best physical theory was the simplest one that completely described all observable phenomena.

Recasting that idea to programming, the best way to implement a solution to any problem is the simplest one that meets all the requirements of that problem. The best code is the simplest code.

---

1 He almost certainly didn't use those exact words—posterity has done Einstein a favor by sharpening up his aphorisms. The closest match in the written record is "It can scarcely be denied that the supreme goal of all theory is to make the irreducible basic elements as simple and as few as possible without having to surrender the adequate representation of a single datum of experience." So, pretty much the same thing, just not as snappy. Also the actual Einstein quote is a little bit long for a Rule title.

Imagine that you're writing code to count the number of bits set in an integer. There are lots of ways to do this. You might use bit trickery[2] to zero out a bit at a time, counting how many bits get zeroed out:

```
int countSetBits(int value)
{
    int count = 0;

    while (value)
    {
        ++count;
        value = value & (value - 1);
    }

    return count;
}
```

Or you might opt for a loop-free implementation, with bit shifting and masking to count the bits in parallel:

```
int countSetBits(int value)
{
    value = ((value & 0xaaaaaaaa) >> 1) + (value & 0x55555555);
    value = ((value & 0xcccccccc) >> 2) + (value & 0x33333333);
    value = ((value & 0xf0f0f0f0) >> 4) + (value & 0x0f0f0f0f);
    value = ((value & 0xff00ff00) >> 8) + (value & 0x00ff00ff);
    value = ((value & 0xffff0000) >> 16) + (value & 0x0000ffff);

    return value;
}
```

Or you might just write the most obvious code possible:

```
int countSetBits(int value)
{
    int count = 0;

    for (int bit = 0; bit < 32; ++bit)
    {
        if (value & (1 << bit))
            ++count;
    }
```

---

2 Apologies to all non-C++ programmers for the bit twiddling in the next three examples. I promise the rest of the book is light on bitwise operations.

```
        return count;
    }
```

The first two answers are clever...and I don't mean that as a compliment.[3] A quick glance isn't enough to figure out how either example actually works—they each have a little morsel of "Wait...what?" code tucked inside the loop. With a little bit of thought you can figure out what's going on, and seeing the trick is kind of fun. But untangling things takes some effort.

And that's with a head start! I told you what the functions did before showing the code, and the function names hammer their purpose home. If you *hadn't* known that the code counted set bits, untangling either of the first two examples would have been even more work.

That's not the case for the final answer. It's obvious that it's counting the bits set. It's as simple as possible, but no simpler, and that makes it better than the first two answers.[4]

Measuring Simplicity

There are many ways to think about what makes code simple.

You might decide to measure simplicity based on how easy code is for someone else on your team to understand. If a randomly chosen colleague can read through a bit of code and understand it with no effort, then the code is appropriately simple.

Or you might decide to measure simplicity by how easy it is to create the code—not just the time to type it, but the time it takes to get the code fully functional and bug-free as well.[5] Complicated code takes a while to get right; simple code is easier to get across the finish line.

These two measures have a lot of overlap, of course. Code that's easy to write tends to be easy to read, too. And there are other valid measures of complexity you might use:

---

3 In a plausible alternate universe, this Rule is named "Cleverness Is Not a Virtue."

4 Modern processors have a dedicated instruction to count the number of bits set in a value—popcnt on x86 processors, for instance, which executes in a single cycle. You can also get carried away with SIMD instructions to count lots of bits even faster than popcnt. But all of these approaches are hard to understand, and which instructions are supported depend on exactly which processor you have. I'd rather see the simplest countSetBits, unless there was a really, really good reason to use something more complicated.

5 Bug-free within experimental error, of course. There are always bugs you haven't found yet.

How much code is written

Simpler code tends to be shorter, though it's possible to jam a lot of complexity into a single line of code.

How many ideas are introduced

Simple code tends to build on the concepts that everyone on your team knows; it doesn't introduce new ways of thinking about problems or new terminology.

How much time it takes to explain

Simple code is easy to explain—in a code review, it's obvious enough that the reviewer zooms right through. Complicated code takes explanation.

Code that seems simple against one measure will seem simple against the other measures as well. You just need to choose which of the measures provides the clearest focus for your work—but I recommend starting with ease of creation and ease of comprehension. If you focus on getting easy-to-read code working quickly, you're creating simple code.

...But No Simpler

It's better for code to be simpler, but it still needs to solve the problem it intends to solve.

Imagine that you're trying to count how many ways there are to climb a ladder with some number of rungs, given the stipulation that you gain one, two, or three rungs with each step. If the ladder has two rungs, there are two ways to climb it—either you step on the first rung or not. Similarly, there are four ways to climb a three-rung ladder—step on the first rung, step on the second rung, step on the first and second rungs, or step directly to the top rung. A four-rung ladder can be climbed in seven ways, a five-rung ladder in thirteen ways, and so on.

You can write simple code to calculate this recursively:

```
int countStepPatterns(int stepCount)
{
    if (stepCount < 0)
        return 0;

    if (stepCount == 0)
        return 1;

    return countStepPatterns(stepCount - 3) +
            countStepPatterns(stepCount - 2) +
```

```
        countStepPatterns(stepCount - 1);
}
```

The basic idea is that any journey up the ladder has to step to the top rung from one of the three rungs below it. Adding the number of ways to climb to each of those rungs gives the number of ways to climb to the top rung. After that, it's just a matter of figuring out the base cases. The preceding code allows negative step counts as a base case to make the recursion simpler.

Unfortunately, this solution doesn't work. Well, it does work, at least for small stepCount values, but countStepPatterns(20) takes about twice as long to complete as countStepPatterns(19). Computers are really fast, but exponential growth like this will catch up to that speed. In my test, the example code started getting pretty slow once stepCount got into the twenties.

If you're expected to count the number of ways up longer ladders, then this code is too simple. The core issue is that all of the intermediate results of count StepPatterns are recalculated over and over, and this leads to exponential run times. A standard answer to this is memoization—hanging onto the calculated intermediate values and reusing them, as in this example:

```
int countStepPatterns(unordered_map<int, int> * memo, int rungCount)
{
    if (rungCount < 0)
        return 0;

    if (rungCount == 0)
        return 1;

    auto iter = memo->find(rungCount);
    if (iter != memo->end())
        return iter->second;

    int stepPatternCount = countStepPatterns(memo, rungCount - 3) +
                           countStepPatterns(memo, rungCount - 2) +
                           countStepPatterns(memo, rungCount - 1);

    memo->insert({ rungCount, stepPatternCount });
    return stepPatternCount;
}

int countStepPatterns(int rungCount)
{
    unordered_map<int, int> memo;
    return countStepPatterns(&memo, rungCount);
}
```

With memoization in place, each value is calculated once and inserted in the hash map. Subsequent calls find the calculated value in the hash map in roughly constant time, and the exponential growth goes away. The memoized code is a smidgen more complicated, but it doesn't hit a performance wall.

You might also decide to use dynamic programming, trading off a bit of conceptual complexity for better code simplicity:

```
int countStepPatterns(int rungCount)
{
    vector<int> stepPatternCounts = { 0, 0, 1 };

    for (int rungIndex = 0; rungIndex < rungCount; ++rungIndex)
    {
        stepPatternCounts.push_back(
            stepPatternCounts[rungIndex + 0] +
            stepPatternCounts[rungIndex + 1] +
            stepPatternCounts[rungIndex + 2]);
    }

    return stepPatternCounts.back();
}
```

This approach runs quickly enough, too, and it's even simpler than the memoized recursive version.

Sometimes It's Better to Simplify the Problem Rather than the Solution

The problems in the original, recursive version of countStepPatterns appeared for longer ladders. The simplest code worked perfectly well for small numbers of rungs, but hit an exponential performance wall for large numbers of rungs. Later versions avoided the exponential wall at the cost of slightly more complexity...but they soon run into a different problem.

If I run the previous code to calculate countStepPatterns(36), I get the right answer, 2,082,876,103. Calling countStepPatterns(37), though, returns –463,960,867. That's clearly not right!

That's because the version of C++ I'm using stores integers as signed 32-bit values, and calculating countStepPatterns(37) overflowed the available bits. There are 3,831,006,429 ways to climb a 37-rung ladder, and that number is too big to fit in a signed 32-bit integer.

So maybe the code is still too simple. It seems reasonable to expect count StepPatterns to work for all ladder lengths, right? C++ doesn't have a standard solution for really big integers, but there are (many) open source libraries that implement various flavors of arbitrary-precision integers. Or given a few hundred lines of code, you could implement your own:

```cpp
struct Ordinal
{
public:

    Ordinal() :
        m_words()
        { ; }
    Ordinal(unsigned int value) :
        m_words({ value })
        { ; }

    typedef unsigned int Word;

    Ordinal operator + (const Ordinal & value) const
    {
        int wordCount = max(m_words.size(), value.m_words.size());

        Ordinal result;
        long long carry = 0;

        for (int wordIndex = 0; wordIndex < wordCount; ++wordIndex)
        {
            long long sum = carry +
                            getWord(wordIndex) +
                            value.getWord(wordIndex);

            result.m_words.push_back(Word(sum));
            carry = sum >> 32;
        }

        if (carry > 0)
            result.m_words.push_back(Word(carry));

        return result;
    }

protected:

    Word getWord(int wordIndex) const
    {
        return (wordIndex < m_words.size()) ? m_words[wordIndex] : 0;
    }

    vector<Word> m_words;
};
```

Dropping `Ordinal` into the last example in place of `int` produces exact answers for longer ladders:

```
Ordinal countStepPatterns(int rungCount)
{
    vector<Ordinal> stepPatternCounts = { 0, 0, 1 };

    for (int rungIndex = 0; rungIndex < rungCount; ++rungIndex)
    {
        stepPatternCounts.push_back(
            stepPatternCounts[rungIndex + 0] +
            stepPatternCounts[rungIndex + 1] +
            stepPatternCounts[rungIndex + 2]);
    }

    return stepPatternCounts.back();
}
```

So…problem solved? With the introduction of `Ordinal`, an exact answer can be calculated for much longer ladders. Sure, adding a few hundred lines of code to implement `Ordinal` isn't great, especially given that the actual `countStep Patterns` function is only 14 lines long, but isn't that the price that must be paid to correctly solve the problem?

Probably not. If there isn't a simple solution to a problem, interrogate the problem before you accept a complicated solution. Is the problem you're trying to solve actually the problem that needs solving? Or are you making unnecessary assumptions about the problem that are complicating your solution?

In this case, if you're actually counting step patterns for real ladders, you can probably assume a maximum ladder length. If the maximum ladder length is, say, 15 rungs, then any of the solutions in this section are perfectly adequate, even the naive recursive example presented first. Add an `assert` to one of them noting the built-in limits of the function and declare victory:

```
int countStepPatterns(int rungCount)
{
    // NOTE (chris) can't represent the pattern count in an int
    // once we get past 36 rungs...

    assert(rungCount <= 36);

    vector<int> stepPatternCounts = { 0, 0, 1 };

    for (int rungIndex = 0; rungIndex < rungCount; ++rungIndex)
    {
        stepPatternCounts.push_back(
```

```
            stepPatternCounts[rungIndex + 0] +
            stepPatternCounts[rungIndex + 1] +
            stepPatternCounts[rungIndex + 2]);
    }

    return stepPatternCounts.back();
}
```

Or if supporting really long ladders is required—handling the inspection ladder for a wind turbine, say—then would an approximate count of steps be enough? Probably, and if so it's easy to replace integers with floating-point values. So easy that I'm not even going to show the code.

Look, everything overflows eventually. Solving the extreme boundary cases for a problem will always lead to an overly complicated solution. Don't get trapped into solving the strictest definition of a problem. It's much better to have a simple solution for the part of the problem that actually needs to be solved instead of a complicated solution to a broader definition of the problem. If you can't simplify the solution, try to simplify the problem.

Simple Algorithms

Sometimes it's a poor choice of algorithm that adds complexity to your code. There are lots of ways to solve any particular problem, after all, some more complicated than others. Simple algorithms lead to simple code. The problem is that the simple algorithm isn't always obvious!

Say you're writing code to sort a deck of cards. An obvious approach is to simulate the riffle shuffle you likely learned as a kid—split the deck into two piles, then fan them into each other, giving the card on each side a roughly equal chance of ending up next into the recombined deck. Repeat until the deck is shuffled.[6]

That might look like this:

```
vector<Card> shuffleOnce(const vector<Card> & cards)
{
    vector<Card> shuffledCards;

    int splitIndex = cards.size() / 2;
    int leftIndex = 0;
```

---

6 A deck of cards is pretty well randomized after seven riffle shuffles. After four or five riffle shuffles the deck isn't randomized at all. And yes, my family gets annoyed with how many times I shuffle a deck of cards before dealing the next hand. "We're here to play cards, Chris, not watch you shuffle." A little knowledge is a dangerous thing.

```
    int rightIndex = splitIndex;

    while (true)
    {
        if (leftIndex >= splitIndex)
        {
            for (; rightIndex < cards.size(); ++rightIndex)
                shuffledCards.push_back(cards[rightIndex]);

            break;
        }
        else if (rightIndex >= cards.size())
        {
            for (; leftIndex < splitIndex; ++leftIndex)
                shuffledCards.push_back(cards[leftIndex]);

            break;
        }
        else if (rand() & 1)
        {
            shuffledCards.push_back(cards[rightIndex]);
            ++rightIndex;
        }
        else
        {
            shuffledCards.push_back(cards[leftIndex]);
            ++leftIndex;
        }
    }

    return shuffledCards;
}

vector<Card> shuffle(const vector<Card> & cards)
{
    vector<Card> shuffledCards = cards;

    for (int i = 0; i < 7; ++i)
    {
        shuffledCards = shuffleOnce(shuffledCards);
    }

    return shuffledCards;
}
```

This simulated-riffle-shuffle algorithm works, and the code I've written here is a fairly simple implementation of that algorithm. You'll have to expend a little energy making sure that all of the index checks are correct, but it's not too bad.

But there are simpler algorithms to shuffle a deck of cards. For instance, you could build a shuffled deck one card at a time. On each iteration, take a new card and swap it with a random card in that iteration's deck. You can do this in place, actually:

```
vector<Card> shuffle(const vector<Card> & cards)
{
    vector<Card> shuffledCards = cards;

    for (int cardIndex = shuffledCards.size(); --cardIndex >= 0; )
    {
        int swapIndex = rand() % (cardIndex + 1);
        swap(shuffledCards[swapIndex], shuffledCards[cardIndex]);
    }

    return shuffledCards;
}
```

By the simplicity measures introduced earlier, this version is superior. It took less time to write.[7] It's easier to read. It's less code. It's easier to explain. It's simpler and better—not because of the code, but because of the better choice of algorithm.

Don't Lose the Plot

Simple code is easy to read—and the simplest code can be read straight through, top to bottom, just like reading a book. Programs aren't books, though. It's easy to end up with code that's hard to follow if the flow through the code isn't simple. When code is convoluted, when it makes you jump from place to place to follow the flow of execution, it's much harder to read.

Convoluted code can result from trying too hard to express each idea in exactly one place. Take the riffle-shuffle code from earlier. The bits of code that deal with the right and left piles of cards look pretty similar to each other. The logic to move one card or a series of cards to the shuffled pile could be split into separate functions, then called from shuffleOnce:

```
void copyCard(
    vector<Card> * destinationCards,
    const vector<Card> & sourceCards,
```

---

7 As measured experimentally; your mileage may vary. I got a little cute with the indexes and conditions when writing the riffle-shuffle code, and it took a few tries to get working. The random selection code worked the first time.

```
        int * sourceIndex)
{
    destinationCards->push_back(sourceCards[*sourceIndex]);
    ++(*sourceIndex);
}

void copyCards(
    vector<Card> * destinationCards,
    const vector<Card> & sourceCards,
    int * sourceIndex,
    int endIndex)
{
    while (*sourceIndex < endIndex)
    {
        copyCard(destinationCards, sourceCards, sourceIndex);
    }
}

vector<Card> shuffleOnce(const vector<Card> & cards)
{
    vector<Card> shuffledCards;

    int splitIndex = cards.size() / 2;
    int leftIndex = 0;
    int rightIndex = splitIndex;

    while (true)
    {
        if (leftIndex >= splitIndex)
        {
            copyCards(&shuffledCards, cards, &rightIndex, cards.size());
            break;
        }
        else if (rightIndex >= cards.size())
        {
            copyCards(&shuffledCards, cards, &leftIndex, splitIndex);
            break;
        }
        else if (rand() & 1)
        {
            copyCard(&shuffledCards, cards, &rightIndex);
        }
        else
        {
            copyCard(&shuffledCards, cards, &leftIndex);
        }
    }

    return shuffledCards;
}
```

The previous version of shuffleOnce was readable top-to-bottom; this one isn't. That makes it harder to read. While reading through the shuffleOnce code you run into the copyCard or copyCards function. Then you have to track down those functions, figure out what they do, pop back to the original function, then match the arguments passed from shuffleOnce to your new understanding of copyCard or copyCards. That's a lot harder than just reading the loops in the original shuffleOnce.

So, the don't-repeat-yourself version of the function took more time to write[8] and is harder to read. It's more code, too! The attempt to remove duplication made the code more complicated, not simpler.

Obviously, there's something to be said for reducing the amount of duplication in your code! But it's important to recognize that there's a cost to removing the duplication—and for small amounts of code and simple ideas, it's better to just leave duplicate copies. The code will be easier to write and easier to read.

One Rule to Rule Them All

Many of the remaining Rules in this book will return to this theme of simplicity, of keeping code as simple as possible but no simpler.

At its heart, programming is a struggle with complexity. Adding new functionality often means making the code more complicated—and as code gets more complicated, it gets harder and harder to work with, and progress gets slower and slower. Eventually, you can reach an event horizon, where any attempt to move forward—to fix a bug or add a feature—causes as many problems as it solves. Further progress is effectively impossible.

In the end, it will be complexity that kills your project.

That means effective programming is about delaying the inevitable. Add as little complexity as possible as features are added and bugs fixed. Look for opportunities to remove complexity, or architect things so that new features don't add much to the overall complexity of the system. Create as much simplicity as possible in how your team works together.

If you're diligent, you can delay the inevitable indefinitely. I wrote the first lines of Sucker Punch code 25 years ago, and the codebase has continuously evolved since then. There's no end in sight—our code is wildly more complicated

---

8 Again, experimentally determined. Took a few tries to get it to compile, actually, as I wavered between using pointers and references.

than it was 25 years ago, but we've been able to stay in control of that complexity, and we're still able to make effective progress.

We've been able to manage complexity, and so can you. Stay sharp, remember that complexity is the ultimate enemy, and you'll do well.

Bugs Are Contagious

There's a truism of programming that the earlier you find a bug, the easier it will be to fix. That's generally true...but I think it's even more true to say that the later you find a bug, the more of a pain in the ass it will be to fix.

Once a bug exists, people will unintentionally write code that relies on that bug. Sometimes that shaky bit of bug-reliant code is nearby, in the same system as the bug. Sometimes it's not nearby—maybe it's downstream, in a bit of code that calls your system and depends on the incorrect results your bug causes. Or it's upstream—a chunk of code that only works because the bug caused you to call it in a particular way.

This is a natural thing—it's impossible to avoid. We notice things that go wrong, not things that go right. When things go wrong, we investigate to figure out why. But when things don't go wrong, we don't investigate. If your code works, or at least seems to work, then there's a natural tendency to assume that it works in the way you think it works, when very often it works for reasons you've never imagined. And since you don't investigate, you never discover the tangled set of circumstances that led to your code accidentally working.

That's true for the code you write, and it's true for the code other people write that calls your code. When you commit a bug to your team's codebase, the codebase will slowly but inevitably accumulate other bits of code that rely on your bug. These hidden entanglements only become visible when you fix an obvious bug and some other part of your project mysteriously stops working.

The sooner you find the bug, the fewer of these entanglements will have time to sprout. That means fewer dependencies to clean up—which is often the most time-consuming part of fixing a bug. It's painfully common to spend more time dealing with the repercussions of a bug fix than fixing the bug itself.

It's useful to think of bugs as being contagious. Each bug in your system tends to create new bugs, as new code works around the bug or relies on its incorrect behavior. The best way to stop the resulting contagion is to eliminate bugs as early as possible, before their evil influence can spread.

Don't Count on Your Users

OK, so we want to detect problems early. How do we do that?

Here's one thing you can't count on—your users. Whether that means teammates calling your code or customers exercising your feature, users aren't a great first line of defense. Sure, sometimes they'll report a problem, but more often they'll assume the behavior they're observing is the behavior you intended. That's where the entanglements come from—unnoticed issues, sure, but also issues that are noticed but then assumed to be part of the design.

You can try to ameliorate this. You can write better user-facing documentation. You can drag your team into a meeting room to explain a new system or feature. You can maintain an up-to-date internal wiki with details about how everything fits together, or put a tech note on your support site. All of these things are worthwhile—they all help, albeit at nontrivial expense and with varying levels of effectiveness—but they don't solve the problem. Fundamentally, your users don't understand your intent as well as you do, so they're going to assume bugs are features no matter what you do.

A better answer is some sort of continuous automated testing. Most programmers would agree that automated testing is a Good Thing. At a minimum, programmers think that automated testing is a Good Thing for *other* programmers to do, whether or not they can be bothered to do it themselves.

There are lots of homegrown variations on the idea of continuous automated testing, as well as more formalized methodologies like test-driven development (*https://oreil.ly/BjsDY*).

Generally speaking, the idea is that your system (or better yet, your whole project) has a set of tests that you can run quickly and conveniently and that thoroughly[1] exercise the system (or project) and report problems. If the tests are truly quick and convenient, they'll get run all the time—like every time you compile or run the project. Any bugs that pop up that early are easy to nip in the bud. If the tests are only *theoretically* quick and convenient, they'll tend to get run as part of the commit process—which is still early enough to avoid the entanglement growth that makes bugs hard to fix.

---

1 ...although perhaps not completely. I won't weigh in on what percentage of your codebase you should aim for covering with automated tests. Keep reading; our percentage at Sucker Punch is very low.

This sort of testing is expensive. Writing the tests for some bit of code can take as much time as writing the code itself. Advocates of automated testing, however, would argue (convincingly!) that this is an illusion. After all, the hidden cost of writing that bit of code is detecting and diagnosing problems later, when they're hard to fix. Coding *is* debugging, right? Testing proponents argue that it's faster to test up front—perhaps even, if you're a diehard, writing a test before you write the code it intends to test.

Continuous automated testing isn't something you can easily adopt as a personal practice. Making it work requires investing in quite a bit of infrastructure—you'll need a nonintrusive testing framework, a testing-friendly deployment system, and a team that's philosophically committed to automated testing. Unless the whole team buys in, you're swimming against the tide. But if you're on a team that buys in, great!

Despite the obvious value in a test-centric approach, we haven't committed to it at Sucker Punch. We do have automated tests for many systems, but collectively they cover only a small part of our codebase. Why is that?

Automated Testing Can Be Tricky

Some projects and some problems lend themselves better to automated testing than others.

Some things are hard to test, either because it's hard to cover all possible inputs or because it's hard to validate the outputs. Imagine you're writing a new lossy audio compression codec. How do you write an automated test for it?

It's easy to verify that your compressor doesn't crash, or to measure how much compression you see against some set of test files. It's not as easy to verify that the decompressed audio actually sounds like the original. You're writing an audio compression codec, so you probably have enough signal processing math to write tests that flag obvious problems, but at some point you'll need to slap headphones on human ears and ask people to pick the compressed sample out of three options. That's not a test you can run quickly or conveniently.

Some code is inherently hard to test because its success is hard to measure—and a lot of the code that gets written at Sucker Punch qualifies. Does a shopkeeper character act like a real shopkeeper would? Does that facial animation actually convey disgust, or does the character just look they're about to burp? Does it feel like I'm firing a bow here, even though I'm really holding a controller?

If you're working on a project that has big chunks of difficult-to-test code, then you're forced into a hybrid model. Test what you can test, control what you can control, and remember that you're not testing everything. Any areas that aren't covered by your automated tests will need to be tested manually: plan accordingly.

That said, you *can* structure your code to make it easier to test.

Imagine you're going to write an external automated test for some bit of code—that is, some bit of testing code, separate from the code you're writing, that will call your code with a set of inputs designed to flex its capabilities, then check that the outputs match expectations. How can you structure your code to make this test easier to write?

Stateless Code Is Easier to Test

One important strategy is to reduce the amount of state in your code. It's a lot easier to test code that doesn't rely on state. Any pure function—a bit of code that relies only on its direct inputs, has no side effects, and has predictable results—is easy to test. Better this:

```
int sumVector(const vector<int> & values)
{
    int sum = 0;
    for (int value : values)
    {
        sum += value;
    }
    return sum;
}
```

Than this:

```
int reduce(
    int initialValue,
    int (*reduceFunction)(int, int),
    const vector<int> & values)
{
    int reducedValue = initialValue;
    for (int value : values)
    {
        reducedValue = reduceFunction(reducedValue, value);
    }
    return reducedValue;
}
```

To test sumVector, you just need a set of inputs and the expected outputs for those inputs. That's exactly the sort of thing that test-driven development frameworks excel at. If there's state involved, the set of inputs required to thoroughly exercise the code gets a lot more complicated.

Testing reduce is harder—in the apparent pursuit of generality, or maybe as a half-step toward threading, it repeatedly calls a passed-in function on the values in vector. You can certainly use reduce to sum the values in the vector:

```
int sum(int value, int otherValue)
{
    return value + otherValue;
}

int vectorSum = reduce(0, sum, values);
```

But testing reduce presents problems. Who knows what the reduceFunction function is going to do, right? Does it rely on some bit of external state? What happens if it has side effects? What if calling that function removes something from the values vector you're iterating over? If you're testing reduce, you've got to anticipate and test all of those things. That's a much more complicated set of tests than you'd need for sumVector.

To thoroughly test code, you need to present it with a thorough representation of all the states it might encounter, then evaluate its outputs against those states. With a pure function, the arguments to the function are the only state that matters. But when you bring in side effects, internal state, or callouts to arbitrary functions, the amount of state that might matter explodes. This forces a compromise—you can accept less thorough test coverage, or write an unmanageable number of test cases.

Let's look at a simple example. Imagine you're tracking a prioritized list of characters. Each character has a priority, and it's easy to get a list of all characters sorted by that priority. The interface is simple:

```
class Character
{
public:

    Character(int priority);
    ~Character();

    void setPriority(int priority);
    int getPriority() const;
```

```
    static const vector<Character *> & getAllCharacters();

protected:

    int m_priority;
    int m_index;

    static vector<Character *> s_allCharacters;
};
```

It's not hard to keep s_allCharacters sorted, with all characters in priority order. You could do this incrementally, tracking where each character lives in your prioritized list and being careful to scoot it back and forth in the list only minimally when its priority changes. That means inserting the character in the right place when it's created:

```
Character::Character(int priority) :
    m_priority(priority),
    m_index(0)
{
    int index = 0;
    for (; index < s_allCharacters.size(); ++index)
    {
        if (priority <= s_allCharacters[index]->m_priority)
            break;
    }

    s_allCharacters.insert(s_allCharacters.begin() + index, this);

    for (; index < s_allCharacters.size(); ++index)
    {
        s_allCharacters[index]->m_index = index;
    }
}
```

Cleaning up indexes when the character is destroyed:

```
Character::~Character()
{
    s_allCharacters.erase(s_allCharacters.begin() + m_index);

    for (; index < s_allCharacters.size(); ++index)
    {
        s_allCharacters[index]->m_index = index;
    }
}
```

And scooting the character back and forth in the list by a minimal amount if its priority changes:

```cpp
void Character::setPriority(int priority)
{
    if (priority == m_priority)
        return;

    m_priority = priority;

    while (m_index > 0)
    {
        Character * character = s_allCharacters[m_index - 1];
        if (character->m_priority <= priority)
            break;

        s_allCharacters[m_index] = character;
        character->m_index = m_index;

        --m_index;
    }

    while (m_index + 1 < s_allCharacters.size())
    {
        Character * character = s_allCharacters[m_index + 1];
        if (character->m_priority >= priority)
            break;

        s_allCharacters[m_index] = character;
        character->m_index = m_index;

        ++m_index;
    }

    s_allCharacters[m_index] = this;
}
```

This works, but testing it is complicated. There's hidden state that an external test can't get at. A test that creates a set of prioritized characters then checks that allCharacters returns them in the proper order will catch some bugs, but it will miss some too. The current index could be screwed up even if the characters are in the right order, and there's no way to check that using the methods Character exposes. Incorrect indexes might cause problems, but there's no guarantee those problems will show up soon (or even ever). And with three separate code paths, each trying to keep the indexes correct, it's easy to slip up.

It's simpler to test a stateless version of Character, one that doesn't try to maintain state:

```
class Character
{
public:

    Character(int priority) :
        m_priority(priority)
    {
        s_allCharacters.push_back(this);
    }

    ~Character()
    {
        auto iter = find(
                        s_allCharacters.begin(),
                        s_allCharacters.end(),
                        this);
        s_allCharacters.erase(iter);
    }

    void setPriority(int priority)
    {
        m_priority = priority;
    }

    int getPriority() const
    {
        return m_priority;
    }

    static int sortByPriority(
        Character * left,
        Character * right)
    {
        return left->m_priority < right->m_priority;
    }

    static vector<Character *> getAllCharacters()
    {
        vector<Character *> sortedCharacters = s_allCharacters;

        sort(
            sortedCharacters.begin(),
            sortedCharacters.end(),
            sortByPriority);

        return sortedCharacters;
    }
```

```
protected:

    int m_priority;

    static vector<Character *> s_allCharacters;
};
```

There's still state here, since you're tracking all the characters in s_all Characters, but it's not hidden. Writing the test for this version of the code might not be as simple as writing the tests for a pure function, but it's a lot simpler than writing the tests for the incremental version of Character you started with.

With the prior state-based approach, you had to be paranoid about what order you did things in. Minus that state, you can just check for expected outputs and feel pretty safe.

This sort of stateless code is easier to get right in the first place, too. That's a hidden advantage of test-driven development—code that's easier to test tends to be easier to write. If you're thinking about how you're going to test some bit of code you're about to write, you'll end up writing something simpler.

Audit State You Can't Eliminate

Let's say that circumstances force you into keeping some state. Maybe the call pattern encourages it—say your sorted list of characters sees minor priority adjustments interleaved with calls to AllCharacters, and all of the sorting in your stateless implementation is thrashing your memory caches.

If it's hard to write an external test because you can't get at some bit of internal state, write an internal test instead.[2] An easy way to do this is to have an auditing method on your data—in this case, an audit function that checks whether the internal state is consistent:

```
void Character::audit()
{
    assert(s_allCharacters[m_index] == this);
}
```

---

2 You could also expose the internal state to your testing code somehow—weakening encapsulation by "friending" your test code, say. It's more maintainable in my experience to add internal tests instead.

This is a pretty short audit function, but that's because I've stripped out anything interesting from this Character class to use it as an example. A real Character class would be likely to have more internal state and a longer audit function.

You can also audit the consistency of your array:

```
void Character::auditAll()
{
    for (int index = 0; index < s_allCharacters.size(); ++index)
    {
        Character * character = s_allCharacters[index];

        if (index > 0)
        {
            Character * prevCharacter = s_allCharacters[index - 1];
            assert(character->m_priority >= prevCharacter->m_priority);
        }

        character->audit();
    }
}
```

There are advantages to this sort of internal testing, especially if you think of internal tests as a complement to external tests. Often you can leave internal tests running all the time, which means they're running on actual real-world test cases, not the artificial ones you built for your unit test.

Someone has to call these internal functions for them to be useful, obviously! A good rule of thumb is calling Character::audit at the end of any method that updates the character's state, and calling Character::auditAll whenever the list changes. You can dial audit frequency up and down based on need.

Don't Trust the Caller

In the normal course of programming, you're going to write code that gets called by other people on your team. Even if you only work on one-person projects, some future version of you will call your code—and that future version of you might as well be a stranger. Future You won't remember the details, and other callers never knew them. So don't trust that the caller is going to get the details right!

The caller will pass incompatible sets of arguments. They'll neglect to call expected initialization functions, and they'll forget to call shutdown functions.

They'll provide a callback function that doesn't actually fulfill the basic requirements expected of that function. They'll get it all wrong...and if you don't detect the mistakes, they won't get fixed. An entanglement will grow instead—this time not from a bug in your code, but from a bug in the calling code.

It might be counterintuitive, but the easiest place to find those bugs isn't in the calling code, it's in the code being called. The caller might be making the mistakes, but *you're* in a better position to catch them.

Now, with good design, you can often make it impossible for callers to get the details wrong. That's the subject of Rule 7, "Eliminate Failure Cases". Sometimes you can't, though. What do you do in those cases?

Here's an example. You're writing a rigid-body physics simulator that's going to be used by three different video games under development at your company. You'll be tracking internal state, like which rigid bodies are in contact with each other, and that state has to get stored somewhere. You can't just call operator new, though, like you would in standard C++ code. Memory is tight, and your clients have their own custom memory managers you need to integrate with.

There's a straightforward answer—have your clients hand over functions to allocate and free the memory you need as part of an initialization step. I'm tempted to start with a few bad examples of how to do initialization, but I'll skip to a decent one instead. If you're actually writing a rigid-body physics simulator, you're likely to have more initialization parameters than the two named in the following code snippet. The gravitational constant, for instance. Collect all of the initialization parameters into a single structure, which is then passed to a single initialization function:

```
struct RigidBodySimulator
{
    struct InitializationParameters
    {
        void * (* m_allocationFunction)(size_t size);
        void (* m_freeFunction)(void * memory);
        float m_gravity;
    };

    void initialize(const InitializationParameters & params);
    void shutDown();
};
```

Expose methods to add and remove new simulated rigid bodies to the system, and to get and set their current state:

```
struct RigidBodySimulator
{
    struct ObjectDefinition
    {
        float m_mass;
        Matrix<3, 3> m_momentOfInertia;
        vector<Triangle> m_triangles;
    };

    struct ObjectState
    {
        Point m_position;
        Quaternion m_orientation;
        Vector m_velocity;
        Vector m_angularVelocity;
    };

    ObjectID createObject(
        const ObjectDefinition & objectDefinition,
        const ObjectState & objectState);
    void destroyObject(
        ObjectID objectID);
    ObjectState getObjectState(
        ObjectID objectID) const;
    void setObjectState(
        ObjectID objectID,
        const ObjectState & objectState);
};
```

The expected usage pattern is pretty obvious, right? Initialize the simulator before you use it, and shut it down when you're done. Add objects, manipulate them, destroy them when you're done. Nothing complicated.

But you can't trust the caller to get even the simple details right. They'll forget to call initialize, they'll ask for object state on objects that have been deleted, or they'll try to set object state on a random ObjectID that you've never handed out.

It's tempting to just ignore these cases—to assume that people will get the details right and let the chips fall where they may—but that's a huge mistake. If you don't detect the error and report it somehow, things will end in tears. Either callers won't notice their mistake, or they'll assume the observed behavior is a feature.

Imagine you've implemented `ObjectID` as a wrapper around a smaller integer, which is then used as an index into a linear list of `ObjectState` structures:

```
struct RigidBodySimulator
{
    struct ObjectID
    {
        int m_index;
    };

    ObjectState getObjectState(
        ObjectID objectID) const
    {
        return m_objectStates[objectID.m_index];
    }

    void setObjectState(
        ObjectID objectID,
        const ObjectState & objectState)
    {
        m_objectStates[objectID.m_index] = objectState;
    }

    vector<ObjectState> m_objectStates;
};
```

This design is simple and easily understood, but it's is pretty shaky. It lets easy-to-make mistakes by the caller go unnoticed. Try to get an object's state after you destroy it and the results will be undefined.

Actually, that's a little misleading, though it's the way people usually talk about interfaces like this. They mean "undefined" in the sense that the interface doesn't promise any particular result when you call `getObjectState` for a destroyed object—but, in practice, the results are completely defined! In the implementation (which I'm not showing you), if you call `getObjectState` immediately after destroying that object with `destroyObject`, you get the state the object had right before it was deleted. It would be easy to assume, implicitly or explicitly, that this was the intended behavior...and from such assumptions do entanglements grow.[3]

Undefined results are the mark of a poorly designed interface.

---

3 This is also a hole in many automated tests, which rarely test unspecified cases as thoroughly as they do specified ones. Your automated tests are unlikely to detect this `destroyObject + getObjectState` example.

Don't let this incorrect usage go unremarked. Anyone calling getObject State after destroyObject should hear about it—but first you need to detect the problem. One easy fix is to supplement the index in ObjectID with a "generation" number:

```
struct RigidBodySimulator
{
    class ObjectID
    {
        friend struct RigidBodySimulator;

    public:

        ObjectID() :
            m_index(-1), m_generation(-1)
            { ; }

    protected:

        ObjectID(int index, int generation) :
            m_index(index), m_generation(generation)
            { ; }

        int m_index;
        int m_generation;
    };

    bool isObjectIDValid(const ObjectID objectID) const
    {
        return objectID.m_index >= 0 &&
            objectID.m_index < m_indexGenerations.size() &&
            m_indexGenerations[objectID.m_index] == objectID.m_generation;
    }

    ObjectID createObject(
        const ObjectDefinition & objectDefinition,
        const ObjectState & objectState)
    {
        int index = findUnusedIndex();

        ++m_indexGenerations[index];
        m_objectDefinitions[index] = objectDefinition;
        m_objectStates[index] = objectState;

        return ObjectID(index, m_indexGenerations[index]);
    }

    void destroyObject(ObjectID objectID)
    {
```

```
        assert(isObjectIDValid(objectID));
        ++m_indexGenerations[objectID.m_index];
    }

    ObjectState getObjectState(ObjectID objectID) const
    {
        assert(isObjectIDValid(objectID));
        return m_objectStates[objectID.m_index];
    }

    void setObjectState(
        ObjectID objectID,
        const ObjectState & objectState)
    {
        assert(isObjectIDValid(objectID));
        m_objectStates[objectID.m_index] = objectState;
    }

    vector<int> m_indexGenerations;
    vector<ObjectDefinition> m_objectDefinitions;
    vector<ObjectState> m_objectStates;
};
```

The generation detects incorrect usage of object IDs. When you create or destroy an object, you bump its generation version number. If you try to destroy an object, then get its state, the generations won't match and this mismatch will be reported.[4] The caller is notified that they've made a mistake and can correct it before it has a chance to fester.

You could easily add code that checks for the other usage mistakes I've identified—forgetting to call initialize, for instance. Or calling it twice. In the preceding code the interface is redesigned a bit to make it harder to create invalid object IDs—the only public constructor creates a valid object ID, so the caller only has easy access to object IDs that are properly constructed and returned.

There's a reasonable discussion to be had about how to flag usage errors like this—you could use asserts, but you could just as easily return error codes or throw exceptions. Your answer will depend on your team's conventions. The important thing is that you flag the error, not how you do the flagging.

---

4 One of the standard paradigms for reporting problems in C is the assert macro. One way or the other, it pops up a message at runtime if the condition it's passed is false. The message varies depending on which compiler and operating system you're using (!), but typically it includes the line number in the source code where the assert failed and the expression passed to the assert.

Keeping Your Code Healthy

Code that's easier to test—or, better yet, continually tests itself—stays healthier longer. It's best to think about this from the start, before you write your first line of code for some new part of the project. You might start with writing an automated test, as with test-driven development. You might opt for a stateless implementation of the functionality, or add continual internal auditing of the functioning of the code.

The result is contagious bugs being discovered early, before they have chance to multiply. That means fewer problems to fix, and easier fixes to make when fixes are necessary.

And there's a hidden benefit! Most of the techniques that make code easier to test also make the code easier to write—having to write tests for all use cases nudges you to simplify to fewer use cases. Eliminating state makes for less fiddly code. Making your interfaces less error-prone makes them simpler.

It's a two-way win. So keep things simple, and keep on testing.

A Good Name Is the Best Documentation

You can't write about programming without quoting Shakespeare, obviously. It's sort of a cliché at this point. Nevertheless, here's *Romeo and Juliet*, a quick recap: Romeo and Juliet are star-crossed teens in love, prevented by the enmity between their two families from spending a joyful life together. It ends poorly for all involved.

Act II, Scene II. Juliet bemoans the situation in the fifth-most famous quote from the play:

What's in a name? That which we call a rose
By any other name would smell as sweet

I've heard similar arguments made about code, typically by colleagues frustrated by my persnickety code review attitude toward how stuff is named. Variables, functions, members, source files, class and structure names—I'll quibble about any of them.

People will argue, typically with an eye roll, that the name doesn't really matter, that what matters is the thing named. The true meaning of the variable (or function, or class, whatever) can only be determined by looking at the code. The truth of a variable is what it represents—how it's set, how it's used, not what it's named. The functionality doesn't change if the name is changed.

So, they declare, just choose something easy to type and get on with coding.

These people are wrong.

The name of a thing is the first and most important documentation you have. It's inescapable. It's always there. Whenever you see any sort of reference to the thing, it's by its name. That continual presence is a glorious opportunity to tell the reader what the thing is, every single time they see it.

This sort of opportunity should never be squandered.

Your goal when choosing the name for something is simple—the name should encapsulate what's important about the thing, and guide the reader in how to think about it. If you're naming a variable, the name should immediately tell the reader what the variable represents. If you're naming a function, the name should tell the reader what the function does.

Sounds simple, right? So how do things go sideways? As many ways as there are stars in the sky, actually, but here are a few common failure modes.

Don't Optimize for Minimal Keystrokes

The first way things go sideways is overly curt names. Remember that code is read much more often than it's written. It's easy when you're writing code to forget this and optimize in favor of names that are easy to type, instead of spending a bit of extra effort to write code that's easy to read.

In extremis, this leads to super short variable names. The older the code is, the more likely you'll see this style. Or, alternatively, if you run into work done by a truly ancient programmer—someone who started programming in the '60s or '70s, say—then you're more likely to see one-letter and two-letter names.[1]

I think of this as *Numerical Recipes* code.[2] I'm a big fan of *Numerical Recipes*, but the coding style is pretty opaque. To paraphrase:

```
void cp(
    int n,
    float rr[],
    float ii[],
    float xr,
    float xi,
    float * yr,
    float * yi)
{
    float rn = 1.0f, in = 0.0f;
    *yr = 0.0f;
    *yi = 0.0f;
    for (int i = 0; i <= n; ++i)
```

---

1 I'm of an age where my first programming language was Applesoft Basic, which allowed long variable names but only paid attention to the first two characters. You read that right; JUDGE$ and JUROR$ are aliases for the same string variable. Good times. My Basic variables were all one or two characters, as in the coding example to follow.

2 *Numerical Recipes* is a classic book explaining all sorts of algorithms for math and science. The Sucker Punch codebase is littered with ideas adapted from it. 10/10, would recommend. William H. Press et al., *Numerical Recipes: The Art of Scientific Computing*, 3rd ed. (Cambridge University Press, 2007).

```
    {
        *yr += rr[i] * rn - ii[i] * in;
        *yi += ii[i] * rn + rr[i] * in;
        float rn2 = rn * xr - in * xi;
        in = in * xr + rn * xi;
        rn = rn2;
    }
}
```

Not immediately obvious what's going on, right? You could puzzle it out—the code evaluates a polynomial over complex numbers—but it's some work. Things are a lot easier with more appropriate names:

```
void evaluateComplexPolynomial(
    int degree,
    float realCoeffs[],
    float imagCoeffs[],
    float realX,
    float imagX,
    float * realY,
    float * imagY)
{
    float realXN = 1.0f, imagXN = 0.0f;
    *realY = 0.0f;
    *imagY = 0.0f;
    for (int n = 0; n <= degree; ++n)
    {
        *realY += realCoeffs[n] * realXN - imagCoeffs[n] * imagXN;
        *imagY += imagCoeffs[n] * realXN + realCoeffs[n] * imagXN;
        float realTemp = realXN * realX - imagXN * imagX;
        imagXN = imagXN * realX + realXN * imagX;
        realXN = realTemp;
    }
}
```

And obviously this particular bit of code is simpler if you have a data type for complex numbers:

```
void evaluateComplexPolynomial(
    vector<complex<float>> & terms,
    complex<float> x,
    complex<float> * y)
{
    complex<float> xN = { 1.0f, 0.0f };
    *y = { 0.0f, 0.0f };
    for (const complex<float> & term : terms)
    {
        *y += xN * term;
        xN *= x;
```

```
    }
}
```

Now the structure of the algorithm is clear, if you remember how complex numbers work. You multiply each term by the domain value x taken to the Nth power, accumulating the results in the range variable y.

Don't Mix and Match Conventions

The second way names go wrong is inconsistency. When code doesn't use consistent rules about how things are named, it's easy for the reader to get confused.

For most projects, some amount of inconsistency is hard to avoid. If you use any external libraries, then you've got trouble—unless all of your dependencies share the same naming rules, and you're willing to work within those rules yourself. Say you're writing a native Windows app, and you're willing to adopt Microsoft's naming conventions—then your code can be consistent. Or you're going to use the C++ standard template libraries and can live with their conventions: still consistent. Otherwise, there will be visible seams as things named with competing conventions are mixed.

Imagine that you've got a vector class that pre-allocates storage for a fixed number of elements. That's useful and not something the C++ standard library provides. Imagine your project has a simple naming scheme for object methods—camel case, starting with a verb. Leaving out a bunch of details, your class looks like this:

```cpp
template <class ELEM, int MAX_COUNT = 8>
class FixedVector
{
public:

    FixedVector() :
        m_count(0)
        { ; }

    void append(const ELEM & elem)
        {
            assert(!isFull());
            (void) new (&m_elements[m_count++]) ELEM(elem);
        }
    void empty()
        {
            while (m_count > 0)
            {
                m_elements[--m_count].~ELEM();
            }
```

```
        }
    int getCount() const
        { return m_count; }
    bool isEmpty() const
        { return m_count == 0; }
    bool isFull() const
        { return m_count >= MAX_COUNT; }

protected:

    int m_count;
    union
    {
        ELEM m_elements[0];
        char m_storage[sizeof(ELEM) * MAX_COUNT];
    };
};
```

This is pretty straightforward.[3] The `append` method adds a new element, the `empty` method empties out the whole array, and you've got some accessors to check the current number of elements in the vector. But if you write code that mixes this `FixedVector` class with a standard C++ container, things aren't so rosy:

```
void reverseToFixedVector(
    vector<int> * source,
    FixedVector<int, 8> * dest)
{
    dest->empty();
    while (!source->empty())
    {
        if (dest->isFull())
            break;

        dest->append(source->back());
        source->pop_back();
    }
}
```

Here you have two consecutive lines that call an `empty` method on a vector, but those two calls do completely different things. The first call empties the

---

3 Well, a zero-sized array isn't straightforward. Support is compiler-dependent; the compiler I use supports them but is grouchy about it. I could write the code without a zero-sized array, but it makes things easier to read and understand, so there you go.

destination vector; the second call checks to see whether the source vector is empty. It's pretty easy to see how this would cause confusion!

Obviously you could adopt Standard Template Library (STL) conventions for the FixedVector class—you could rename it fixed_vector, and use STL-style names for all of its methods—but that just moves the line of confusion elsewhere in your project. Now you're not just asking your programmers to adapt to and use a foreign set of naming conventions—you're asking them to write code with those conventions as well. That's a much bigger undertaking.

It's easy to underestimate the cognitive load of mixing conventions like this. There's a real cost to switching back and forth, constantly reinterpreting what you're reading in terms of which set of conventions it must be using. In this example, that means popping back and forth in the code to figure out which variable has which type, and therefore which set of conventions it uses. Assuming that you know which conventions are used by which type, of course!

At Sucker Punch we avoided the specific problem of inconsistency between our conventions and the standard C++ container conventions by writing our own version of all the container classes instead of using the STL versions. That's a pretty extreme solution, but it does eliminate a lot of cognitive strain—the container classes work just like all the other code we write, so single-stepping into a container class's method doesn't drop you into a foreign landscape. Like, say, the STL's jungle of macros and truly unhinged template magic. Not to judge, but still.

Even so, we're not entirely free of foreign conventions, because we use code we didn't write, like the PlayStation platform libraries. For most projects, some degree of mixed conventions is inevitable. The key is to minimize the mixing where possible. Ring fence the foreign bodies if you can, in hopes that their conventions won't leak out into the code everyone deals with all the time.

Don't Shoot Yourself in the Foot

Avoid self-inflicted wounds—if the programmers on your team aren't using consistent naming conventions, you're all creating entirely avoidable problems for yourselves. A jumble of conventions makes even straightforward code a challenge to sort out:

```
int split(int min, int max, int index, int count)
{
    return min + (max - min) * index / count;
}
```

```
void split(int x0, int x1, int y0, int y1, int & r0, int & r1)
{
    r0 = split(x0, x1, y0, y1);
    r1 = split(x0, x1, y0 + 1, y1);
}

void layoutWindows(vector<HWND> ww, LPRECT rc)
{
    int w = ww.size();
    int rowCount = int(sqrtf(float(w - 1))) + 1;
    int extra = rowCount * rowCount  - w;
    int r = 0, c = 0;
    HWND hWndPrev = HWND_TOP;
    for (HWND theWindow : ww)
    {
        int cols = (r < extra) ? rowCount - 1 : rowCount;
        int x0, x1, y0, y1;
        split(rc->left, rc->right, c, cols, x0, x1);
        split(rc->top, rc->bottom, r, rowCount, y0, y1);
        SetWindowPos(
            theWindow,
            hWndPrev,
            x0,
            y0,
            x1 - x0,
            y1 - y0,
            SWP_NOZORDER);
        hWndPrev = theWindow;
        if (++c >= cols)
        {
            c = 0;
            ++r;
        }
    }
}
```

I feel a little queasy right now. That was rough for me to type; I'm taking one for the team here.

The algorithm isn't that complicated—I'm just arranging windows to fill a target rectangle by dividing them into columns and rows, keeping roughly the same aspect ratio as the target rectangle. But I've made it unnecessarily hard to figure out what's going on with the naming choices.

The most obvious problem is the jumble of three or four different naming styles, which is bad enough. But there's another issue that pops up even in more consistently named code—the name of something changing as it's passed into a function. The first time I call split, I pass x0 and x1 as the last two arguments.

They'll receive the right and left sides of the window's new rectangle. Inside the split function, though, x0 and x1 mean something completely different.

That's a problem. If you're single-stepping through LayoutWindows, you've got a mental model of what x0 and x1 are. If you single-step into split, you still see x0 and x1—but now they mean something completely different. This function is using x and y as generic variable names, just like in algebra class. They're not connected in any way with a coordinate system, like x and y are in the LayoutWindows function. Algebra in one function, Cartesian coordinates in the next—that's cognitive load, which slows you down and creates mistakes.

Some amount of this renaming in function calls is unavoidable. Function arguments are often the result of expressions, not just passing another variable. In this example the first two arguments to split are rc->left and rc->right, which can't be the names for those concepts inside the split function. You'll have to create variable names—but if you're smart, those variable names will be left and right, which makes it easier to track what's what as you single-step into the function.

Here's the same function reorganized a bit to make it more consistent and readable:

```
int divideRange(int min, int max, int index, int count)
{
    return min + (max - min) * index / count;
}

void layoutWindows(vector<HWND> windows, LPRECT rect)
{
    int windowCount = windows.size();
    int rowCount = int(sqrtf(float(windowCount - 1))) + 1;
    int shortRowCount = rowCount * rowCount - windowCount;

    HWND lastWindow = HWND_TOP;
    int rowIndex = 0, colIndex = 0;

    for (HWND window : windows)
    {
        int colCount = (rowIndex < shortRowCount) ?
                        rowCount - 1 :
                        rowCount;

        int left = divideRange(
                        rect->left,
                        rect->right,
                        colIndex,
                        colCount);
```

```
        int right = divideRange(
                        rect->left,
                        rect->right,
                        colIndex + 1,
                        colCount);
        int top = divideRange(
                        rect->top,
                        rect->bottom,
                        rowIndex,
                        rowCount);
        int bottom = divideRange(
                        rect->top,
                        rect->bottom,
                        rowIndex + 1,
                        rowCount);

    SetWindowPos(
        window,
        lastWindow,
        left,
        top,
        right - left,
        bottom - top,
        SWP_NOACTIVATE);

    lastWindow = window;
    if (++colIndex >= colCount)
    {
        colIndex = 0;
        ++rowIndex;
    }
    }
}
```

Still the same algorithm, but much easier to understand. Consistent naming patterns make it easier to track what's going on. It's easier to identify the concept represented by a variable solely from its name, without inspecting the code to infer its meaning—you may not know everything about a variable named rowIndex, but you can be pretty sure it's the index of a row. Which row and of what is not as clear, but knowing it's a row index is a big head start.

Consistently naming indexes and counts has some positive side effects. When you step into the divideRange function, it also uses index and count as argument names. It's easy to mentally translate the colIndex and colCount variables in layoutWindows to the index and count arguments of divideRange. I've minimized the cognitive load, especially compared to the x0/x1 mess of my first version of this function.

This is common. If you have a consistent set of rules for naming things, then as you pass between different functions, or different sections of the codebase, similar things will have similar names. Identical things will usually have identical names. As you single-step through code, or try to understand how different bits of code interact with each other, you don't have to juggle a bunch of names for a single thing. There's only one name—or only a small number of obviously and closely related names, like the index + count example earlier.

Don't Make Me Think

Actually, you can go further with rules to create consistency.

The key to consistency is for everything to be *as mechanical as possible*. If your team's conventions for how things are named require judgment calls or careful thought, then they won't work. Different programmers will make different judgment calls, and everyone's names will be different.

You'd much rather be in a happy spot where everyone just naturally chooses the same names for the same things, because that makes working with everyone's code much easier. And the easiest way to create this level of consistency is to have mechanical rules that everyone follows.

The Sucker Punch rules for variable naming are especially mechanical. I haven't used them for the examples in this book, mostly in the interest of approachability. Our rules work well for us, but that's because we all use them constantly. They're a little strange-looking if you're seeing them for the first time.

Instead, I've used gentler conventions for this book's examples—if I've got a class representing a character, the class is named Character and a variable holding a character is typically named character, while a vector full of characters would be named characters.[4] Simple conventions chosen for readability, but consistently used.

The Sucker Punch codebase is similar in spirit, just with a more thorough set of rules and a little bit more terseness. We use a variant of Microsoft's Hungarian standard for variable naming. This is...divisive. Not so much with Sucker

---

4 Unsurprisingly, the class would be implemented in files named *character.h* and *character.cpp*.

Punch programmers, who adapt pretty quickly, but outside of the Microsoft ecosystem, the Hungarian naming standard is commonly a target of derision.[5]

The core idea of the Hungarian standard is that the type (or sometimes usage) of a variable mechanically determines all or part of the variable's name. If you have an index into an array of factions, then that variable is named iFaction. If you have a vector of pointers to characters, then the variable is named vpCharacter.

In many cases, that's where the story stops. The variable name is entirely mechanical, and as a result everyone uses exactly the same name for the variable. That's what we're hoping for!

If you have multiple variables with the same type, you tack a qualifier onto the end of the variable name. If you have two character pointers, they might be called pCharacter and pCharacterOther. This does introduce judgment calls, but the conventions we have about common qualifier patterns limit the inconsistency introduced.

The important thing isn't the details of our naming conventions—it's that we *have* strict conventions, that they're as mechanical as we can make them, and that they're both well-documented and enforced. That puts us in a happy place where everyone chooses the same names for the same things, and working with someone else's code feels like working with your own.

Figure out which of your own project conventions you can make more mechanical and do it. You'll reap the benefits for years to come.

---

5 I think the negativity misconstrues the advantages of the Hungarian standard. Originally, using it was a workaround to the lack of type-safe linking in early C compilers. Embedding type names into variable and function names added a degree of type safety, if only by convention. That's unimportant at this point, but it's the center of most of the derision. There's also criticism that code using the convention is hard to read, but that's like saying Icelandic is hard to read—sure, if you don't speak it! The real value of the Hungarian standard for us now is that following its rules lets us all naturally create the same names for things, and that leads to an easier-to-work-with codebase.

Generalization Takes Three Examples

We're all taught as new programmers that general solutions are preferable to specific ones. Better to write one function that solves two problems than to write separate functions for each problem.

You're unlikely to write this code:

```cpp
Sign * findRedSign(const vector<Sign *> & signs)
{
    for (Sign * sign : signs)
        if (sign->color() == Color::Red)
            return sign;

    return nullptr;
}
```

When it would be easy to write this code:

```cpp
Sign * findSignByColor(const vector<Sign *> & signs, Color color)
{
    for (Sign * sign : signs)
        if (sign->color() == color)
            return sign;

    return nullptr;
}
```

It's natural to think in terms of generalization, especially for such a simple example. If you need to find all the red signs in the world, your natural instinct as a programmer is to write the code to find signs of an arbitrary color, then pass in red as that color. Nature abhors a vacuum; programmers abhor code that only solves one problem.

It's worth thinking about why this feels so natural. At some level, the instinct to write `findSignByColor` instead of `findRedSign` is based on a prediction. Given that you're looking for a red sign, you can confidently predict that at some point you'll want to look for a blue sign and write the code to handle that case too.

In fact, why stop there? Why not write an even more general solution for finding signs?

You could create a more general interface that lets you query any aspect of the sign—color, size, location, text—so that searching for a sign by color is just a special subcase. You might do this by creating a structure defining the acceptable values for each aspect of a sign:

```cpp
bool matchColors(
    const vector<Color> & colors,
    Color colorMatch)
{
    if (colors.empty())
        return true;

    for (Color color : colors)
        if (color == colorMatch)
            return true;

    return false;
}

bool matchLocation(
    Location location,
    float distanceMax,
    Location locationMatch)
{
    float distance = getDistance(location, locationMatch);
    return distance < distanceMax;
}

struct SignQuery
{
    SignQuery() :
        m_colors(),
        m_location(),
        m_distance(FLT_MAX),
        m_textExpression(".*")
    {
        ;
    }

    bool matchSign(const Sign * sign) const
    {
```

```
        return matchColors(m_colors, sign->color()) &&
            matchLocation(m_location, m_distance, sign->location()) &&
            regex_match(sign->text(), m_textExpression);
    }

    vector<Color> m_colors;
    Location m_location;
    float m_distance;
    regex m_textExpression;
};
```

Designing the query parameters requires some judgment calls, since each aspect forces a different query model. In this example, the judgment calls I made were:

- Rather than specifying a single color, you can provide a list of acceptable colors. An empty list specifies that any color is acceptable.

- Internally, a Location stores latitude and longitude as floating-point values, so looking for an exact match isn't useful. Instead, you would specify a maximum distance from some location.

- You could use a regular expression to match the text or partial text of the sign, which would handle a lot of obvious cases.

The actual code to find a matching sign is simple:

```
Sign * findSign(const SignQuery & query, const vector<Sign *> & signs)
{
    for (Sign * sign : signs)
        if (query.matchSign(sign))
            return sign;

    return nullptr;
}
```

Finding a red sign with this model is still pretty straightforward—create a SignQuery, specify red as the only acceptable color, then call findSign:

```
Sign * findRedSign(const vector<Sign *> & signs)
{
    SignQuery query;
    query.m_colors = { Color::Red };
    return findSign(query, signs);
}
```

Remember that the design of SignQuery is based on one example: finding a single red sign. The rest is all conjecture. At this point there aren't other examples to build on, so you're just predicting what other kinds of signs you'll need to find.

And that's the problem—your predictions are likely to be wrong. If you're lucky, they'll only be a little bit wrong...but you probably won't be lucky.

YAGNI

Most obviously, you'll anticipate and solve for cases that never occur in practice. Maybe the first few sign-finding use cases look like this:

- Find a red sign.

- Find a sign near the corner of Main Street and Barr Street.

- Find a red sign near 212 South Water Street.

- Find a green sign.

- Find a red sign near 902 Mill Street.

You can solve all of these cases with SignQuery and findSign, so in that sense the code does a decent job predicting the use cases. But I don't see any cases where you're accepting multiple sign colors, and none of the use cases looks at the sign's text. All the actual use cases look for a single color, at most, and some restrict to a location. The SignQuery code solves for cases that aren't occurring in practice.

This is a common pattern, common enough that the Extreme Programming philosophy has a name for it—YAGNI, or "You Ain't Gonna Need It." The work you did to define a list of acceptable colors rather than the single color in your known use case? Wasted time and effort. The experiments you did with the C++ regular expression class, figuring out how to distinguish complete matches from partial? That's time you're not getting back.

What's more, the extra complexity of SignQuery imposes a cost on anyone using it. It's pretty obvious how to use the findSignByColor function, but find Sign requires a little more investigation. There are three different querying models packed into it, after all!

Is a partial match of the regular expression sufficient, or does the expression need to match the entire text of the sign? It's not obvious how the three conditions interact—is this an "and" or an "or"? If you read the code, it's clear that a sign matches the query only if *all* of the conditions match, but that requires reading the code. Which introduces a new bit of confusion—which SignQuery fields are required? As written, an empty query straight out of the constructor matches all signs, so you only need to set fields that you're filtering on—but learning this required some investigation.

Given the clear pattern in the real-world use cases, it would have been better to have just solved the *actual problem*:

```
Sign * findSignWithColorNearLocation(
    const vector<Sign *> & signs,
    Color color = Color::Invalid,
    Location location = Location::Invalid,
    float distance = 0.0f)
{
    for (Sign * sign : signs)
    {
        if (isColorValid(color) &&
            sign->color() != color)
        {
            continue;
        }

        if (isLocationValid(location) &&
            getDistance(sign->location(), location) > distance)
        {
            continue;
        }

        return sign;
    }

    return nullptr;
}
```

Your response at this point might be to accuse me of cheating. Sure, now that the first few use cases are on the table, it seems like findSignWithColorNearLocation is a better solution than SignQuery—but you couldn't have predicted that after the first use case. Writing findSignWithColorNearLocation as a general solution wasn't any more likely to succeed than writing SignQuery turned out to be. One of the use cases might have allowed multiple colors or might have referred to the text of the signs.

That's exactly my point! *No* general solution was predictable after one use case, so it was a mistake to try to write one. Both findSignWithColorNearLocation and SignQuery are mistakes. There's no winner here, just two losers.

Here's the best way to find a red sign:

```
Sign * findRedSign(const vector<Sign *> & signs)
{
    for (Sign * sign : signs)
        if (sign->color() == Color::Red)
            return sign;

    return nullptr;
}
```

Yes, I'm serious. I might pass in the color to match, but that's as far as I'd go. If you've got one use case, *write code to solve that use case.* Don't try to guess what the second use case will be. Write code to solve problems you understand, not ones you're guessing at.

An Obvious Objection to This Strategy, in Response to Which I Double Down

"Wait a second," you may say at this point. "Doesn't writing code that barely meets the requirements of the use case guarantee that you'll run into use cases that the code won't handle? What do you do when the next use case that pops up doesn't fit the code you've written? That seems inevitable."

"And isn't this an argument for writing more general code? Sure, the first five use cases we ran into with SignQuery didn't exercise all of the code we wrote, but what if the sixth use case did? Wouldn't we be glad to have the SignQuery code all written and ready to go when that happened?"

No, not really. Save your effort. When a use case pops up that your code doesn't handle, write code to handle it. You might cut and paste your first effort, making adjustments to handle the new use case. You might start again from scratch. Both are fine.

The first use case in the list of five was "Find a red sign," and I wrote code to do exactly that and no more. The second use case was "Find a sign near the corner of Main Street and Barr Street," so now I'll write code to do exactly that and no more:

```
Sign * findSignNearLocation(
    const vector<Sign *> & signs,
    Location location,
    float distance)
{
    for (Sign * sign : signs)
    {
```

```
        if (getDistance(sign->location(), location) <= distance)
        {
            return sign;
        }
    }

    return nullptr;
}
```

The third use case was "Find a red sign near 212 South Water Street," and this isn't handled by either of the two functions I've written. This is the inflection point—now that we've got three independent use cases, it's starting to make sense to generalize. With three independent use cases, we can more confidently predict the fourth and fifth.

Why three? What makes three a magic number? Nothing, really, except for the fact that it's not one or two. One example isn't enough to guess the general pattern. Based on my experience, two usually isn't either—after two examples, you'll just be more confident in your inaccurate generalization. With three different examples, your prediction of the pattern will be more accurate *and* you're likely to be a little bit more conservative in your generalization. Nothing like being wrong after examples one and two to leave you humble!

Still, there's no *requirement* that you generalize at this point! It would be perfectly fine to write a third function without folding the first two functions into it:

```
Sign * findSignWithColorNearLocation(
    const vector<Sign *> & signs,
    Color color,
    Location location,
    float distance)
{
    for (Sign * sign : signs)
    {
        if (sign->color() == color &&
            getDistance(sign->location(), location) >= distance)
        {
            return sign;
        }
    }

    return nullptr;
}
```

This three-separate-functions approach has one important benefit—the functions are very simple. It's obvious which one of them to call. If you have a color and a location, call `findSignWithColorNearLocation`. If you just have a color, it's `findSignWithColor`; if you just have a location, it's `findSignNearLocation`.[1]

If your sign-finding use cases continue to check for a single color and/or location, those three functions will be fine forever. The approach doesn't scale very well, of course—with two separate arguments and three separate `findSign` functions the approach isn't a disaster, but with more possible arguments it quickly becomes ridiculous. If at some point you have a use case that involves looking at the sign text, you'll probably shy away from creating seven variations of the `findSign` function.

There's nothing wrong at this point with combining the three `findSign` functions into a single function that handles all three cases. Once you have three separate use cases it's safer to generalize. But generalize only if you think it makes the code easier to write and read, based *solely* on the use cases you have in hand. Never generalize because you're worried about the next use case—only generalize on the use cases you know.

Writing generalized code in C++ for this is a little painful because C++ doesn't really have optional arguments, only default values for arguments. That means inventing some way to mark our arguments as "not present." One solution is to add `Invalid` values for color and location to use when we don't care about them. Repeating the first version of `findSignWithColorNearLocation`:

```
Sign * findSignWithColorNearLocation(
    const vector<Sign *> & signs,
    Color color = Color::Invalid,
    Location location = Location::Invalid,
    float distance = 0.0f)
{
    for (Sign * sign : signs)
    {
        if (isColorValid(color) &&
            sign->color() != color)
        {
            continue;
        }

        if (isLocationValid(location) &&
            getDistance(sign->location(), location) > distance)
        {
            continue;
```

---

1 Or, if you're using a language like C++ that supports function overloading, you could call all three versions of `findSign` and let the compiler sort things out.

```
        }

        return sign;
    }

    return nullptr;
}
```

With this function written, all the calls to `findSignWithColor` and `findSign` `NearLocation` could be replaced with calls to `findSignWithColorNearLocation`.

It's Actually Worse than YAGNI

So far you've seen that generalizing prematurely means you're likely to write code that never gets exercised, and that's bad. The less obvious problem is that generalizing prematurely makes it harder to adapt to unanticipated use cases. That's partly because the generalized code you've written is more complicated and therefore takes more work to adjust, but there's also something more subtle that happens. Once you've established the template for generalization, you're likely to extend that template for future use cases instead of reevaluating it.

Roll back the clock a bit. Imagine that you generalized early with the `Sign` `Query` class, but this time the first few use cases look like this:

- Find a red sign.
- Find a red "STOP" sign near the corner of Main Street and Barr Street.
- Find all the red or green signs on Main Street.
- Find all white signs with text "MPH" on Wabash Avenue or Water Street.
- Find a sign with the text "Lane" or colored blue near 902 Mill Street.

The first two use cases in this list fit `SignQuery` pretty well, but then things start to fall apart.

The third use case, "Find all the red or green signs on Main Street," adds two new requirements. First, the code needs to return all matching signs instead of a single sign. That's not hard:

```
vector<Sign *> findSigns(
    const SignQuery & query,
    const vector<Sign *> & signs)
{
    vector<Sign *> matchedSigns;

    for (Sign * sign : signs)
```

```
    {
        if (query.matchSign(sign))
            matchedSigns.push_back(sign);
    }

    return matchedSigns;
}
```

The second new requirement is to find all signs along a street, and that's trickier. Assuming streets can be represented as a series of line segments connecting locations, both locations and streets can be packaged into a new `Area` struct:

```
struct Area
{
    enum class Kind
    {
        Invalid,
        Point,
        Street,
    };

    Kind m_kind;
    vector<Location> m_locations;
    float m_maxDistance;
};

static bool matchArea(const Area & area, Location matchLocation)
{
    switch (area.m_kind)
    {
    case Area::Kind::Invalid:
        return true;

    case Area::Kind::Point:
        {
            float distance = getDistance(
                            area.m_locations[0],
                            matchLocation);
            return distance <= area.m_maxDistance;
        }
        break;

    case Area::Kind::Street:
        {
            for (int index = 0;
                index < area.m_locations.size() - 1;
                ++index)
            {
```

```
                Location location = getClosestLocationOnSegment(
                                area.m_locations[index + 0],
                                area.m_locations[index + 1],
                                matchLocation);

                float distance = getDistance(location, matchLocation);
                if (distance <= area.m_maxDistance)
                    return true;
            }

            return false;
        }
        break;
    }
    return false;
}
```

Then the new `Area` struct can replace the location and maximum distance in `SignQuery`:

```
struct SignQuery
{
    SignQuery() :
        m_colors(),
        m_area(),
        m_textExpression(".*")
    {
        ;
    }

    bool matchSign(const Sign * sign) const
    {
        return matchColors(m_colors, sign->color()) &&
                matchArea(m_area, sign->location()) &&
                regex_match(sign->m_text, m_textExpression);
    }

    vector<Color> m_colors;
    Location m_location;
    float m_distance;
    regex m_textExpression;
};
```

The fourth use case asks for all speed-limit signs on either of two streets, which doesn't fit. It's easy enough to support a list of areas:

```
bool matchAreas(const vector<Area> & areas, Location matchLocation)
{
    if (areas.empty())
```

```
            return true;

    for (const Area & area : areas)
        if (matchArea(area, matchLocation))
            return true;

    return false;
}
```

Then you can replace the single area in SignQuery with a list:

```
struct SignQuery
{
    SignQuery() :
        m_colors(),
        m_areas(),
        m_textExpression(".*")
    {
        ;
    }

    bool matchSign(const Sign * sign) const
    {
        return matchColors(m_colors, sign->color()) &&
            matchAreas(m_areas, sign->location()) &&
            regex_match(sign->m_text, m_textExpression);
    }

    vector<Color> m_colors;
    vector<Area> m_areas;
    regex m_textExpression;
};
```

Use case five really mixes things up—it's looking for a sign to mark a point of historical interest. Those signs are usually blue, so it looks for that, but it also might be green with particular text. That doesn't fit the model in SignQuery.

Again, not impossible. Adding Boolean operations to SignQuery addresses the new use case:

```
struct SignQuery
{
    SignQuery() :
        m_colors(),
        m_areas(),
        m_textExpression(".*"),
        m_boolean(Boolean::None),
        m_queries()
    {
```

```
    ;
}

~SignQuery()
{
    for (SignQuery * query : m_queries)
        delete query;
}

enum class Boolean
{
    None,
    And,
    Or,
    Not
};

static bool matchBoolean(
    Boolean boolean,
    const vector<SignQuery *> & queries,
    const Sign * sign)
{
    switch (boolean)
    {
    case Boolean::Not:
        return !queries[0]->matchSign(sign);

    case Boolean::Or:
        {
            for (const SignQuery * query : queries)
                if (query->matchSign(sign))
                    return true;

            return false;
        }
        break;

    case Boolean::And:
        {
            for (const SignQuery * query : queries)
                if (!query->matchSign(sign))
                    return false;

            return true;
        }
        break;
    }

    return true;
}
```

```
bool matchSign(const Sign * sign) const
{
    return matchColors(m_colors, sign->color()) &&
            matchAreas(m_areas, sign->location()) &&
            regex_match(sign->m_text, m_textExpression) &&
            matchBoolean(m_boolean, m_queries, sign);
}

vector<Color> m_colors;
vector<Area> m_areas;
regex m_textExpression;
Boolean m_boolean;
vector<SignQuery *> m_queries;
};
```

Whew. That was a more demanding set of use cases than the set we saw in the beginning of this Rule. After making a lot of changes, though, the QuerySign model can handle a broad range of requests. There are reasonable requests that still can't be answered—"find two signs within 10 meters of each other," say— but it's easy to imagine that we've covered the important cases. Victory, right?

This Is Not What Success Looks Like

Actually, it's not clear that extending SignQuery so much has put us in a good spot, even though I was being scrupulously fair—there's no YAGNI in any of the extensions, and I kept everything as neat and tidy as I could.

When you continue to extend a general solution, you can lose sight of the context. That's exactly what has happened here.

Let's compare solving that last use case using SignQuery with doing the same thing directly. Here's the SignQuery solution:

```
SignQuery * blueQuery = new SignQuery;
blueQuery->m_colors = { Color::Blue };

SignQuery * locationQuery = new SignQuery;
locationQuery->m_areas = { mainStreet };

SignQuery query;
query.m_boolean = SignQuery::Boolean::Or;
query.m_queries = { blueQuery, locationQuery };

vector<Sign *> locationSigns = findSigns(query, signs);
```

And here's the direct version:

```
vector<Sign *> locationSigns;
for (Sign * sign : signs)
{
    if (sign->color() == Color::Blue ||
        matchArea(mainStreet, sign->location()))
    {
        locationSigns.push_back(sign);
    }
}
```

The direct solution is better. It's simpler, it's easier to understand, it's easier to debug, it's easier to extend. All the work we did on `SignQuery` just led us further and further away from the simplest and best answer. And that's the real danger in premature generalization—not just that you'll implement features that never get used, but that *your generalization establishes a direction that will be hard to change.*

Generalized solutions are really sticky. Once you establish an abstraction to solve a problem, it's hard to even conceive of alternatives. Once you use `find Signs` to find all the red signs, your instinct will be to use `findSigns` whenever you need to find signs of any sort. The very name of the function tells you to do that!

So if you've got a case that doesn't quite fit, the obvious answer is to extend `SignQuery` and `findSigns` to cover the new case. The same goes for the next case that doesn't fit, and the one after that. As the general solution becomes more expressive, it also becomes more cumbersome...and unless you're very careful, you won't even notice that you've extended your generalization past its natural bounds.

When you're holding a hammer, everything looks like a nail, right? Creating a general solution is handing out hammers. Don't do it until you're sure that you've got a bag of nails instead of a bag of screws.[2]

---

2 You can use a hammer to drive a screw, by the way. You just have to swing the hammer harder. At the risk of being painfully obvious, the same is true of code. You can get things to work with an awkward abstraction—you just have to swing the abstraction harder.

The First Lesson of Optimization Is Don't Optimize

My favorite programming task is optimization. Usually that means making some code system run faster, though sometimes I'm optimizing memory usage or network bandwidth or some other resource.

It's my favorite task because it's simple to measure success. For most coding work, what constitutes success is fuzzy. Books like this one try hard to define what good code or a good system looks like, but what makes a line of code good is always imprecise.

That's not true for optimization. There, the answers are crisper. If you're trying to make something run faster, you can measure your success directly. The same goes for the cost of that success in terms of increased code size or complexity. No worrying about semi-defined long-term benefits, no trusting that someone reading your new code a few years from now will understand it immediately and be swept away in a wave of emotional appreciation for you as a programmer. Just immediate, tangible results.

I'm not alone in this fondness for optimization. In fact, it's seductive enough to have prompted the one programming adage that every programmer knows:

Premature optimization is the root of all evil.

That's not the whole quote, by the way. The original version, as written down by Donald Knuth in 1974, is more nuanced:

We should forget about small efficiencies, say about 97% of the time: premature optimization is the root of all evil.

It's important to note the context.[1] In 1974, compilers were much less sophisticated than they are now. The "small efficiencies" Knuth talks about were often tricky little bits of code to get the compiler to generate the code you wanted, like caching end points to eke out a little bit of performance:

```
int stripNegativeValues(int count, int * data)
{
    int * to = data;

    for (int * from = data, * end = data + count;
         from < end;
         ++from)
    {
        if (*from >= 0)
            *to++ = *from;
    }

    return to - data;
}
```

Or using macros to avoid the cost of a function call:[2]

```
typedef struct
{
    float x, y, z;
} Vector;

#define dotProduct(A, B) (A.x * B.x + A.y * B.y + A.z * B.z)
```

Fortunately, these days the compiler is smart enough to generate the right instructions for your source code, at least if you're writing simple and straightforward code. The trickier you try to get, the less likely it is that the compiler will be able to figure out what you mean, so old-school tricks and extravagant C++ magic often end up generating worse code than just writing out the simplest expression of your logic.

---

1 The origin of the quote is disputed, though Knuth's version is the first known published form of it. It's also attributed to Tony Hoare, who thought it sounded more like something Edsger Djikstra would have said. All three parties appear to be unsure of the actual origin, attributing it to common folk wisdom at the time. This is the perfect recipe for an unending argument (*https://oreil.ly/feSrN*) on the internet.

2 Note the archaic syntax here, which I threw in to take the old-timers down Memory Lane.

Having smart compilers hasn't saved us from ourselves, though. It's instinctive in programmers to worry about resources, whether that's time or storage or bandwidth—and that can lead to trying to solve performance problems before they pop up.

Let's say you're choosing a random item from a list, something games do a lot. The items aren't equally likely—each has a weighted chance of being chosen:

```
template <class T>
T chooseRandomValue(int count, const int * weights, const T * values)
{
    int totalWeight = 0;
    for (int index = 0; index < count; ++index)
    {
        totalWeight += weights[index];
    }

    int selectWeight = randomInRange(0, totalWeight - 1);
    for (int index = 0;; ++index)
    {
        selectWeight -= weights[index];
        if (selectWeight < 0)
            return values[index];
    }

    assert(false);
    return T();
}
```

This is pretty simple. Sum up all the weights, then choose a random number no larger than the sum. As you subtract weights, one of them will cause the sum to go negative, selecting that weighted value. The chance of that happening is proportional to the weight—done!

But it's easy to look at this and decide it could be faster. The second loop through the values doesn't seem necessary. If you hang on to the running sum of weights, you could divide-and-conquer your way to the answer, making the second loop much faster:

```
template <class T>
T chooseRandomValue(int count, const int * weights, const T * values)
{
    vector<int> weightSums = { 0 };
    for (int index = 0; index < count; ++index)
    {
        weightSums.push_back(weightSums.back() + weights[index]);
    }
```

```
    int weight = randomInRange(0, weightSums.back() - 1);

    int minIndex = 0;
    int maxIndex = count;

    while (minIndex + 1 < maxIndex)
    {
        int midIndex = (minIndex + maxIndex) / 2;
        if (weight >= weightSums[midIndex])
            minIndex = midIndex;
        else
            maxIndex = midIndex;
    }

    return values[minIndex];
}
```

This is a rookie mistake. Actually, it's a whole list of rookie mistakes all nested inside each other. Yes, the second loop is O(log N) now, not linear, but that doesn't really matter when the first loop is still linear. You haven't made a dent in overall performance.

Even that isn't really the issue. Unless you know that you've got a *lot* of weighted random choices, the simple linear loop is going to be faster. Until you get to 200(!) or so choices, the linear loop is faster than the binary search, at least as measured on my PC. That's a bigger number than you would have guessed, right? Up until that point, simpler logic and better memory-access patterns trump algorithmic efficiency.

But that's not the real issue, either. It doesn't matter how fast you do the lookup—the second version allocates memory, which is much slower than anything else you do. If you actually run the two functions as written earlier, the first version is twenty times faster than the second one. *Twenty times!*

Wait—that's still not the real issue! The *real* issue is that it doesn't matter how fast chooseRandomValue is, as you would quickly learn with a little bit of profiling. You might call it hundreds of times every second, but the profiler would tell you it represents a meaningless fraction of your overall runtime. The Sucker Punch engine has functions that are called millions of times every second; if you're writing a game, you do too. When it comes to performance, those functions matter, and chooseRandomValue doesn't.

The First Lesson of Optimization

So that's the first lesson of optimization—*don't optimize.*

Make your code as simple as possible. Don't worry about how fast it will run. It'll be fast enough. And if it's not, it will be easy to make it fast. That last bit—that it will be easy to make simple code fast—is the second lesson.

The Second Lesson of Optimization

Imagine you've got some simple, solid code that you took ordinary care writing. Your section of the project is running a little slow, so you instrument it and discover that this small bit of code is soaking up half of your performance.

This discovery is great news! If you can fix the performance of that one bit of code, you can double your overall performance.

This is pretty typical, by the way. The first time you look at the performance of some bit of code that's never been optimized, there's invariably good news. It's obvious what you need to work on.

Bad news would be discovering that nothing is obviously slow, but that's rare for code that hasn't survived a few rounds of optimization.

Here's a rule of thumb—if you've never optimized some bit of code, you can make it five to ten times faster without a lot of work. That may seem optimistic, but it isn't. In practice, there's lots of low-hanging fruit in unoptimized code.

Putting the Second Lesson to the Test

Let's put that rule of thumb to the test. Imagine that I was wrong about choose RandomValue. It's getting called so often, and with so many choices, that it's actually taking up half of your processor time.

Now, if you were starting with the second implementation, my rule of thumb would be easy to prove. Just switch to a simpler, no-allocation model like your first implementation and it runs 20 times faster. Rule of thumb proven!

That's too easy, though. Let's assume you're starting with the first implementation, so you don't have the easy solution of removing memory allocation. That's a bit unrealistic, actually—usually the first thing you discover when you look at performance is that someone is allocating memory inside a loop, and it's easy to fix. But let's assume you got unlucky and it's not something simple.

Here's a five-step process for optimizing something. I'm going to focus on performance ("processor time," to be explicit), but the same steps work for any resource. Just substitute network bandwidth, memory usage, power consumption, or whatever measurable thing you're trying to optimize for in the following steps.

STEP 1: MEASURE AND ATTRIBUTE PROCESSOR TIME

That is, measure how much processor time is being spent and attribute it to functions, or objects, or whatever is convenient. In the preceding example, I must have done this already because I know that `chooseRandomValue` is consuming half of my processor time.

STEP 2: MAKE SURE THERE'S NOT A BUG

It's pretty common to find out that what looks like a performance problem is actually a bug. In this case, with `chooseRandomValue` actually soaking up half of your cycles, I would strongly suspect a bug somewhere. I'd look pretty hard at whether all of these calls to `chooseRandomValue` are appropriate.

Maybe someone is getting a loop condition wrong and a counter is wrapping all the way around. Instead of a handful of iterations, it's looping 2^{32} times, plus or minus. That's a lot of calls to `chooseRandomValue`! (And yes, I've fixed this exact bug.)

STEP 3: MEASURE YOUR DATA

Don't even think about optimizing until you know what your data looks like. How many calls are made to `chooseRandomValue`? How many options are you choosing between? Are you repeatedly choosing from a small number of weighted distributions, or is it less predictable? How many zero weights are in the list? Do the lists of values you're choosing from have repeated values?

Most optimizations exploit some aspect of the data or how you use it. You can't make good decisions about optimization without thoroughly understanding the shape of your data.

STEP 4: PLAN AND PROTOTYPE

If your optimization worked perfectly—if it drove processor time all the way to zero—then what would overall performance look like? In this case, that would mean that `chooseRandomValue` ran in zero time. If it did, would you hit your performance target?

If not, then your plan isn't good enough. You'll need to identify other bits of code that can be optimized. Don't start working on an optimization until you know it's part of a plan that can succeed.

Sometimes it's hard to project what overall performance will look like with a perfect optimization. Code interacts with other code in unpredictable ways. Maybe `chooseRandomValue` is pulling weight values into the processor's data cache, and some other function is also using those values. In the worst case, you drive `chooseRandomValue` to zero cycles and overall performance doesn't change. The core problem was loading the weight values into the data cache—you've just shifted the blame to a new culprit.

Look for an opportunity to prototype your optimization. In this case, maybe you can just have `chooseRandomValue` return the first value in the list of choices every single time. That's not correct, but it's likely to give you a good idea of what performance would be with a perfectly optimal solution.

STEP 5: OPTIMIZE AND REPEAT

Once you're through the first four steps, you can start thinking about optimization. You've got ideas about how expensive various parts of the code ought to be, based on how much logic is involved and how much memory is accessed. Maybe some of this code or memory access could be simplified or skipped. If there's not some simple way to speed up the code, look for things you can exploit in the data. For instance, if most of the weights passed to `chooseRandomValue` are zero, you can exploit that. If there are duplicate values, then that might be something you can work with.

Don't just dive in, though. A one-step optimization plan of "look for some bit of code that looks slow and make it faster" is not going to work. Your instincts are wrong about where the problem is, they're wrong about what the data looks like, and they're wrong about what the right fix will be.[3]

Once you've completed Step 5, measure your performance again. If you've hit your target, great! Declare victory and stop optimizing. Otherwise, back to Step 1 you go. Some of the steps may go more quickly the second time through, but it's worth pausing at each of them to think about what you've learned so far.

Applying the Five-Step Optimization Process

OK, I'm ready to apply the process! I'm setting aside the word processor and firing up the development environment. I'll start with the first implementation of `chooseRandomValue`, apply the five-step optimization process, and see how much effort it takes to get a 10x speedup.

---

3 Unless your instinct is that someone is allocating memory somewhere. Then you're probably right.

The first implementation of `chooseRandomValue` is a solid example of taking ordinary care while writing code—it's optimized for simplicity and clarity, which is always the place to start. If my rule of thumb is correct, then I should be able to get a 5x to 10x speedup without too much work.

I admit to a bit of nervousness as I type this. This has the potential to be really embarrassing.

I've already done Step 1—I know that I'm spending half of my cycles in `chooseRandomValue`.

For Step 2, I put in a gallant effort but don't find any bugs. All the callers have legitimate reasons to call, and they're not doing anything obviously wrong.

In Step 3, I discover the problem—I'm making a lot of calls to `chooseRandom Value` and in most cases passing long lists of weights and values. The data looks pretty random, though the weights are small. Most of the values are less than 5 and none is greater than 15. Interestingly, there are lots of calls, but they're all from a small, static number of distributions—that is, the same lists of thousands of weights and values are getting passed over and over.

For Step 4, I create a perfect-performance version of `chooseRandomValue`. In this case, I substitute a version that returns a random value from the list while ignoring the weights—hard to imagine anything simpler than that. You could just return the first value in the list, but that would skip the random-number generation call that seems inevitable, so returning an unweighted random choice seems like a better prototype.

I'm testing it now...and the code runs roughly 50 times faster than my baseline implementation. Looks like there's room for the 5x to 10x speedup I predicted. On to Step 5—making the code run faster!

Your first impulse when you need to make code run faster might be to actually, you know, *make the code run faster*. Do the same stuff, just do it faster: unroll a loop, use multimedia instructions to process multiple entries at once, write some assembly language, move some bit of math outside a loop.

That's a bad impulse. Those sorts of optimizations are the *last* thing you should try, not the first thing. In the two million or so lines of code in *Ghost of Tsushima*, there are only a few dozen places where we've done those sorts of microoptimizations. It's not that we don't spend a lot of effort optimizing—everything we do has to complete in a sixtieth of a second, after all.[4] We sweat

---

4 Or thirtieth of a second, depending on the game. I'm not committing us to any specific performance numbers for future games, mind you.

bullets to get the game to run that fast. But with rare exceptions, doing the same thing faster isn't how we improve performance.

The way to make code run faster is to do less, not to do the same things faster. Figure out what the code is doing that it doesn't need to be doing, or what it's doing multiple times that could be done once. Eliminate those bits of code and things will run faster.

In this case, an obvious candidate is calculating the total weight for a distribution. In the first implementation of chooseRandomValue I'm doing that on every call...but when I measured the data in Step 3 I discovered that I was generating random values from a limited number of distributions. I could easily calculate the total weight once for each distribution, then reuse it in choose RandomValue:

```
struct Distribution
{
    Distribution(int count, int * weights, int * values);

    int chooseRandomValue() const;

    vector<int> m_weights;
    vector<int> m_values;
    int m_totalWeight;
};

Distribution::Distribution(int count, int * weights, int * values) :
    m_weights(),
    m_values(),
    m_totalWeight(0)
{
    int totalWeight = 0;

    for (int index = 0; index < count; ++index)
    {
        m_weights.push_back(weights[index]);
        m_values.push_back(values[index]);

        totalWeight += weights[index];
    }

    m_totalWeight = totalWeight;
}

int Distribution::chooseRandomValue() const
{
    int select = randomInRange(0, m_totalWeight - 1);
```

```
    for (int index = 0;; ++index)
    {
        select -= m_weights[index];
        if (select < 0)
            return m_values[index];
    }

    assert(false);
    return 0;
}
```

Allocating memory is expensive—that's why the ill-fated first attempt to optimize chooseRandomValue failed. It allocated memory on every call, which completely dominated the overall cost of the function. Here, though, I'm only doing the allocation once per distribution, not once per call. If I was creating new distributions all the time then these allocations would be a disaster, but I know from Step 3 (where I measured the data) that I've got a relatively short list of distributions. Allocating a chunk of memory for each distribution in that short list is fine.

I run the code again...and it's about 1.7 times faster than the baseline. Encouraging, but not a complete victory. If you think about the math here, though, you'll realize that at best I might have hoped for a 3x speedup. I walked through the list of weights 1.5 times on average before—all the way through once to calculate the total weight, then on average halfway through to look up the random value. Now I'm only doing the lookup.

The difference is the memory access. Before, the full pass through the weights pulled them all into some level of the data cache, so the second lookup pass had quick access to them. Now it takes more time for the second pass to retrieve the values, so I get a 1.7x speedup instead of a 3x speedup.

There's an obvious next step—now that memory allocation is plausible, a binary search makes more sense. That isn't hard to get right, just a bit fiddly:

```
struct Distribution
{
    Distribution(int count, int * weights, int * values);

    int chooseRandomValue() const;

    vector<int> m_weights;
    vector<int> m_values;
    vector<int> m_weightSums;
};

Distribution::Distribution(int count, int * weights, int * values) :
```

```
        m_weights(),
        m_values(),
        m_weightSums()
    {
        int totalWeight = 0;

        for (int index = 0; index < count; ++index)
        {
            m_weights.push_back(weights[index]);
            m_values.push_back(values[index]);
            m_weightSums.push_back(totalWeight);

            totalWeight += weights[index];
        }

        m_weightSums.push_back(totalWeight);
    }

int Distribution::chooseRandomValue() const
{
    int select = randomInRange(0, m_weightSums.back() - 1);

    int minIndex = 0;
    int maxIndex = m_weights.size();

    while (minIndex + 1 < maxIndex)
    {
        int midIndex = (minIndex + maxIndex) / 2;
        if (select >= m_weightSums[midIndex])
            minIndex = midIndex;
        else
            maxIndex = midIndex;
    }

    return m_values[minIndex];
}
```

Testing this attempt...and it's about 12 times faster than the baseline. Rule of thumb validated! Imagine an audible sigh of relief from the author here as I return, vindicated, to the word processor.

Most of the time a 12x speedup is enough. Once you've picked the low-hanging fruit, move on to other things. Resist the temptation to keep optimizing. It's easy to get caught up in the joy of tangible success and chase more performance wins you don't need. The function that was a performance problem is no longer a performance problem. At this point it's no different than any other function in the project. It doesn't need more optimization.

Look, I'm dealing with that temptation right now. I've got more ideas about how `chooseRandomValue` could be faster. I'm curious about which ones will actually work, and I'm fighting the urge to satisfy that curiosity. But the right thing to do once you hit your performance target is to add your optimization ideas as comments to the code, then set it aside. Declare victory and move on.

There's an obvious question that I haven't addressed. The first lesson of optimization was "Don't optimize," right? Take ordinary care, write simple and clear code, and trust that if you need to be able to make the code 5 to 10 times faster it will be easy to do so.

But what if 5 to 10 times faster isn't enough? What if you make a huge mistake in your initial design for a system, a mistake big enough that you need things to be 100 times or 1,000 times faster?

There Is No Third Lesson of Optimization

You might argue that there's a third lesson of optimization: "But don't do anything stupid." If you're going to build a high-frequency trading application where microseconds matter, then don't build it in Python. If you're defining some result structure you're going to be passing around all over your C++ code, don't design it so every copy does a memory allocation.

Honestly, I think the third lesson doesn't exist. Programmers worry too much about performance, full stop.

I get it. I have the same weakness. I'll build complexity into code for the sake of performance without a shred of evidence that performance will matter. I catch myself doing this All. The. Time.

Maybe the third lesson is "Don't worry about making mistakes, because you won't be able to make mistakes you can't fix."

If you *do* write your high-frequency trading app in Python and then run into trouble, there's still hope. Convert the stuff that needs to go fast to C++ and leave the stuff that can go slow in Python. Converting from Python to C++ will get you (another rule of thumb) a 10x speedup, and per our experiment in this Rule, we can expect an easy 5x to 10x speedup once it's in C++. Presto, a 50x to 100x speedup.

This is a pretty frequent upgrade path for us at Sucker Punch, actually—writing the first version of something in our lovely but relatively slow scripting language, then converting it to C++ if it becomes a bottleneck. We get the benefits of trying ideas quickly, knowing that there's an escape path to better performance if that proves necessary.

Remember, if you actually make a mistake so bad that you'll need to find a 100x performance win, then you're going to know about it early. Mistakes that bad don't lurk in the weeds. They're obvious from the start, so you're not going to get in too deep before you discover them. So, again, don't worry about them.

Trust in the two lessons of optimization. Write simple and clear code, and trust that solutions will appear for any performance problems you run into.

Interlude: In Which the Previous Chapter Is Criticized

I stand behind the message of the previous chapter—the first lesson of optimization is, in fact, "Don't optimize." However! This strongly expressed point of view, alone among the many strongly expressed points in this book, prompted immediate dissent from a large subset of my teammates at Sucker Punch.

It's only fair to give their well-reasoned objections a hearing! I now present the opposing points of view in the form of an imagined Socratic dialogue between me and the many dissenters, whom I've merged into a single character for dramatic purposes. They have all been given a chance to review this chapter to make sure their views are fairly represented.

The Dissenter: I formally lodge my disagreement with the premise of this chapter.[1]

Chris: I thought this chapter was just common sense. Didn't you see the Knuth quote? "We should forget about small efficiencies, say about 97% of the time: premature optimization is the root of all evil!"

The Dissenter: That quote has been used to justify all sorts of code with atrocious performance, and you're just encouraging more of it.

Chris: Wow. There's an emotional undercurrent to that feedback. Perhaps that's because you've had to spend too much time reworking other people's code to fix performance problems that shouldn't have been there to begin with? And also waiting for popular video games to boot?

The Dissenter: Yes. And yes.

---

1 This is a direct quote.

Chris: And you work on performance-critical parts of our codebase, which probably leads to a different set of priorities than someone working on, say, the logic behind our user interface.

The Dissenter: That is true, though I'd note that we both know of a game[2] whose user-interface architecture was so ill-conceived that its performance problems were deemed unfixable. The entire user interface had to be thrown out and rebuilt, and the game missed its ship date by six months as a result.

Chris: Yes. Rule 20, "Do the Math", applies to that case. In retrospect, they should have realized how bad their architecture was and fixed it much earlier in the project. Really big performance problems tend to show up right away—but only if you measure them. I could imagine a fourth rule of optimization: "Assume your code will be fast enough, but measure it anyway."

The Dissenter: I would be slightly mollified by this. The biggest reason our end-of-project optimization challenges have been manageable is that we have accurate profiling tools and use them as part of our day-to-day engineering loop.

Chris: Yes. I think this is the Sucker Punch equivalent to the testing focus a lot of coding teams have. We don't have a lot of unit tests because we're willing to let a few bugs sneak in, but we're less willing to be surprised by performance problems.

The Dissenter: Still, I think your argument for Rule 5 misses an important point. It would be easy to read it as "Don't worry about optimization," but what you're really saying is, "Simple code is easy to optimize, so write simple code."

Chris: Yes, that's right. This fits into Rule 1 and the overall theme of the book: make your code as simple as possible, but no simpler. One of the benefits of this approach is that your code will be easy to optimize.

The Dissenter: But even given that, when you write simple code, you're thinking about how it could be faster if it had to be. This has definitely come up when I've done a code review on your code. Or when you did a code review on my code. Actually, probably both.

Chris: Absolutely, we all think about that. That's not the first priority for code—correctness and simplicity are—but scouting out your escape route for optimization is good practice, even if it doesn't prove necessary. And it usually doesn't.

The Dissenter: It's true that optimization often isn't free. If an optimization makes the code more complicated, uses more memory, or adds some

---

2 Which we will not name.

pre-processing step, then the performance payoff better be worth it. Faster code isn't strictly better code. On that we agree.

Chris: Good!

The Dissenter: I'd also like to say that while simple code may be easy to optimize, being slow doesn't make code simple. In fact making code too complicated is one of the easiest ways to make it slow.

Chris: Absolutely.

The Dissenter: I've got to say, this Rule doesn't really capture what most of the optimization work I do is like. Generally, I'm not optimizing some bit of new code—I'm trying to squeeze more performance out of some code that's already been optimized. That's a lot harder.

Chris: Yes. The chapter really is about writing new code.

The Dissenter: Right, but even then, when I'm adding new code to some system I already know is performance critical, I have to think about performance from the start. I can't just write simple code and hope for the best.

Chris: That's probably true, or true at least enough of the time to make it a reasonable first step. Would you agree that worrying about performance from the start has probably led to at least some code that was more optimized than it needed to be?

The Dissenter: I grudgingly accept this, but I think it's uncommon. I still save time overall by not writing code that immediately needs to be optimized.

Chris: I'd buy that. Even Knuth's rule stops at 97%, right? If you're confident based on past experience that you're working in the 3%, then it's reasonable to consider performance in your first implementation. Just don't get carried away until you've measured your code and discovered a problem. And if everyone on your team thinks they're working on the 3%, then you all need to do a better job profiling the code.

The Dissenter: The other thing about working on optimized code is that the gains are smaller. I'll buy the idea that you can usually make new code 5 or 10 times faster without a lot of work. But at some point you exhaust the easy ideas, and then performance gains are a lot harder to find.

Chris: Yes, and at that point the rules change. You're more likely to halve your execution time with five small changes than with one big change. But even then, you've got to be alert to the idea that there could be a bigger algorithmic fix. For example, we spent weeks of effort optimizing the main draw loop in the first *Sly Cooper* game. We were eking out tiny fractions of performance at a time—only to discover that switching to a spatial partitioning system quintupled its performance.

The Dissenter: That was before my time. Cool story, though.

Chris: How about the five-step optimization process?

The Dissenter: Pretty solid. I was OK with that part of the chapter.

Chris: I can't believe none of you commented on the brilliant insight of "Step 2: Make Sure There's Not a Bug". I was proud of that step.

The Dissenter: I indicated my appreciation of Step 2 by not criticizing it. Don't expect a lot of praise, Chris. None of us want to deal with an even more self-confident version of you.

Chris: Fair enough.

Code Reviews Are Good for Three Reasons

One of the biggest changes in the thirty-something years I've been programming full time is the gradual acceptance of code reviews of various forms.

I'd never even heard of code reviews until the early '90s. I'm not saying they didn't happen, because of course they did, but they weren't widespread outside of failure-is-not-an-option situations, like medical-device firmware or control code in rockets. You know, the sort of thing where bugs kill people.[1]

For most programmers 30 years ago, the thought of someone else looking through your code felt...invasive. Sure, if you're collaborating with people, you have to at least look at the interface to your teammate's code to figure out how to interface with it, and you'll probably end up single-stepping through someone else's code—but actually walking line-by-line through code and passing judgment on it felt deeply weird. Like reading someone's diary, or (in modern terms) stumbling onto someone's browsing history.

Anyhow, in the early '90s I transferred into a team at Microsoft that had a code review policy. Lucky for me, my project was so inconsequential in that team's grand scheme of things that my project team and I were completely ignored. Among other things, we were left to decide what our code review process was. I'm not even sure what the actual official code review process for the big team was; we just did what we thought made sense and nobody ever checked up on us. I certainly wasn't going to ask for guidance, in fear of having

---

1 Real people, not virtual ones. I'm a video game programmer: virtual people die from my bugs all the time.

some horrible process imposed on us. Much better to ask for forgiveness than permission.

To my shock, I found code reviews immediately and undeniably useful. I've been doing them with my teams ever since—but not for the reasons I expected.

The most obvious reason to do code reviews is to detect bugs before they're checked into the project. If your code review process is at all rational, the person doing the review is well-prepared to understand the code that's being checked in. Maybe they've been part of the implementation of that section of the code, or they're an expert in some other bit of code that the new code relies on, or they're a frequent user of the code they're reviewing. In any case, they might be able to spot problems like an assumption you've missed or broken, a misuse of some bit of code you're calling, or maybe a change to the system's behavior that will break some other bit of code the reviewer is working on.

Does this happen? Do code reviews *actually* turn up bugs? Sure, a few—at least in my experience, given the way we conduct code reviews on my team.

That's an important caveat. *The value you're going to get out of code reviews is going to depend on how much time and effort you invest into them and how you conduct them.* Here's a quick description of how most Sucker Punch code reviews work these days:

- It's real time—two people sitting down at the same computer (at least in pre-pandemic times).

- It's informal. When you have code ready for review, you walk over to a plausible reviewer's office and ask them for a review. Our social contract is that when someone asks for a review, you agree, barring really pressing circumstances.

- The reviewer walks through the change in a diff utility while the reviewee provides commentary on the changes. It's a dialogue, with the reviewer asking questions until they're satisfied they understand the changes being made, suggesting changes, identifying things that need to be tested, and discussing alternate approaches. Having the reviewee drive the review is usually a mistake; it's too easy for the reviewer to just accept what the reviewee says instead of thinking things through for themselves.

- The reviewee is responsible for taking notes on all the suggested changes and extra tests to run. The social contract is that all suggestions are incorporated, at least by default.

- Depending on the scope of the change, the code review can take five minutes or five hours. It's rare to have a code review that doesn't result in at least a change or two before check-in. A big code review can result in pages and pages of notes to incorporate.

- Usually one code review is enough. After the appropriate changes are made and extra tests run, the reviewee commits the code. Sometimes, if it's a big change with lots of review notes, the reviewer might re-review the updated changes. If the original code reviewer isn't confident they understand some part of the change, they might suggest that another person on the team also review the code. But most often it's code review + incorporate changes + commit.

With this process, we do find bugs...but again, not in the way that you'd expect. Here are the three basic ways we find bugs in code reviews, roughly sorted by how often bugs are found, most common to least common:

- Before you ask for a review, you walk through the diff yourself to make sure you've tidied up anything embarrassing before showing it to someone else. In the process of self-reviewing, you find a bug: say, an error case you've missed. You fix the problem before anyone sees it.

- During the review, you're talking the reviewer through a particular section of the code...and being forced to explain your approach helps you understand why it's flawed. You point out the bug to the reviewer, discussion ensues, and you make a note and move on. Or, if the flaw you've discovered is big enough, you just bail on the code review entirely, restarting it once you've made the wholesale changes you need.

- During the review, the reviewer sees a problem you've missed. Or the way you describe what you've done makes it clear that you're misunderstanding some bit of code you're calling. You discuss the possible issue, agree that it's a problem, and make a note.

It's rare that the reviewer finds a bug just by staring at the code in question and applying deep insight. The code review process itself tends to surface them, either during preparation or as a result of talking through the change. That's why it's useful for code reviews to be dialogues—the process of explaining things and understanding that explanation illuminates any mismatched assumptions between reviewer and reviewee. That's good for finding bugs, but it's also good for knowing where a comment is needed or a name needs to be changed.

It's important to point out the inarguable limitations of our code review process. Every single bug in our code managed to sneak through a code review, and we have thousands of bugs! We don't make exceptions to the code review requirement—every single line of code that gets checked in has been reviewed—so every bug was missed by multiple people before it got checked in. Code reviews find bugs, but they certainly don't find all of them.

Code reviews are an inefficient way to find bugs. Yet we're still doing them. That's because finding bugs is only *one* of the reasons we do code reviews, and it's not even the most important reason.

Code Reviews Are About Sharing Knowledge

Here's a more important reason to do code reviews—properly conducted, they're an excellent way to propagate knowledge across your team.

That's particularly important for the team at Sucker Punch, because we're flexible about assignments, with coders moving pretty freely between different parts of our codebase. That works a lot better if each of the coders has basic knowledge of how the different parts of the codebase work. Code reviews are a good way of spreading this knowledge.

Imagine arbitrarily dividing the programmers on your team into "junior" and "senior" groups, based roughly on familiarity with the codebase. Senior coders know the codebase well, while junior coders are still learning its ins and outs. Our code reviews involve two people, so there are four possible combinations of seniority for the reviewer and reviewee. Only three of them are useful, as shown in Table 6-1.

Table 6-1. Code review taxonomy

	Senior reviewer	Junior reviewer
Senior reviewee	Useful	Useful
Junior reviewee	Useful	FORBIDDEN

If a senior coder reviews a junior coder's work, they're well-positioned to see problems—not just bugs in the code being reviewed, but general misunderstandings the junior coder has. Perhaps the junior coder hasn't followed the team's formatting standards correctly, or they've generalized their solution too early, or they've written a complicated solution to a simple problem. None of these are bugs, per se, but violating the Rules of Programming degrades the quality of the code, so the senior coder should note this to be fixed in the code review.

If a junior coder reviews a senior coder's work, they're less likely to find problems, but they're more likely to ask questions in order to figure out what's going on. In the process of answering those questions, the reviewee helps the reviewer understand the context for the code, leaving them with a better under-standing of how all the pieces of the codebase fit together. The reviewer sees and can ask about examples of good code—correctly formatted, appropriately engineered, and clearly structured and named.

Think of these two junior–senior interactions as part of the education pro-cess for new coders on your team. To be effective, new people need to know how all the pieces fit together, how code gets written on your team, and why things are done the way they are. Code reviews are an excellent way to transfer all of this informal knowledge to new members of the team.

Useful combination number three is a senior coder reviewing another senior coder's code. This is a good chance to find bugs and to check both coders' assumptions about how the changes fit into the overall scope of things, discuss future work in the area, identify extra tests that might be run, and ensure that at least two people understand the lines of code being checked in.

The Forbidden Code Review

The last combination, a junior coder reviewing another junior coder's work, is not useful. In fact, it can be really destructive. All of the benefits I just discussed evaporate when both coders are junior. There's no knowledge transfer, there's not enough context to find bugs, and there's no using the code review as a springboard to talk about future directions. At worst, the two junior coders reflect half-formed opinions back and forth until they seem like official team policy. When weird paradigms and conventions pop up in Sucker Punch code (which happens, despite our best efforts), it's often a result of two junior coders ping-ponging reviews back and forth. So we ban this sort of code review.

The True Value of the Code Review

We find bugs and we transfer knowledge. That's probably enough to justify the effort we put into code reviews—which usually amounts to maybe 5% to 10% of the time spent writing the code in the first place. But there's one more important benefit of code reviews, probably the most important one of all, and it's entirely social:

Everyone writes better code if they know someone is going to look at it.

They'll follow formatting and naming conventions better. They won't take shortcuts or leave tasks for later. Their comments will be clearer. They'll solve problems the right way, not with hacks and workarounds. They'll remember to take out temporary code used to diagnose a problem.

All of this happens before the code review itself—it's a result of the pressure we put on ourselves as programmers to do work we're proud of and are happy to show to our peers. It's a healthy form of peer pressure. We write better code, and over time this results in a healthier codebase and a more productive team.

Code Reviews Are Inherently Social

Summing up, well-conducted code reviews are good for three reasons:

- You'll find some bugs.
- Everyone will understand the code better.
- People will write code they're happy to share.

Look, code reviews are like any process. If you're going to spend time on them, you want them to be productive. That means thinking through what you're getting out of them and why. Get rid of the parts of the process that aren't helping, and double down on the things that work. Either you get more out of the time you're spending, or you spend less time to get the same value.

Unless you're doing something like pair programming, writing and debugging code is usually a solitary act. One lone warrior, alone at their keyboard, triumphing over bugs and recalcitrant libraries.

Code reviews aren't solitary. Most of their value comes from the social interactions between the reviewer and reviewee. You realize you've got a bug while explaining a line of code, you explain a section of code well enough that the reviewer uses it correctly the next time they call it, you clean up the hack you don't want anyone to see before asking for a review, or you learn a simpler way of doing something from the reviewee's explanation of the technique they're using.

Knowing that the value in a code review springs from social interaction, from two people talking through a change, you should make sure your code review process encourages that interaction. If the review is quiet—if the reviewer silently flips through a diff and occasionally grunts while the reviewee silently watches—then something is wrong. Yes, it's still a code review, but you're missing out on the real value that the review could provide.

And if all of your code reviews turn into arguments, you're doing them wrong! A reviewee who isn't open to the reviewer's input won't learn anything; neither will a reviewer who doesn't make the effort to understand why the reviewee wrote the code the way they did. And, in any case, code reviews are not the forum for arguing about the project direction, or about the team's conventions or philosophy. Work out those issues as a team; you won't resolve anything in a series of two-person spats.

A healthy code review strengthens your codebase while it strengthens the bonds of your team. It's a professional and open dialogue where both participants leave having learned something.

Eliminate Failure Cases

That title seems optimistic, doesn't it? What does it even mean?

Some failure cases are unavoidable, right? If I try to open a file, that file might not exist, or it might be locked by some other user. No interface-design cleverness can avoid the possibility of failing to open the file. So that can't be it. This must be more about eliminating the failures that actually are avoidable, not intrinsic to file operations—perhaps usage mistakes, like writing to a file after you've closed the handle to that file, or calling methods on an object before you've fully initialized it.

Maybe I could design systems that make it impossible to make usage mistakes, but that doesn't sound easy. And it isn't. It's pretty hard to design a system that's impossible to misuse. If you expose a feature to users, they'll find a bizarre way to use it that eventually causes everything to explode, like building a functioning 8-bit processor entirely out of *Minecraft* blocks.[1]

And if you expose a feature to other programmers on your team—they *will* misuse it. The misuse might be intentional, a desperate attempt to get something working—say, closing a file handle after calling the filesystem shutdown routine because that's the only way to avoid an unwanted callback. More likely it will be entirely unintentional, a misinterpretation of how your interface expects to be called.

The key question to ask yourself about your design is: "How hard am I making it for users of this feature or interface to shoot themselves in the foot?"

The proper answer, of course, is "Very hard," but too often we create features or interfaces that make inadvertent usage easy.

---

1 No kidding (*https://oreil.ly/rjKQT*).

And if it's easy to misuse a feature or interface, then mistakes are inevitable. In some sense, mistakes are designed into that feature or interface. What we'd like to do is to design mistakes out, rather than designing them in. But first let's look at some examples of functions that have failures designed in.

A Function That Makes It Easy to Shoot Myself in the Foot

Every C programmer knows at least one example of a function that's easy to get wrong—printf. There's a fundamental problem with how printf is designed—it expects the format string it's given to match the argument types passed, with unspecified mayhem occurring if the two don't agree.

This code works because the types agree:

```
void showAuthorRoyalties(const char * authorName, double amount)
{
    printf("%s is due $%.2f this quarter.\n", authorName, amount);
}
```

But if we tweak the format string, things fall over:

```
void showAuthorRoyalties(const char * authorName, double amount)
{
    printf("remit $%.2f to %s this quarter.\n", authorName, amount);
}
```

Roughly speaking, printf tries to interpret authorName (which is a string) as a float (uh oh). That's going to have unpredictable results. Not a crash, probably—since all 2^{64}-bit combinations can be interpreted as doubles, something will get formatted, even if it's "NaN." Next, though, printf interprets amount (which is a double) as a string (uh oh) and this is very likely to crash.

Actually, this isn't what happens when I compile and run the preceding code. Mismatching arguments like this is such an easy mistake to make that modern C compilers have hacked in an extra set of checks for printf. When I try to compile the broken example, I get compile errors (!) for both arguments. If the format string to printf is a constant, the compiler can (and does) check for type agreement.

This hack sort of proves my point—the design of printf is so bad that the compiler has to include special checks to hide the problem. Those special checks won't happen for any of the code you're writing, obviously. If you roll your own formatting function using a `printf`-style format string, the compiler is not going to check for type agreement.[2]

Shooting Myself in the Foot via a Ricochet

To actually get the crash, I sidestep the compiler's type-agreement hack:

```
void showAuthorRoyalties(const char * authorName, double amount)
{
    printf(
        getLocalizedMessage(MessageID::RoyaltyFormat),
        authorName,
        amount);
}
```

Instead of specifying a format string directly, I'm pulling it from a list. Our games get translated into lots of languages, so any user-visible string is going to come from a database of localized strings. The compiler has no way of knowing what the string is, so it can't check type agreement like it does for a literal string.

The net result is a disaster—a bad idea wrapped inside a worse one. I start with the type shakiness of `printf`, then make it worse by entirely separating the format string from its use while keeping the hidden dependence on parameter order. Inevitably, some poor translator is going to swap the order of the two parameters in the course of translating that line due to expected word ordering in their language,[3] and our code will crash.

Perhaps we can forgive `printf` its inadequacies, given that its design dates back to the beginning of time.[4] But requiring separate arguments to match in some way is widespread, despite being a bad idea. You might write a routine that expects two array-valued arguments to have the same size:

```
void showAuthorRoyalties(
    const vector<string> & titles,
    const vector<double> & royalties)
{
    assert(titles.size() == royalties.size());
```

---

2 OK, in very limited cases this isn't true. If you're using format strings that *exactly* match `printf` format strings and are willing to dive deep into your compiler's documentation, you can probably find a way to leverage the compiler's `printf` support for your case. I wouldn't recommend this. You're throwing good money after bad.

3 In this case, Irish. Per an undisclosed translation app, "Tá $%.2f dlite do %s an ráithe seo."

4 Literally—the C language and `printf` were invented very shortly after Unix time value zero. And `printf` is still used 50 years later, an unlikely fate for any code I've ever written.

```
for (int index = 0; index < titles.size(); ++index)
{
    printf("%s,%f\n", titles[index].c_str(), royalties[index]);
}
}
```

You could also include arguments whose interpretation depends on another argument: say, flagging identity matrices in a coordinate-space conversion function in an (arguably misguided) attempt to avoid the cost of a matrix inversion and a couple of matrix multiplications:

```
Point convertCoordinateSystem(
    const Point & point,
    bool isFromIdentity,
    const Matrix & fromMatrix,
    bool isToIdentity,
    const Matrix & toMatrix)
{
    assert(!isFromIdentity || fromMatrix.isZero());
    assert(!isToIdentity || toMatrix.isZero());

    Point convertedPoint = point;
    if (!isFromIdentity)
        convertedPoint *= fromMatrix;
    if (!isToIdentity)
        convertedPoint *= Invert(toMatrix);

    return convertedPoint;
}
```

At best, you'll detect these kinds of problems when you run the code—they'll sail right through compilation.

When you detect a problem, the alternatives aren't great. If you return an error for mismatched arguments, then you're stuck writing error-handling code in the caller. Writing error-handling code to account for a mistake you made in calling the function is a sign that something is seriously wrong.

Alternatively, you could add an assert that the arguments match. Depending on how you use asserts, the effect of this could range from an immediate hard crash to a message you can ignore at your own risk. No point along that spectrum is pleasant.

Enlisting the Compiler's Aid to Avoid Shooting My Foot

It would be better to design the interface to make incorrect usage impossible— or at least to make the compiler reject it. You could combine parallel arrays to eliminate the possibility of mismatched lengths:

```
void showAuthorRoyalties(const vector<TitleInfo> & titleInfos)
{
    for (const TitleInfo & titleInfo : titleInfos)
    {
        printf("%s,%f\n", titleInfo.m_title.c_str(), titleInfo.m_royalty);
    }
}
```

You could also collapse related arguments into a single argument:

```
Point convertCoordinateSystem(
    const Point & point,
    const Matrix & fromMatrix,
    const Matrix & toMatrix)
{
    Point convertedPoint = point;
    if (!fromMatrix.isIdentity())
        convertedPoint *= fromMatrix;
    if (!toMatrix.isIdentity())
        convertedPoint *= Invert(toMatrix);

    return convertedPoint;
}
```

The localized `printf` nightmare is trickier to fix. If you want to both make things type safe and also give correct results when arguments are reordered during translation, the simple solution of using strings for all the arguments to the formatting function isn't quite enough.

If you create helper functions that format a single argument, returning a field name and the formatted argument, you can solve both problems:

```
void showAuthorRoyalties(const char * authorName, double amount)
{
    // Eg "{AuthorName} is due {Amount} this quarter."

    printMessage(
        MessageID::RoyaltyFormat,
        formatStringField("AuthorName", authorName),
        formatCurrencyField("Amount", "#.##", amount));
}
```

Now you can at least detect any lack of agreement between the localized format string and the arguments you're passing, though unfortunately not at compile time. The format string can specify the arguments in whatever order makes sense for the target language and printMessage will sort things out. If the format string names a field you're not providing or doesn't name a field you do provide, that can be logged at runtime. Better yet, the mismatch could be flagged in whatever tool the localization team uses to do localization, so that they can fix it before the code even runs.

Timing Is Everything

A key point in creating failure-proof interfaces is to detect usage mistakes as early as possible.

In the worst case, the mistaken usage isn't detected at all—the feature just generates incorrect results. It relies on the caller to realize their mistake and sort things out. They won't; they'll just wonder how their foot got full of holes.

If a mistake is detected when the code runs—well, that's not great, though it's better than continuing blithely on without noting the problem. Ideally the mistake is reported in some unmissable way.

It would be better if the compiler detected the mistake instead. It's hard to miss code that fails to compile.

Or best of all, the design of the system might make it impossible to express the mistaken idea at all!

A More Complicated Example

Another place where failure is often designed in rather than out is the construction of complex objects.

Here's an example. At Sucker Punch, we write a lot of code that draws visualizations in our game world to help with debugging. For example, we have code that shows a wireframe outline of the places characters are allowed to walk. We also have code to draw little markers over the heads of NPCs that are currently aware of the player, meaning that the AI system is modeling that the NPC knows exactly where the player is. We have code that draws little numeric scores above the various places an enemy swordsman is thinking about moving to in a fight.

Debug drawing like this is more complicated than it sounds. Our debug-rendering tech supports 30 separate drawing options, all expressed on a debug-drawing context object. The 30 options determine how the program will turn simple drawing calls—like a call to draw a triangle when given three points—into actual drawing primitives. What coordinate space are those points in? Should the triangle be drawn as a wireframe or opaque? Should the triangle be visible if it's behind a wall? And so on, for another 27 options.

We could pass 30 options to a constructor, but that's pretty unwieldy. If we did that for an adapted and simplified version of our actual debug-drawing parameter structure, we might end up with something like this:

```
struct Params
{
    Params(
        const Matrix & matrix,
        const Sphere & sphereBounds,
        ViewKind viewKind,
        DrawStyle drawStyle,
        TimeStyle timeStyle,
        const Time & timeExpires,
        string tagName,
        const OffsetPolys & offsetPolys,
        const LineWidth & lineWidth,
        const CustomView & customView,
        const BufferStrategy & bufferStrategy,
        const XRay & xRay,
        const HitTestContext * hitTestContext,
        bool exclude,
        bool pulse,
        bool faceCamera);
};
```

All of these options are used by some bit of Sucker Punch code, but most callers specify only one or two options. The default choices are usually correct. We do most of our debug drawing in the same 3D coordinate space we use for the game itself, for instance. If we wanted to draw a simple sphere above a character's head, as in our example showing which NPCs are aware of the player, we might write something like this:

```
void markCharacterPosition(const Character * character)
{
    Params params(
        Matrix(Identity),
        Sphere(),
        ViewKind::World,
        DrawStyle::Wireframe,
        TimeStyle::Update,
        Time(),
        string(),
        OffsetPolys(),
        LineWidth(),
```

```
        CustomView(),
        BufferStrategy(),
        XRay(),
        nullptr,
        false,
        false,
        false);

    params.drawSphere(
        character->getPosition() + Vector(0.0, 0.0, 2.0),
        0.015,
        Color(Red));
}
```

This is pretty bad. It's an inconvenient design to use, and it has too many inherent failure points. You're never going to remember the order of 16 arguments, leaving you at the mercy of your IDE to remind you of what goes where. For arguments with unique types, the compiler will likely bail you out if you guess wrong, but good luck keeping track of which of the four random Boolean arguments at the end of the list does what. If you're just reading through mark CharacterPosition, they're a total mystery.

And keep your fingers crossed that you'll never add or remove an argument from the constructor. A quick review of the Sucker Punch codebase shows 850 or so places where we build debug-rendering parameters. I wouldn't want to be the person who removed a parameter from each of them!

Here's the thing about functions with lots of parameters—they're unwieldy to use, and the unwieldiness grows over time. That's because you're fighting a positive feedback loop. The function that's most likely to grow another parameter is the one that already has a bunch of parameters. If a function takes eight arguments, you've got pretty strong evidence that at some point you'll decide to add a ninth. The worst offenders tend to get even worse. It's best to plan an escape route when you feel like a function is starting to have too many parameters.

The most common workaround for parameter-heavy constructors is to break the construction process up into multiple calls. The actual constructor fills in default values, then you call construction-phase-only methods to fill in any non-default values. When you're done, you cap things off with some sort of commit call.

Let's imagine we want the character marker to be visible through walls, but dimmed down by 50%. A phased constructor approach might look like this:

```
void markCharacterPosition(const Character * character)
{
    Params params;
    params.setXRay(0.5);
    params.commit();

    params.drawSphere(
        character->getPosition() + Vector(0.0, 0.0, 2.0),
        0.015,
        Color(Red));
}
```

This is much better than the 16-argument version, but we've designed in a new failure point—we've introduced ordering requirements. One set of methods, like setXRay, is called while we're constructing the params. The other set of methods, like drawSphere, is called *after* we've fully constructed the params. We haven't defined what happens if we call them out of this expected order—calling setXRay after commit, or calling drawSphere before commit—so the editor and compiler can't help us. The mistake won't be detected until runtime, in this case probably as an assert inside setXRay or drawSphere.

Catching mistakes that late isn't optimal. Better than not catching them at all, but we'd like to catch them earlier, or design away the possibility.

You might use conventions to help people avoid ordering mistakes. Your team could define a set of conventions about how to build multiphase constructors—say, that there are never any arguments to the constructor, there's always a commit method, and asserts are used to flag usage mistakes. If you see a commit method, then you recognize the pattern and know how to build and use the object. That's better than no conventions, of course, but it's not the best we can do.

In the ideal case, we wouldn't rely on conventions; we'd get the compiler to enforce correct usage. It's better to make an incorrect usage impossible, not just avoidable.

Making Ordering Mistakes Impossible

One way to do this is to divide the two phases into separate objects—build the parameters, then draw using those parameters. To spice things up, let's add a couple of extra parameters. We'll draw a solid version of the sphere instead of the default wireframe, and pulse the sphere's size a bit to make it more visible. Separating the phases into objects, that looks like this:

```
void markCharacterPosition(const Character * character)
{
    Params params;
    params.setXRay(0.5);
    params.setDrawStyle(DrawStyle::Solid);
    params.setPulse(true);

    Draw draw(params);
    draw.drawSphere(
        character->getPosition() + Vector(0.0, 0.0, 2.0),
        0.015,
        Color(Red));
}
```

With this structure, ordering is implied. You need a Params object to create a Draw object, so it's natural to create it first.

There's an idiomatic C++ trick you can use to make things a little bit more concise. If you return a reference to the object itself from the set functions, you can chain the set calls together. You might want to avert your eyes if you're squeamish:

```
void markCharacterPosition(const Character * character)
{
    const Params params = Params()
                    .setXRay(0.5)
                    .setDrawStyle(DrawStyle::Solid)
                    .setPulse(true);

    Draw draw(params);
    draw.drawSphere(
        character->getPosition() + Vector(0.0, 0.0, 2.0),
        0.015,
        Color(Red));
}
```

Unless you're used to this idiom, that doesn't look like C++ code, which is not a plus. If you're a believer in the Principle of Least Astonishment—in this context, the belief that the least surprising expression of an algorithm is its best expression—then it isn't great to drop in some code that happens to be legal but looks really weird.

There is one big plus here, though. Since all the monkeying about with Params happens in our method chaining, we can make the Params object constant with C++'s const keyword. That means the compiler will stop us from mucking with it once it's built. This fixes a lingering bit of ambiguity—it isn't clear what happens if you alter a `Params` object after constructing a `Draw` object from it. Making the `Params` object `const` makes this moot.

Still, though, defining two objects is a pain. Separating the classes makes it clearer to some Sucker Puncher writing debug visualization code that they shouldn't call the set functions after the draw functions...but it would be even better if it were truly impossible, not just clear. Given how I've created the preceding code, we can do exactly that:

```
void markCharacterPosition(const Character * character)
{
    Draw draw = Params()
                .setXRay(0.5)
                .setDrawStyle(DrawStyle::Solid)
                .setPulse(true);

    draw.drawSphere(
        character->getPosition() + Vector(0.0, 0.0, 2.0),
        0.015,
        Color(Red));
}
```

Now the weird "method chain" idiom makes more sense! We don't expose the `Params` object to the rest of the code at all. It only exists long enough to construct the `Draw` object, so there's no copy of it for us to accidentally reference. This is actually pretty tight code—written like this, we've designed out failure.

Like all weird little idioms, this one is best when it's widely used on your project. Then it doesn't seem weird. Everyone on your team recognizes the idiom when it's used, and you don't violate the Principle of Least Astonishment. If your team isn't already using this idiom, then don't introduce it to solve one object-construction problem. If I saw this in a code review, I'd reject it on principle, because we don't use the method chaining idiom at Sucker Punch, but I can easily imagine another instance of Sucker Punch somewhere in the multiverse where method chaining is the standard way to solve problems like this.

Using Templates Instead of Method Chaining

The weird little idiom we *do* accept at Sucker Punch is using C++ templates to do this sort of type-safe optional argument stuff. This isn't the only problem we have that involves a big bucket of parameters, only a few of which are used by most callers, so we've established conventions about how to handle those problems.

The code we'd actually write for a `Params` object might look like this:

```
void markCharacterPosition(const Character * character)
{
    Draw draw(XRay(0.5), DrawStyle::Solid, Pulse());

    draw.drawSphere(
        character->getPosition() + Vector(0.0, 0.0, 2.0),
        0.015,
        Color(Red));
}
```

This isn't better or worse than the method-chaining model, just different. For us, it's better because it's the idiom we use; to a team that uses method chaining, it would seem opaque and weird. In the end, though, any idiom that eliminates usage errors—that stops a programmer from shooting themself in the foot—is a big step up from an idiom that relies on users to get all the details right on their own.

Coordinated Control of State

This Rule has looked at two common examples so far—argument matching and complicated constructors—and how we can design interfaces to them to eliminate usage errors. Here's a third example that pops up repeatedly in Sucker Punch games: coordinating all the code that wants to manage the state of our game's characters.

Let's say that we're deciding whether a character is going to react to some damaging event, like getting hit with an arrow. Generally, if a character is hit by an arrow, they need to react. But not always! If the game has launched into a scripted cut scene with the player walking up to talk to an NPC, then we'd rather just ignore a stray arrow flying in and hitting the player. It might look dumb, but it's better than the alternative—inflicting damage on the player when they're not in control is a cardinal sin of game design. Cut scenes are also pretty fragile, so having the player take damage could throw off everything else that's supposed to happen in the cut scene. Better just to have the arrow bounce off.

The tricky bit is that there are lots of reasons why a character might be temporarily invulnerable. It's not just cut scenes! The character might have just chugged an invulnerability potion. We might make them briefly invulnerable after getting hit by an arrow to avoid animation issues. Maybe it's convenient to make the player invulnerable while we're testing new attacks, so we add a debug menu option for player invulnerability. We end up with dozens of places where characters are temporarily marked invulnerable.

The most obvious approach is to focus on the character's invulnerability. At any point, the character is either invulnerable or not—why not just expose that? That seems simple:

```
struct Character
{
    void setInvulnerable(bool invulnerable);
    bool isInvulnerable() const;
};
```

Then we might make the player invulnerable for cut scenes like this:

```
void playCelebrationCutScene()
{
    Character * player = getPlayer();
    player->setInvulnerable(true);
    playCutScene("where's chewie's medal.cut");
    player->setInvulnerable(false);
}
```

This works, but only as long as only one bit of code at a time is monkeying with the player's invulnerability. We probably have similar code for the invulnerability potion:[5]

```
void chugInvulnerabilityPotion()
{
    Character * player = getPlayer();
    player->setInvulnerable(true);
    sleepUntil(now() + 5.0);
    player->setInvulnerable(false);
}
```

It's easy for these two bits of code to get tangled up, because the design makes usage errors easy. If the player pops the cork on an invulnerability potion during a cut scene, then we've got trouble. The cut scene starts and makes the player invulnerable via setInvulnerable, then the potion is chugged and calls setInvulnerable again. This doesn't have any effect since the player is already invulnerable. Five seconds later, the potion wears off and calls setInvulnerable (false)...while the cut scene is still rolling. Not good.

---

5 I adapted these examples from equivalent code written in our scripting language, which has built-in support for asynchronous programming through co-routines. The sleepUntil call doesn't block other code from running; neither does playCutScene in the last example. That can lead to complications, as we shall see.

If we were going to generalize based on one example, we might try to fix the problem like this:

```
void playCelebrationCutScene()
{
    Character * player = getPlayer();
    bool wasInvulnerable = player->isInvulnerable();
    player->setInvulnerable(true);
    playCutScene("where's chewie's medal.cut");
    player->setInvulnerable(wasInvulnerable);
}

void chugInvulnerabilityPotion()
{
    Character * player = getPlayer();
    bool wasInvulnerable = player->isInvulnerable();
    player->setInvulnerable(true);
    sleepUntil(now() + 5.0);
    player->setInvulnerable(wasInvulnerable);
}
```

This code tries to restore the original state of the flag to avoid entanglements. This sort of works—Sucker Punch has shipped games with solutions like this—but it falls apart once we don't have strict nesting. That could happen if the player chugs the invulnerability potion right before the cut scene starts, for instance, leaving the potion to wear off after the cut scene starts.

So how to eliminate these usage errors? Well, we could think about separating the various bits of invulnerability code. If we maintained separate invulnerability flags for each bit of interested code, then those bits of code wouldn't get entangled:

```
void playCelebrationCutScene()
{
    Character * player = getPlayer();
    player->setInvulnerable(InvulnerabilityReason::CutScene, true);
    playCutScene("it's anti-fur bias, that's what it is.cut");
    player->setInvulnerable(InvulnerabilityReason::CutScene, false);
}

void chugInvulnerabilityPotion()
{
    Character * player = getPlayer();
    player->setInvulnerable(InvulnerabilityReason::Potion, true);
    sleepUntil(now() + 5.0);
    player->setInvulnerable(InvulnerabilityReason::Potion, false);
}
```

With this approach, we check all of the invulnerability flags instead of a single flag. The player is invulnerable if any of them is set. As long as there's only one bit of code setting each individual flag we don't have to worry about the separate bits of code tripping over each other.

This approach can work, but it takes discipline. If someone gets lazy and reuses an `InvulnerabilityReason` in a different bit of code, then everything can come crashing down. And adding a new value to the `InvulnerabilityReason` enum every time we have a new bit of code that wants to tweak invulnerability will quickly get annoying.

We might think about eliminating entanglement by tracking an invulnerability count. Instead of a single flag, we count how many bits of code want the character to be invulnerable. If any bit of code wants the character invulnerable, then they're invulnerable. This leads to a pretty simple push-pop model:

```
void playCelebrationCutScene()
{
    Character * player = getPlayer();
    player->pushInvulnerability();
    playCutScene("I'm getting my own ship.cut");
    player->popInvulnerability();
}

void chugInvulnerabilityPotion()
{
    Character * player = getPlayer();
    player->pushInvulnerability();
    sleepUntil(now() + 5.0);
    player->popInvulnerability();
}
```

A push-pop model like this works. Once you're used to the idiom, it's easy to understand. It's easily extended when a new bit of code wants to monkey with damage, and different bits of code can push and pop the invulnerability count independently without breaking things.

We've still left easy usage mistakes, though. If your code forgets to call `popInvulnerability`, the character stays invulnerable forever. That's an easy mistake to make—maybe you add an early exit to your function, not realizing that cleanup is required. Or maybe you try to fix this by popping in your early exit case and end up accidentally popping twice, with even more mysterious results.[6]

---

6 I've made both of these mistakes more than once, for the record.

Better to eliminate the usage mistake entirely. The easiest way to do this is to wrap the push-pop in a constructor-destructor pair. Then the compiler becomes our ally:

```
void playCelebrationCutScene()
{
    Character * player = getPlayer();
    InvulnerableToken invulnerable(player);

    playCutScene("see you later, losers.cut");
}

void chugInvulnerabilityPotion()
{
    Character * player = getPlayer();
    InvulnerableToken invulnerable(player);

    sleepUntil(now() + 5.0);
}
```

This is pretty tight. We've made it hard to get things wrong. It's still possible to screw things up, of course. If you create an `InvulnerableHandle` someplace where it's not going to be destroyed (embedded in a structure you've stored on the heap, say), things can still go sideways. In practice, though, we've found that object lifetimes are something our programmers typically get right, and leveraging it to provide robust management of shared state works really well for us.

Detecting Mistakes Is Good, but Making Them Impossible to Express Is Better

In these examples, we were able to eliminate most of the ways to screw up, usually by enlisting the compiler to lend a hand. Anything the compiler catches makes the programmer's job easier. The techniques we used aren't complicated. We've applied them to lots of disparate problems in Sucker Punch games. And if things are structured so that you can't even express the error, even better! But Douglas Adams has something to say about the matter:[7]

A common mistake that people make when trying to design something completely foolproof is to underestimate the ingenuity of complete fools.

---

[7] Douglas Adams, *Mostly Harmless* (Del Rey, 1993).

He's right, of course. There's no perfect answer, no way to prevent all possible usage errors. We can stop the user from shooting themselves directly in the foot, but it's hard to stop all the possible ricochets. Our goal isn't a completely foolproof design—just a design that makes it really easy to get things right and really hard to get things wrong.

Despite our inability to make our designs completely foolproof, every bit of foolishness we can prevent makes our systems more robust. So look for opportunities to eliminate failure cases from your design from the start.

Code That Isn't Running Doesn't Work

Any big codebase, especially one that's been around a while, has dead ends in it: lines of code, or functions, or subsystems, that aren't getting exercised any more. Presumably they were added for a reason—at one point, those lines of code were getting called. Things change, though, and at some point whatever code was calling no longer needs to. The calls stop coming. The code has been orphaned.

Sometimes the orphaning is obvious, like a function that isn't called from anywhere else in the program. If your language and toolchain are robust enough, you might even get a warning about this particular kind of dead code.

More typically, the orphaned code isn't that obvious. It might still be mechanical, like a virtual method defined in a base class that is never called for a particular derived class. Static analysis can't pick up that sort of thing up. Or there's code written to handle some special edge case in a function, a scenario that requires special conditional handling. At some point, things change and that scenario can no longer occur. The edge case code is still sitting there, but it's never called.

The closer you look at any mature codebase, the more orphaned code you find—like enumerated values that are defined but never used, or special-case code targeted at an old version of a library you haven't used for years.

This sort of evolution of code is both natural and inevitable. The codebase is a river, winding its way back and forth through its floodplain, occasionally shifting course. Sometimes when the course changes enough, an old part of the river is cut off. It still looks like a river, but now it's a lake.

Let's look at a simplified example of code evolution. Imagine you've got some code that tracks all the characters in a game. Through the course of the game's development, your requirements for character tracking evolve, and the code evolves with it. We'll check in at four points in this evolution.

Step 1: A Simple Beginning

Things start off simple. Your game instantiates an object for each character in the game, and that object exposes some simple querying methods, mostly about whether that character considers another character a threat or an ally:

```
struct Person
{
    Person(Faction faction, const Point & position);
    ~Person();

    bool isEnemy(const Person * otherPerson) const;

    void findNearbyEnemies(
        float maxDistance,
        vector<Person *> * enemies);
    void findAllies(
        vector<Person *> * enemies);

    Faction m_faction;
    Point m_point;

    static vector<Person *> s_persons;
    static bool s_needsSort;
};
```

You maintain a list of all the characters in the game:

```
Person::Person(Faction faction, const Point & point) :
    m_faction(faction),
    m_point(point)
{
    s_persons.push_back(this);
    s_needsSort = true;
}

Person::~Person()
{
    eraseByValue(&s_persons, this);
}
```

A "faction" is assigned to each character, and characters from different factions are considered enemies:

```
bool Person::isEnemy(const Person * otherPerson) const
{
    return m_faction != otherPerson->m_faction;
}
```

You frequently need to find a character's nearby enemies, so there's a method for that:

```
void Person::findNearbyEnemies(
    float maxDistance,
    vector<Person *> * enemies)
{
    for (Person * otherPerson : Person::s_persons)
    {
        float distance = getDistance(m_point, otherPerson->m_point);
        if (distance >= maxDistance)
            continue;

        if (!isEnemy(otherPerson))
            continue;

        enemies->push_back(otherPerson);
    }
}
```

You also need to know who a character's allies are, so there's a method for that, too. That method has a little bit of trickery—characters are sorted by faction, which puts all of the character's allies together. You can early exit when you hit the end of the character's allies:

```
bool compareFaction(Person * person, Person * otherPerson)
{
    return person->m_faction < otherPerson->m_faction;
}

void Person::findAllies(vector<Person *> * allies)
{
    if (s_needsSort)
    {
        s_needsSort = false;
        sort(s_persons.begin(), s_persons.end(), compareFaction);
    }

    int index = 0;
```

```
for (; index < s_persons.size(); ++index)
{
    if (!isEnemy(s_persons[index]))
        break;
}

for (; index < s_persons.size(); ++index)
{
    Person * otherPerson = s_persons[index];
    if (isEnemy(otherPerson))
        break;

    if (otherPerson != this)
        allies->push_back(otherPerson);
}
}
```

This all works—so you trundle along with a simple faction-based hostility model. Games can get pretty far with something this simple, by the way—if you added a function to decide which factions are hostile to which other factions, you'd have the exact hostility model for Sucker Punch's *inFamous* series of games.

But while the hostility model seems to be sufficient, you soon outgrow the two query functions we started with, findNearbyEnemies and findAllies. Both are useful, but new problems arise that they don't address. Maybe you want to find all allies to whom the player has a clear line of sight. You could do this by finding the player's allies, then filtering out the ones the player can't see:

```
vector<Person *> allies;
player->findAllies(&allies);

vector<Person *> visibleAllies;
for (Person * person : allies)
{
    if (isClearLineOfSight(player, person))
        visibleAllies.push_back(person);
}
```

You also might create more methods in Person to handle cases like this—easy enough to add a findVisibleAllies method, right? Then you wouldn't need the intermediate list allies; you could skip straight to visibleAllies. But that approach gets unwieldy as the number of find functions mounts. If you add a dozen increasingly specialized find functions to Person, most of which are called from exactly one place, then you're not doing yourself any favors.

Step 2: Generalizing a Common Pattern

You've accumulated enough examples of this pattern ("find characters that match a certain set of criteria") to feel confident generalizing,[1] so you add a template function to the Person class:

```
template <class COND>
void Person::findPersons(
    COND condition,
    vector<Person *> * persons)
{
    for (Person * person : s_persons)
    {
        if (condition(person))
            persons->push_back(person);
    }
}
```

That lets you sidestep the extra memory allocations while still having reasonably legible code:[2]

```
struct IsVisibleAlly
{
    IsVisibleAlly(Person * person) :
        m_person(person)
        { ; }

    bool operator () (Person * otherPerson) const
    {
        return otherPerson != m_person &&
                isClearLineOfSight(m_person, otherPerson) &&
                !m_person->isEnemy(otherPerson);
    }

    Person * m_person;
};

player->findPersons(IsVisibleAlly(player), &allies);
```

Once the template is solid, you sweep through all the calls to Person::find NearbyEnemies and Person::findAllies in your codebase. When you find the multistage filtering idiom you used in the first line of sight example, you convert it to use the new findPersons template.

---

1 Where "enough" is "at least three," per Rule 4, "Generalization Takes Three Examples".

2 You could use a lambda here, too, of course, if your team has joined the Lambda Generation.

In this process of doing this sweep, you discover that every single one of the places you called findAllies was doing extra filtering, so you convert them all to findPersons. That's a good thing—the code is simpler, faster, and easier to read. You're happy with the results of this step. Your codebase is easier to read without all the multistage filtering. You keep trundling forward with a few findNearbyEnemies calls, a lot of findPersons calls, and zero findAllies calls.

But eventually you decide that your simple hostility model isn't good enough. You decide to let players put on disguises. Your goal is to let the player put on a security guard's uniform, then walk through a secured area without getting shot.

Step 3: Adding Disguises

Adding disguises also exposes the shortcomings of the simple hostility model you've used so far. Dividing the world into allies and enemies isn't working so well. You really need to add something in between, to reflect the ambivalence many of the characters feel for each other. A security guard considers another security guard their ally, but a random tourist falls somewhere in between being an ally or an enemy.

It's easy to abstract this more nuanced hostility model into a virtual interface:

```
enum class Hostility
{
    Friendly,
    Neutral,
    Hostile
};

struct Disguise
{
    virtual Hostility getHostility(const Person * otherPerson) const = 0;
};
```

You add a new method on Person to set the character's current disguise, using nullptr to indicate the lack of any disguise:

```
void Person::setDisguise(Disguise * disguise)
{
    m_disguise = disguise;
}
```

Obviously the isEnemy method is going to have to change a bit:

```
bool Person::isEnemy(const Person * otherPerson) const
{
    if (otherPerson == this)
        return false;

    if (m_disguise)
    {
        switch (m_disguise->getHostility(otherPerson))
        {
        case Hostility::Friendly:
            return false;

        case Hostility::Hostile:
            return true;

        case Hostility::Neutral:
            break;
        }
    }

    return m_faction != otherPerson->m_faction;
}
```

And...that's it, actually. All the other code we've written seems to work fine—no new bugs pop up, and disguises work as expected.

But there's a problem lurking—the old Person::findAllies method no longer works. And we have no idea that it's stopped working, because nobody is calling it. Adding disguises broke a subtle assumption in findAllies. It assumes that if we sort the whole list of characters on faction, then all of our allies will be adjacent to each other in the array. With disguises, that's often the case, but not always the case.

You can't count on code reviews to catch this sort of problem. Code reviews are good at finding problems in code that has changed, because that's what the review focuses on. They're not good at finding problems in code that hasn't changed, because reviewers usually skip over all of that stuff.

This particular bug is nasty because it's not even guaranteed to show up once we start creating and using disguises. As long as your allies form a contiguous range in the list of characters, everything works fine. And even when findAllies doesn't work, it still returns a partial list of allies, so the failure isn't necessarily obvious.

It's entirely possible that this bug will stay hidden forever! I still find occasional bugs in code I wrote 25 years ago, and I'm pretty sure they weren't the last bugs in that code. There are always more bugs still hiding in old code, waiting for things to change enough that these latent bugs become active ones. But things might never change in a way that exposes the latent bugs...so is this really a problem?

Step 4: The Chickens Return Home to Roost

In this case, yes, because many months later your example evolves again. Someone is writing some debugging code that lists all of the player's allies. The Person::findAllies method is perfect for this—so they call it in the obvious way:

```
vector<Person *> allies;
player->findAllies(&allies);

for (Person * ally : allies)
{
    cout << ally->getName() << "\n";
}
```

This code certainly looks fine! If disguises haven't been set, then it works perfectly. Even if disguises are being used, this code won't break in an obvious way. Even when it doesn't work perfectly, it will still list allies...it might not list all the player's allies, but you're less likely to notice a missing ally than an enemy popping up in the ally list. It's entirely possible that this change sails through your code review process, too.

But in all those months where nobody was calling findAllies, some code was written that assumed the results returned from findPersons would be in a stable order. That was an easy assumption to make—the order was perfectly stable, after all! So the new code found a couple of nearby allies and had them follow in single file behind the player, and everything worked great. Now, for some bizarre reason, on rare and unpredictable occasions the followers all panic, scrambling to new places in the single file order. Which is unshippable.

The problem, of course, is that innocuous-looking findAllies call. If new characters have been added, then findAllies re-sorts the list of characters, unpredictably scrambling the order of the results of any call to findPersons. It's going to be a serious hassle to review all of the places findPersons is called to look for problems.

Assigning Blame

So where did things go wrong?

It would be easy to point at Step 3 as the problem, because we clearly made a mistake in that step. We added disguises, but didn't update findAllies to match. That was an easy mistake to make, though—the code we wrote worked perfectly, and nothing seemed to break. No amount of product testing would find the problem in findAllies since it's not called anywhere. Even reviewing findAllies itself might not have helped—the assumption is a subtle one.[3]

You might argue that there's a mistake in Step 4, where we wrote new code that resurrected the use of the unused findAllies. That's the name of this Rule, after all—"Code That Isn't Running Doesn't Work." If I know that findAllies hasn't been getting called, then I should definitely assume it doesn't work.

That's not the general assumption you'd make as a programmer, though, at least not if you're working in a healthy codebase. When you're writing some new bit of code or fixing some problem, you have to assume that the rest of the codebase pretty much works. If you see a bit of functionality, you expect it to operate as intended. It's impossible to make progress otherwise.

The real mistake in this example was made in Step 2. When you orphaned findAllies, you created a problem. When you stopped calling it, it stopped working.

Now, that may sound ridiculous. At the point you orphaned it, the function still worked exactly as intended. Why would you discard perfectly functional code, throwing away the work it took to get it to that point? It clearly didn't stop working until Step 3, right?

Maybe. It's Schrödinger's cat, right? Once we got past Step 2, the code wasn't running anymore, so you don't know whether it was working or not. In this example, it seems simple to spot the mistake—our orphaned function stopped working in Step 3, and we discovered this (at great cost) in Step 4. But in the real world, there were dozens of steps between Steps 2 and 4. I edited out all the ones that didn't have an effect...but any one of them could have broken the orphaned function and we wouldn't have known.

It's simpler to assume that when we orphan something, it immediately stops working. Over time, this is almost certainly true. We just won't know when it happens.

---

3 If you just shouted "Where's your unit test?!?" at the book, hang tight. I'll get there.

If we make this assumption, then the mistake in Step 2 wasn't orphaning findAllies. It was not deleting findAllies when we orphaned it. When we stopped calling it, it stopped working. In Step 2, we made Steps 3 and 4 inevitable—the unexercised code was eventually going to break, and someone would eventually call it again. Much better to delete the orphaned code immediately.

The Limits of Testing

That's not the standard answer to this problem, of course. If you work on a testing-centric team, you may have wondered why the unit tests didn't catch the problem. If we have a full and complete set of unit tests, then findAllies isn't really orphaned. It's still getting called by our unit tests, so we wouldn't have to assume that it immediately stopped working.

Unit tests are imperfect, though. There are good reasons why some teams don't have unit tests for every bit of code. For one, testing is much more effective for some sorts of code than others. It's easier to test simple stateless functions with obvious effects than more complicated, stateful stuff. If you're testing the C standard libraries, it's a lot easier to test strcpy than it is to test malloc.[4] Once things are stateful it's a lot harder for your unit tests to exactly replicate the ways in which the codebase actually exercises things. Use cases will slip past your unit tests.

The test cases for findAllies were written when we wrote findAllies, long before we thought about adding disguises to the Person class. As a result, those test cases don't exercise disguises. The findAllies function works fine as long as there are no disguises in place, so no problems are reported. It's possible that the person adding disguises also realizes that the unit tests for findAllies need updating, and that they'll add tests with the particular kind of disguises that break findAllies, and that the order of everything will exhibit the problem...but that's a big ask.

There's also a cost involved for the unit test. We have to keep the unit tests for findAllies up-to-date. There's going to be some cost to running those tests. And for what? To make sure a function that no one is calling keeps working?

Ah, you say...but didn't I just claim that Step 2 (orphaning findAllies) made Step 3 (breaking findAllies) and Step 4 (tripping over the broken code)

---

4 The standard function strcpy copies a C-style string to a new home. It's simple and completely stateless. The standard function malloc is the general-purpose memory allocator for C. It manages all dynamically allocated objects (plus or minus) in your code. It's very complicated and nothing but state.

inevitable? When we orphaned the code in Step 2, we made it inevitable that we would create a bug in the orphaned code, and that someone would eventually call the orphaned code and trigger the bug. Surely it would be good to write a solid unit test so that we're more likely to detect any bugs we create, and to make it more likely that the orphaned function still works when someone eventually calls it?

Well—no. That's the point of deleting the orphaned code in Step 2. Since the code has been deleted, we don't have to worry about bugs sprouting in it, so there's no Step 3. We also don't have to worry about coders deciding to call it—it doesn't exist, so there's nothing to call, so there's no Step 4.

Instead, the coders will call findPersons, which works perfectly:

```
struct IsAlly
{
    IsAlly(Person * person) :
        m_person(person)
        { ; }

    bool operator () (Person * otherPerson) const
    {
        return otherPerson != m_person &&
                !m_person->isEnemy(otherPerson);
    }

    Person * m_person;
};

vector<Person *> allies;
player->findPersons(IsAlly(player), &allies);
```

Recognizing that a bit of code has been orphaned and can be safely removed should spark joy.[5] Seriously, this should be the happiest moment in your week. You're reducing the amount of code in your project, which makes everything easier, without reducing functionality in any way. It's quick, it's easy, and everyone is better off.

---

5 If it helps, remind yourself that you can always retrieve the deleted code from your source control system. You won't, but maybe the fact that you *could* will lead you to do the right thing.

Write Collapsible Code

I end up spending a lot of time looking through code, trying to figure out what it's doing. The subject might be code I'm trying to debug, some bit of code I'm thinking about calling from some code I'm writing, or some bit of code that's calling code I'm responsible for. And frequently the thing the code is *trying* to do isn't what it's *actually doing*, which is what makes the exercise interesting.

At its best, reading code is just like reading any other language. You sail along through the narrative, top to bottom, eagerly following the twists and turns of the plot, and reach the end of the code with a full understanding of what it does and why.

Actually, at its easiest, you sight-read code just like you'd sight-read a single word:

```
int sum = 0;
```

Or maybe:

```
sum = sum + 1;
```

There's no thinking or reasoning involved for these two examples—a glance at the code is enough to understand it. You can do the same thing for bigger chunks of code, if they neatly fit some common paradigm:

```
Color Flower::getColor() const
{
    return m_color;
}
```

You might even be able to sight-read a whole loop:

```
int sum = 0;
for (int value : values)
```

```
{
    sum += value;
}
```

That's pushing things, though. As blocks of code get bigger, it becomes harder to sight-read them—or if you're a cynical old programmer like me, it gets harder to trust your ability to sight-read them, having made the mistake of glancing at code and thinking I understood it way too many times.

When code gets too big to sight-read, you start reasoning about it. Think about what your brain is doing when you look at this code:

```
vector<bool> flags(100, false);  ❶
vector<int> results;  ❷

for (int value = 2; value < flags.size(); ++value)  ❸
{
    if (flags[value])  ❹
        continue;  ❹

    results.push_back(value);  ❺

    for (int multiple = value;  ❻
            multiple < flags.size();  ❻
            multiple += value)  ❻
    {
        flags[multiple] = true;  ❼
    }
}
```

You almost certainly didn't sight-read this—that is, you didn't glance at it and immediately think "Sieve of Eratosthenes" (*https://oreil.ly/mgEXO*). Instead, you read through the code, top to bottom, sight-reading a line or so at a time, reasoning through what each line did and how it fit with the lines that had come before.

Maybe, in detail, your thought process went something like this:

❶ flags is a vector filled with 100 falses.

❷ Looks like we're going to collect results in this array.

❸ OK, just a loop over the flags array, kind of fun to start a loop index at two, not sure what that's about.

❹ Hmm, skipping if the flags array is set for the current value, not sure what that's about either...

❺ Pushing the values we don't skip into the `results` array? That must be the output.

❻ Another loop, this time over the multiples of value.

❼ Ah, OK, we're marking all the multiples, this is the Sieve of Era-whatever... Erathosanes? That's why we started with two instead of zero or one. I understand this now: the `results` vector ends up with a list of prime numbers.

The reasoning process involved some mental juggling—seeing something you didn't quite understand, then setting it aside for a moment until you figured out how it fit together with later code, just like a juggler tosses a ball into the air knowing that they'll need to catch it a bit later. In this case, you juggled two mysteries—why the loop started at two, and why the outer loop skipped flagged values. The loop over multiples resolved the two mysteries—you caught the juggled balls and understood the code.

Jugglers can only juggle so many balls—three, in my case. The number of balls you can *mentally* juggle is a bit bigger, but it's still limited. There's a surprisingly low limit to how many thoughts you can set aside at once. If you try to track too many, you'll start losing track of a random subset of the things you're trying to remember.

That's because "mental juggling" or "cognitive load" is really just short-term memory.[1] To simplify things, there's a difference between your *long-term memory*, the things you remember permanently, and your *short-term* memory. Think about memorizing a shopping list, which exercises your short-term memory—if there are two or three items on your list, you just remember them. If there are a dozen, you'll need to write them down.

That's because there's a limit to how many things fit in short-term memory. You may have heard the approximation that you can only fit seven (plus or minus two) thoughts into your short-term memory. Try to fit any more, and the new thoughts bump out the old ones. This is just as true when you're reading code as it is when you're trying to remember all of the items on your shopping list at the grocery store.

---

1 Or maybe *working memory*, if you've chosen that side in the ongoing debate among cognitive scientists. I'm actually on Team Working Memory, but *short-term memory* is a more widely known term, so that's what I'm using.

For most of us, that seven (plus or minus two) number is a fairly hard limit.[2] Juggling three separate coding thoughts is easy—it takes no special effort to hold onto a few mysteries about some bit of code you're reading. Tracking a dozen thoughts, on the other hand, is pretty much impossible. If there are a dozen things you don't understand about some bit of code, you're in deep trouble. In programming terms, your cache overflows, and you lose track of some of the things you're trying to figure out.

This Is What Failure Feels Like

As programmers, we've all had the experience of trying and failing to figure out how some bit of complicated code works. You look through the code and see stuff you don't understand. In an attempt to understand it, you pop elsewhere in the code, searching for the function that gets called, or the structures that are defined, or looking for some comment that at least gives some context. And that search leads to another search. By the time you actually figure something out about the code, you've lost track of where you were to begin with. You're forgetting things at approximately the same rate you're learning things. Frustrating!

The Role of Short-Term Memory

Good code doesn't set its reader up for this sort of failure. Code gets written once but read many times, after all; if you want to write good code, you need to think about the person reading it later. Don't ask that person to juggle too many new ideas at once.

If some bit of code forces the reader to keep more than seven (plus or minus two) balls in the air, then balls will get dropped. And everything the reader is trying to fit into their short-term memory counts as a ball. It's not just unresolved mysteries, though those obviously count. It's also the accumulated facts and connections they're managing, hoping to see connections to the unresolved mysteries. If the total count of mysteries and facts and connections goes above your reader's limit, then things will get dropped.

Those drops make the code hard to read. If the reader drops some fact that's necessary to solve a mystery, then that mystery won't get solved. And neither you nor the reader has control over which thought gets dropped—so the one fact key to unraveling the mystery goes missing, and the mystery isn't resolved.

---

2 I have experimentally determined that coffee does not affect the limit.

Let's count the amount of running thoughts required for the code example:

```cpp
vector<bool> flags(100, false); ❶
vector<int> results; ❷

for (int value = 2; value < flags.size(); ++value) ❸
{
    if (flags[value]) ❹
        continue; ❹

    results.push_back(value); ❺

    for (int multiple = value; ❻
            multiple < flags.size(); ❻
            multiple += value) ❻
    {
        flags[multiple] = true; ❼
    }
}
```

❶ flags is a vector of 100 bools, all false to begin with (+1). Count = 1.

❷ The result looks like the output of the loop (+1). Count = 2.

❸ It's a loop with index value starting at two (+1). Count = 3.

❹ We're skipping values for some reason (+1). Count = 4.

❺ Ah, OK, we're storing the values into results. Theory confirmed (+0). Count = 4.

❻ Another loop, this time over multiples of value (+1). Count = 5.

❼ Everything collapses down to "the results vector is full of primes." Count = 1.

The thought count stays safely below the limit, even if we're counting thoughts conservatively, so there's no danger of overflowing the reader's ability to keep track of things. And the count doesn't just go up—it can also go down. When a variable goes out of scope, say, there's no point in worrying about it anymore. Or, more importantly, when a whole collection of ideas collapses into a single thought.

In this example, that happened when you realized that the code generates a list of prime numbers. You were juggling a bunch of details about the code, then realized how they fit together. Once you knew how they fit together, you stopped worrying about the details and just held onto the result. All the details collapsed into a single thought.

Good code makes this process easy. It's collapsible. It stays within the limits of short-term memory. It presents its ideas in small, related chunks, with each chunk carefully written to fit inside the reader's short-term memory, be put together, then collapse down to a single thought.

There are some easy techniques for doing exactly that. Let's look at a longer example:

```
void factorValue(
    int unfactoredValue,
    vector<int> * factors)
{
    // Clear flags marking multiples of primes

    vector<bool> isMultiple;
    for (int value = 0; value < 100; ++value)
        isMultiple.push_back(false);

    // Find primes by skipping multiples of primes

    vector<int> primes;

    for (int value = 2; value < isMultiple.size(); ++value)
    {
        if (isMultiple[value])
            continue;

        primes.push_back(value);

        for (int multiple = value;
             multiple < isMultiple.size();
             multiple += value)
        {
            isMultiple[multiple] = true;
        }
    }

    // Find prime factors of value

    int remainder = unfactoredValue;

    for (int prime : primes)
    {
```

```
        while (remainder % prime == 0)
        {
            factors->push_back(prime);
            remainder /= prime;
        }
    }
}
```

The middle section of this function is exactly the same logic as the last example—but this version is much easier to understand.[3] That's because it's more collapsible.

Good names help immensely. The names primes and isMultiple give you a head start on collapsing the loop—it's no surprise that the array ends up containing prime numbers. You might have spotted the Sieve of Eratosthenes a lot earlier if the array in the first example had been named primes—that's the power of a good name.

The name primes is also a mighty convenient handle for the idea that the array does in fact hold prime numbers. If the variable had been named xx instead, you'd have needed to burn a precious short-term memory slot remembering that xx is an array of primes. Remembering that primes contains primes is trivial. At worst, it pushes your short-term memory budget toward seven plus two, instead of seven minus two; at best, it's so self-explanatory that it's free, placing zero burden on your short-term memory.

The comments also collapse the details, since they tell you what each chunk of code is trying to do. And the comments have a second function—they mark the chunks for you. Between each pair of comments there's a chunky little code puzzle, small enough to fit inside your short-term memory, which collapses down to a single thought. The comment at the start of each chunk tells you what that chunk is going to collapse to. Reading the code in the chunk just confirms the comment.

This is the power of abstraction. It's how you manage to understand complicated things. Sure, you can only remember seven (plus or minus two) new things at a time, but you can aggregate those things into new concepts, then build things out of those aggregated concepts. Instead of remembering all the details, you remember the abstraction—and remembering a simple abstraction only soaks up one of your short-term memory slots.

---

3 This is not a smart way to factor a number, by the way. It's just an example. Rule 19 has a smarter version.

Where to Draw the Line

Marking the abstractions with function boundaries can also help readability. In
this case, that might mean splitting the three commented sections of `getFactors`
into separate functions:

```cpp
void clearFlags(
    int count,
    vector<bool> * flags)
{
    flags->clear();
    for (int value = 0; value < count; ++value)
        flags->push_back(false);
}

void getPrimes(
    vector<bool> & isMultiple,
    vector<int> * primes)
{
    for (int value = 2; value < isMultiple.size(); ++value)
    {
        if (isMultiple[value])
            continue;

        primes->push_back(value);

        for (int multiple = value;
             multiple < isMultiple.size();
             multiple += value)
        {
            isMultiple[multiple] = true;
        }
    }
}

void getFactors(
    int unfactoredValue,
    const vector<int> & primes,
    vector<int> * factors)
{
    int remainder = unfactoredValue;

    for (int prime : primes)
    {
        while (remainder % prime == 0)
        {
            factors->push_back(prime);
            remainder /= prime;
        }
```

```
        }
}
```

Then `factorValue` can be rewritten in terms of these three functions:

```
void factorValue(
    int unfactoredValue,
    vector<int> * factors)
{
    vector<bool> isMultiple;
    clearFlags(100, &isMultiple);

    vector<int> primes;
    getPrimes(isMultiple, &primes);

    getFactors(unfactoredValue, primes, factors);
}
```

Is this easier to read?

Yes and no! The functions define clear concepts, and once you understand what they do, the names help fix the concepts in your head.

But instead of a simple linear progression of code, reading top to bottom, you're hopping around from function to function. If you start by digging into `factorValue`, the first thing you run into is a call to `clearFlags`. You have to find that function and read it to see what it does. While you're looking at `clearFlags`, you have to remember where you came from in `factorValue`, track which variables correspond to which arguments, then put everything back together when you pop out of `clearFlags`.

So there's more to track, and that makes it harder to collapse the concepts. Remembering all the contextual details soaks up short-term memory slots, and you've only got seven (plus or minus two) slots to work with. Remembering where you are in a nested call chain can overload your short-term memory all by itself.

There's a thought in programming that *abstraction is always a net positive*— that anything that can be pulled into a function should be pulled into a function. The more functions, the better. Since abstraction is the tool we use to understand complicated things, it seems to follow that anything that can be abstracted should be abstracted.

The Cost of Abstraction

This is silly. There's a cost to abstraction, and a cost to separating out logic into functions. This cost can outweigh the benefits. Here's an example:

```
int sum = 0;
for (int value : values)
{
    sum += value;
}
```

That's pretty simple code to understand, if you already know that values is a vector of integers. It collapses easily—loop over the values, add them all up, and you've got the sum.

You might see this instead:

```
int sum = reduce(values, 0, add);
```

Hmm. This is certainly concise. You might infer from the names of sum and add that it's calculating some sort of sum, but that's just a guess. To know for sure, you'd need to start investigating.

To start with, it's not clear what the reduce function (or at least something that looks like a function) is doing, nor is it clear what add is, and the 0 passed as an argument is a mystery too. Searching for reduce in your codebase produces a lot of hits, but it looks like this is the one that's important:

```
template <class T, class D, class F>
D reduce(T & t, D init, F func)
{
    return reduce(t.begin(), t.end(), init, func);
}
```

OK, that's a start. Looks like the first argument to reduce is a container class, since begin and end are standard bits of C++ iteration goo. You need to find the four-argument version of reduce:

```
template <class T, class D, class F>
D reduce(T begin, T end, D init, F func)
{
    D accum = init;
    for (auto iter = begin; iter != end; ++iter)
    {
        accum = func(accum, *iter);
    }
```

```
        return accum;
    }
```

Things become a little bit clearer! The reduce function loops over a collection, successively applying a function (or function-like thing) to each element and an accumulated value. Popping back out a few levels, you expect that add will add two values, and it does:

```
int add(int a, int b)
{
    return a + b;
}
```

Now the last pieces click into place. This use of reduce is calculating the sum of the values in the array, just like the simple loop you started with...but the simple loop is *much* easier to read and understand. It collapsed easily, where this more abstracted version of the algorithm required real effort to collapse. The extra layers of abstraction aren't helping, they're just obscuring what's going on. You had to find and interpret four separate bits of code to understand things, stretching your short-term memory to do so.

Use Abstraction to Make Things Easier to Understand

I think there's a good rule of thumb hidden here for making abstraction decisions, whether that's to break logic out as a function, or to use some general-purpose abstraction to solve your specific problem. The rule is simple—will this change make the code simpler and easier to understand? Will the code collapse more easily with the change? If so, create the function or employ the abstraction. If not, don't.

The Role of Long-Term Memory

This chapter has been pretty bleak so far! A budget of seven (plus or minus two) thoughts in short-term memory is pretty stingy. It's hard to see how you could build anything even half-complicated with a conceptual budget that small, even if you're focused on collapsing thoughts into more abstract thoughts at every opportunity.

So that can't be the whole story! I know for certain that I'm completely familiar with way more than seven (plus or minus two) things in our engine.

There are dozens and dozens[4] of methods on the main Sucker Punch character class, and I know what they all do. What's going on?

Well, it's simple. All of the details I know about our game tech are stored in my long-term memory, and there's not a fixed budget for that. I am certain you have quick recall for a truly impressive amount of stuff about your projects—concepts, facts, names, development history, the person to talk to when something goes wrong, funny stories about a bug you had to fix in that one function. All of that lives in your long-term memory.

You use short-term memory to figure stuff out—it's the working storage for any reasoning you do, the place the pieces hang out while you try to figure out how they fit together. Once the puzzle pieces fit together, once the conclusions have time to settle, once you've collapsed the details into the abstraction, then the result can move into your long-term memory. That's where all the details about your project live—you're not figuring them out every time afresh, you're just remembering your conclusions from earlier.

That means that despite the obvious similarity, there's a big difference between this code:

```
sort(
    values.begin(),
    values.end(),
    [](float a, float b) { return a < b; });
```

And this code:

```
processVector(
    values.begin(),
    values.end(),
    [](float a, float b) { return a < b; });
```

I know what sort does. I know the abstraction, it's in my long-term memory. I can nearly sight-read it—the only work is looking at the comparison function to see what the sort order will be. As a result, it doesn't really take up a new short-term-memory slot to read sort. I knew values was a vector of floats; now I know values is a sorted vector of floats. That's still one thought in my cache.

My reaction to processVector is entirely different. I haven't seen it before, and I don't know what it does. The name isn't helpful—it's a good demonstration of the power of a weak name. My only recourse is to go look at the

---

4 Actually there are dozens *of* dozens. That's too many methods. We need to do some housekeeping.

processVector code, maybe by single-stepping into it,[5] in order to start figuring things out. I'm back to my painfully small budget of seven (plus or minus two) thoughts while I'm collapsing it to something simpler.

Common Knowledge Is Free; New Concepts Are Expensive

Your goal when writing code is to make it easy to understand, so it's important to keep the difference between sort and processVector in mind. A reference to sort doesn't stress the reader's short-term memory, because they already know what sort does. A reference to processVector is different—in order to understand the code, the reader needs to dive into processVector to collapse it, and that's going to stress their cache.

Code that uses abstractions or patterns that everyone on the team understands is much easier to read than code that invents new abstractions or patterns.

One takeaway from this is obvious—if you're writing code, use the standard abstractions and patterns common on your team. Don't invent new ones...unless you're confident that the newly invented abstraction or pattern is strong enough that it will become standardized across your team.

For instance, in the Sieve of Eratosthenes example, I kept an array of flags (imaginatively named isMultiple) marking which integers were known not to be prime because they were multiples of other numbers. This was a plain-old C-style array of bool values. It's easy to see that it would be possible to abstract this into a "vector of bits" class, eking out a bit of storage and very slightly better memory-access patterns.

With a BitVector class,[6] the Sieve code might look like this:

```
vector<int> primes;
BitVector isMultiple(100);

for (int value = 2; value < isMultiple.size(); ++value)
{
    if (isMultiple[value])
        continue;

    primes.push_back(value);
```

---

5 Stepping through code in the debugger is an excellent way to understand it better. 10/10, would recommend. It doesn't fundamentally change the need for short-term memory, but the debugger can be a crutch to help you remember or quickly regenerate thoughts, like what all the variables are and what values they hold.

6 The BitVector class in this chapter is (in spirit, at least) a simplified version of C++'s vector<bool>.

```
    for (int multiple = value;
         multiple < isMultiple.size();
         multiple += value)
    {
        isMultiple[multiple] = true;
    }
}
```

Is this easy to read? Well, if the BitVector class is a standard part of your team's armamentarium, something that everyone knows, then sure! It might even be easier than the version of the code that stored these flags as a simple array of bools.

Someone who doesn't know BitVector is in a different boat. Well, a reckless programmer might just assume it's, you know, a vector of bits, and sail forward. Reckless programmers tend to vote themselves off the island, though. A prudent programmer would investigate the BitVector class to make sure they understand it...and it's not trivial, even in the simplest possible version that fits the preceding usage pattern:

```
class BitVector
{
public:

    BitVector(int size) :
        m_size(size),
        m_values()
    {
        m_values.resize((size + 31) / 32, 0);
    }

    int size() const
    {
        return m_size;
    }

    class Bit
    {
        friend class BitVector;

    public:

        operator bool () const
        {
            return (*m_value & m_bit) != 0;
        }
```

```
        void operator = (bool value)
        {
            if (value)
                *m_value |= m_bit;
            else
                *m_value *= ~m_bit;
        }

        unsigned int * m_value;
        unsigned int m_bit;
    };

    Bit operator [] (int index)
    {
        assert(index >= 0 && index < m_size);
        Bit bit = { &m_values[index / 32], 1U << (index % 32) };
        return bit;
    }

protected:

    int m_size;
    vector<unsigned int> m_values;
};
```

A real BitVector class would be more functional than this—and also bigger and more complicated, of course! Even at this level of functionality there's trickiness, like creating a temporary object that wraps the ability to read and write a single bit, then relies on C++ operators to handle getting and setting the value.[7]

That's clever,[8] and it lets us write code that looks like simple array access even though it compiles to something more complicated. But sorting out the trick is going to use up slots in the reader's short-term memory—their goal is to understand the Sieve code, not sort out the details of this weird BitVector class. For programmers who haven't internalized what BitVector does—for programmers who haven't collapsed and committed the BitVector abstraction to long-term memory—its use made the Sieve code harder to understand, not easier.

---

7 The primary function of C++ sometimes seems to be allowing you to pack a universe of complexity into every raindrop of code. But I digress.

8 Not a compliment.

So if you were writing the Sieve code,[9] would it make sense to introduce a new BitVector class to handle the array of flags? No, almost certainly not! It's unnecessary work, and it makes the code harder to read.

The only justification for introducing BitVector is if you know that it's going to be used broadly enough in the codebase that everyone on the team will add it to their long-term memory, and that using it will have important advantages over preexisting solutions. And the only way you can know that is if you've identified a lot of places in the codebase where an array of bits is used, and you have identified (and hopefully measured!) the advantages and have a good reason for not just using vector<bool>. Then, and only then, does it make sense to introduce BitVector.

For what it's worth, we do have a bit vector class at Sucker Punch, used in roughly 120 places in our fairly large codebase. It's comfortable tech for most of the team—they've internalized what it does, so a reference to the bit vector class isn't going to trigger an investigation. It's part of our common knowledge, so it's safe to use. But it wasn't introduced based on one use case—we wrote it based on lots of examples of code working with large arrays of bits.

Putting It All Together

The best code—which is to say, the easiest code to read and understand—leverages how short-term and long-term memory work together. It leverages the standards and conventions of your team, because all of that stuff is already in everyone's long-term memory. When new thoughts are introduced, they pop up in small-to-medium-sized chunks, small enough to fit inside the reader's short-term memory. Those chunks have simple, easily abstracted functionality and carefully chosen names, which makes them easy to collapse and commit to long-term memory.

The result? A codebase that is easy to read and easy to learn—that makes it easy to collapse new ideas into simple abstractions, then does the same thing with those abstractions recursively until the whole codebase is clear.

---

9 Please don't generate prime numbers this way, though. Humanity has invented much better ways of generating primes in the intervening 2,250 years. Hats off to Eratosthenes, though! The Sieve is the third or fourth most impressive thing on his resume, and I still know what it is.

Localize Complexity

Complexity is the enemy of scale.

You know that simpler code is better—as simple as possible, but no simpler, per Rule 1—but that Rule becomes harder to follow as the scale of your project increases. It's easy to keep your code simple for simple problems, but as code grows and matures it naturally grows more complicated. And as it grows more complicated, it becomes harder to work with—you lose the ability to keep all the details in your head. Every time you attempt to fix a bug or add a new feature, you trip over unpredictable side effects—every step forward is matched by an unexpected step backward.

Part of the solution is to look for opportunities to keep things simple or make things simple. That's Rule 1. But complexity can't be eliminated entirely; any moderately functional and long-lived bit of software is going to have to weather the complexity inherent in the problems the software solves. But complexity can be managed.

To borrow a sports cliché: you can't stop complexity, you can only hope to contain it.

Along those lines, a useful strategy is to isolate any complexity you can't eliminate. If the internal details of some bit of code are complicated, but its external interface is simple, the complexity presents less of a problem. When you're inside that bit of code you have to cope with its internal complexity, but outside the code you don't have to worry about it.

A Simple Example

Consider the sine and cosine functions in your language of choice. The external interface is simple—call the function, get the sine or cosine of the angle passed in. The internal details are complicated, though.

I was many years old before I wondered how these functions were actually implemented. Until then, as far as I was concerned, they just magically produced the right answer[1]...and this blissful ignorance was perfectly OK! Whatever complexity existed inside of the implementation of the sine and cosine functions didn't affect how I used them. They just worked in the way I expected.

You can draw a circle without knowing the implementation details of sine and cosine:

```
void drawCircle(Point center, float radius, Color color)
{
    int count = int(ceil(pi / acos((radius - 1.0) / radius)));
    Point previousPoint = center + Vector(radius, 0.0, 0.0);
    for (int index = 1; index <= count; ++index)
    {
        float angle = 2.0 * pi * index / count;
        Point nextPoint = center +
                          radius * Vector(cosf(angle), sinf(angle), 0.0);

        drawLine(previousPoint, nextPoint, color);

        previousPoint = nextPoint;
    }
}
```

There's complexity somewhere inside sinf and cosf (the C standard library's sine and cosine functions for 32-bit floats), but it doesn't leak out through the simple abstraction of those functions into the rest of your code.[2] The complexity is safely localized.

Hiding Internal Details

The same rule applies to your own code. Whenever possible, you should isolate complexity, confining it to clearly defined sections of your code.

---

1 As I recall, my naive guess the first time my curiosity was piqued amounted to "big tables and linear interpolation." I'm a little embarrassed by this guess; I knew what a Taylor series was at the time.

2 Both sinf and cosf are implementation-dependent and can be surprisingly complicated. I've tried to write short explanations here and failed; the important thing to keep in mind is that the functions don't need to calculate an *exact* value, only a value that's accurate to the resolution of a floating-point value, and that modulus math can reduce the angle to a convenient range for the approximation. Interestingly, there are x86 instructions to calculate sine and cosine, but modern compilers don't use them unless explicitly ordered to do so. Those instructions, introduced in 1987, have known flaws that can't be fixed for the sake of backward compatibility. Sigh.

Imagine that you've got a list of customer records, and you're writing a function to return a list of customers who've recently purchased something. The customer records look like this:

```
struct Customer
{
    int m_customerID;
    string m_firstName;
    string m_lastName;
    Date m_lastPurchase;
    Date m_validFrom;
    Date m_validUntil;
    bool m_isClosed;
};
```

The complexity here is that not all customer records in your list are valid. Some customer accounts have expired or haven't been activated yet, and other accounts have been closed by the customers. Your function will need to exclude those invalid customer records:

```
void findRecentPurchasers(
    const vector<Customer *> & customers,
    Date startingDate,
    vector<Customer *> * recentCustomers)
{
    Date currentDate = getCurrentDate();

    for (Customer * customer : customers)
    {
        if (customer->m_validFrom >= currentDate &&
            customer->m_validUntil <= currentDate &&
            !customer->m_isClosed &&
            customer->m_lastPurchase >= startingDate)
        {
            recentCustomers->push_back(customer);
        }
    }
}
```

The complexity introduced by invalid customer records isn't localized—it has leaked into this unrelated function. Every loop through the customer list now has to check for invalid customer records. And if the rules determining validity change, every one of those loops will have to be updated.

The code in the previous example is pretty bad design, honestly. There's no reason to duplicate the customer validity check in every loop—one of the promises of object-oriented design was making it easier to hide exactly this sort of complexity. At a minimum, the eligibility rule should be encapsulated:

```
struct Customer
{
    bool isValid() const
    {
        Date currentDate = getCurrentDate();

        return m_validFrom >= currentDate &&
               m_validUntil <= currentDate &&
               !m_isClosed;
    }

    int m_customerID;
    string m_firstName;
    string m_lastName;
    Date m_lastPurchase;
    Date m_validFrom;
    Date m_validUntil;
    bool m_isClosed;
};
```

That makes the loop a little bit simpler:

```
void findRecentPurchasers(
    const vector<Customer *> & customers,
    Date startingDate,
    vector<Customer *> * recentCustomers)
{
    Date currentDate = getCurrentDate();

    for (Customer * customer : customers)
    {
        if (customer->isValid() &&
            customer->m_lastPurchase >= startingDate)
        {
            recentCustomers->push_back(customer);
        }
    }
}
```

That's only a half-measure, though. A better solution lies upstream: instead of looping over all customers, it should loop over *valid* customers. Whatever bit of your code provides a list of customers should also provide a list of valid customers, likely computed from the list of all customers. Then your code will be appropriately simple:

```
void findRecentPurchasers(
    const vector<Customer *> & validCustomers,
    Date startingDate,
    vector<Customer *> * recentCustomers)
{
    Date currentDate = getCurrentDate();

    for (Customer * customer : validCustomers)
    {
        if (customer->m_lastPurchase >= startingDate)
        {
            recentCustomers->push_back(customer);
        }
    }
}
```

With this change, all the complexity is localized to the function that returns a list of valid customers. Code like findRecentPurchasers doesn't need to worry about customer validity, and is easier to write and understand as a result.

Distributed State and Complexity

Object-oriented design can help localize complexity, but it's not a panacea. It's easy to get in trouble, especially when you've distributed state across a set of objects instead of localizing it in a single object.

Distributing state isn't necessarily a problem! Sometimes the most natural way of modeling a system is to create multiple objects that jointly manage the system's state. The promise of object-oriented design is that this sort of multiple-object design can still hang together—each object manages its own state, with well-defined interactions between the objects.

That promise of an easy-to-understand object-oriented design won't be fulfilled without some careful coding, though. It's easy to end up with pretty rickety code if you're trying to do something that depends on the current state of multiple objects.

Here's an invented example. You're building a stealth game, in which part of the fun is skulking around without getting spotted by your enemies. In this family-friendly example, the player is trying to sneak up behind other characters in order to tape "kick me" signs to their backs. To make this easier, you want to show a little "eye" icon on screen. The eye is closed when none of the player's enemies can see them, but opens when an enemy has a clear line of sight to the player. A closed eye means the player is safe, while an open eye means they're at risk of being spotted.

You've got a handful of objects and classes to model this: an object for the player, objects for all the other characters, an object for the eye icon, and an object that tracks which characters have a clear line of sight to which other characters. The last object, the awareness manager, provides a way for you to register a callback function that is called whenever a particular character is spotted by another character, and a second callback function that is called when that other character loses sight of the registered character.

Given these objects, an obvious way to implement this feature centers on the player object. The player object can implement an awareness callback function, then use that callback to keep count of how many other characters have spotted the player. If that count is zero, the player object sets the eye icon to closed; otherwise, it sets it to open.

The awareness manager looks like this:

```
class AwarenessEvents
{
public:

    virtual void OnSpotted(Character * otherCharacter);
    virtual void OnLostSight(Character * otherCharacter);
};

class AwarenessManager
{
public:

    int getSpottedCount(Character * character);
    void subscribe(Character * character, AwarenessEvents * events);
    void unsubscribe(Character * character, AwarenessEvents * events);
};
```

The eye icon is even simpler:

```
class EyeIcon
{
public:

    bool isOpen() const;
    void open();
    void close();
};
```

Given these objects, the player code is easy to write. Get an initial count from the awareness manager when the player object is created and implement the AwarenessEvents interface to catch changes. With an accurate count of other characters who can see the player, the eye icon can be opened or closed appropriately:

```
class Player : public Character, public AwarenessEvents
{
public:

    Player();

    void onSpotted(Character * otherCharacter) override;
    void onLostSight(Character * otherCharacter) override;

protected:

    int m_spottedCount;
};

Player::Player() :
    m_spottedCount(getAwarenessManager()->getSpottedCount(this))
{
    if (m_spottedCount == 0)
        getEyeIcon()->close();

    getAwarenessManager()->subscribe(this, this);
}

void Player::onSpotted(Character * otherCharacter)
{
    if (m_spottedCount == 0)
        getEyeIcon()->open();

    ++m_spottedCount;
}

void Player::onLostSight(Character * otherCharacter)
{
    --m_spottedCount;

    if (m_spottedCount == 0)
        getEyeIcon()->close();
}
```

This isn't bad code. There's not a lot of it, and the code itself is pretty easy to read. There's a bit of subtlety in choosing when to compare m_spottedCount to 0, but it's not hard to figure out. I think this code is defensible.

Capacitated?

Like all designs, though, this example evolves. To add a bit of a challenge for the player, we give it a twist: the eye icon should be open whenever the player is incapacitated. Or, to put it another way, the eye icon should be closed when none of the enemies have spotted the player *and* the player isn't incapacitated.

In this case, the Player class has a setStatus method that's called to mark changes in the player's overall well-being. It's easy enough to insert some code into setStatus to catch cases where the player becomes incapacited or recovers to be fully...um, capacitated? Unincapacitated? Whatever. You only care about a change in the player's status when m_spottedCount is zero, since otherwise the eye icon is already open. Similarly, when the spotted count's zero-ness changes, you only have to worry about the eye icon if the player isn't incapacitated:

```
enum class STATUS
{
    Normal,
    Blindfolded
};

class Player : public Character, public AwarenessEvents
{
public:

    Player();

    void setStatus(STATUS status);

    void onSpotted(Character * otherCharacter) override;
    void onLostSight(Character * otherCharacter) override;

protected:

    STATUS m_status;
    int m_spottedCount;
};

Player::Player() :
    m_status(STATUS::Normal),
    m_spottedCount(getAwarenessManager()->getSpottedCount(this))
{
    if (m_spottedCount == 0)
```

```
        getEyeIcon()->close();

    getAwarenessManager()->subscribe(this, this);
}

void Player::setStatus(STATUS status)
{
    if (status == m_status)
        return;

    if (m_spottedCount == 0)
    {
        if (status == STATUS::Normal)
            getEyeIcon()->close();
        else if (m_status == STATUS::Normal)
            getEyeIcon()->open();
    }

    m_status = status;
}

void Player::onSpotted(Character * otherCharacter)
{
    if (m_spottedCount == 0 && m_status == STATUS::Normal)
        getEyeIcon()->open();

    ++m_spottedCount;
}

void Player::onLostSight(Character * otherCharacter)
{
    --m_spottedCount;

    if (m_spottedCount == 0 && m_status == STATUS::Normal)
        getEyeIcon()->close();
}
```

This has added some complexity, especially in how the two overlapping conditions for showing the health indicator interact with each other. It still doesn't seem disastrous, though.

The assumptions the code makes to minimize work—like only updating the eye icon in CPlayer::setStatus when the spotted count is zero—are more subtle now. It's not too hard to figure out what's going on, but there's a price in complexity being paid for a little bit of efficiency.

Things Start to Get Foggy

The design evolves again, surprising absolutely no one. This time you're adding weather effects. If the weather is foggy, then the eye icon should be open, just like when the player has been spotted or is incapacitated.

The weather system, like the awareness system, provides a simple query and callback API:

```
enum class WEATHER
{
    Clear,
    Foggy
};

class WeatherEvents
{
public:

    virtual void onWeatherChanged(WEATHER oldWeather, WEATHER newWeather);
};

class WeatherManager
{
public:

    WEATHER getCurrentWeather() const;
    void subscribe(WeatherEvents * events);
};
```

This fits into the pattern you used for awareness. Implement a weather callback, add some initialization code, mix some new logic into the existing checks, and you've got a working system:

```
class Player :
    public Character,
    public AwarenessEvents,
    public WeatherEvents
{
public:

    Player();

    void setStatus(STATUS status);

    void onSpotted(Character * otherCharacter) override;
    void onLostSight(Character * otherCharacter) override;

    void onWeatherChanged(WEATHER oldWeather, WEATHER newWeather) override;
```

```
protected:

    STATUS m_status;
    int m_spottedCount;
};

Player::Player() :
    m_status(STATUS::Normal),
    m_spottedCount(getAwarenessManager()->getSpottedCount(this))
{
    if (m_spottedCount == 0 &&
        getWeatherManager()->getCurrentWeather() != WEATHER::Foggy)
    {
        getEyeIcon()->close();
    }

    getAwarenessManager()->subscribe(this, this);
    getWeatherManager()->subscribe(this);
}

void Player::setStatus(STATUS status)
{
    if (status == m_status)
        return;

    if (m_spottedCount == 0 &&
        getWeatherManager()->getCurrentWeather() != WEATHER::Foggy)
    {
        if (status == STATUS::Normal)
            getEyeIcon()->close();
        else if (m_status == STATUS::Normal)
            getEyeIcon()->open();
    }

    m_status = status;
}

void Player::onSpotted(Character * otherCharacter)
{
    if (m_spottedCount == 0 &&
        m_status == STATUS::Normal &&
        getWeatherManager()->getCurrentWeather() != WEATHER::Foggy)
    {
        getEyeIcon()->open();
    }

    ++m_spottedCount;
}

void Player::onLostSight(Character * otherCharacter)
```

```
    {
        --m_spottedCount;

        if (m_spottedCount == 0 &&
            m_status == STATUS::Normal &&
            getWeatherManager()->getCurrentWeather() != WEATHER::Foggy)
        {
            getEyeIcon()->close();
        }
    }

    void Player::onWeatherChanged(WEATHER oldWeather, WEATHER newWeather)
    {
        if (m_spottedCount == 0 &&
            m_status == STATUS::Normal)
        {
            if (oldWeather == WEATHER::Foggy)
                getEyeIcon()->close();
            else if (newWeather == WEATHER::Foggy)
                getEyeIcon()->open();
        }
    }
```

Again, if you've just written code like this, it can feel reasonable. I've certainly written code like this and not felt bad about it!

It's an evolution of the approach of the first version—look at the state of the world when the player object is initialized, then track changes in the world's state to keep the eye icon up-to-date.

Conceptually, at least, there's a common, repeated theme that grew out of the initial implementation—don't bother updating the eye icon when its state shouldn't change. When the weather changes, there's no need to update the eye icon unless the spotted count is zero and the player isn't incapacitated. If the spotted count is nonzero or the player is incapacitated, then the eye icon is already open and should remain so.

There are three variations of that idea in the code: for line of sight, player status, and current weather. The idea is expressed slightly differently for each of them, but it's still just one idea, so it doesn't seem that complicated.

Take a step back, though. It's easy to see the shared idea when you're writing the code—it's your idea, after all! Imagine a teammate was looking at the last example. Will the basic idea be obvious to them? Uh...not so much.

If you know the idea—that is, don't bother updating the eye icon when its state shouldn't change—then you can see how the idea gets expressed in each of its repetitions. If you're trying to go the other direction, to infer the basic idea from all the ways it's expressed...well, then it's not so obvious.

Rethinking the Approach

There's a bigger problem here, though. The user-visible design of this feature is pretty simple—the eye icon should be closed when three conditions are met:

- No enemy has spotted the player.
- The player isn't incapacitated.
- The weather isn't foggy.

As written earlier, you have five (!) separate implementations of this logic, all expressing those three conditions in different ways. That's confusing. And there's no simple, straightforward implementation of the rules—no place where you just check the three conditions. All five implementations are variations, all using bits of context to minimize the work done.

If your design changes in any way, you need to update each of the five implementations to match. For example, if you add a new WEATHER:HeavyFog state for the weather system, then you have to add checks for it in all the places you checked for WEATHER:Foggy.

More dangerously, what if the methods you've added change in some other way? Maybe you decide the player model should turn his head to look at any enemy that spots him, which means more code in CPlayer::onSpotted. Now you have to make sure that you're not inadvertently breaking the stealth indicator.

There's a pretty big problem underlying this code—it fails to localize the complexity of the design. You've got a simple design—the three conditions outlined at the start of the section—but you've scattered the implementation of that design across five separate implementations, all written slightly differently. Each condition adds a bit of complexity, and each bit of complexity interacts with all the other bits of complexity. They get tangled up very quickly.

If you've got a complicated idea, like the rules for when the eye icon is open or closed, then aim to express that complicated idea in one place.

In this case, that means one straightforward implementation of the three conditions. Then you can build the rest of the code around that implementation. Leaving the rest of the system alone, you might end up with something like this:

```cpp
enum class STATUS
{
    Normal,
    Blindfolded
};

class Player :
    public Character,
    public AwarenessEvents,
    public WeatherEvents
{
public:

    Player();

    void setStatus(STATUS status);

    void onSpotted(Character * otherCharacter) override;
    void onLostSight(Character * otherCharacter) override;

    void onWeatherChanged(WEATHER oldWeather, WEATHER newWeather) override;

protected:

    void refreshStealthIndicator();

    STATUS m_status;
};

Player::Player() :
    m_status(STATUS::Normal)
{
    refreshStealthIndicator();

    getAwarenessManager()->subscribe(this, this);
    getWeatherManager()->subscribe(this);
}

void Player::setStatus(STATUS status)
{
    m_status = status;

    refreshStealthIndicator();
}

void Player::onSpotted(Character * otherCharacter)
```

```
{
    refreshStealthIndicator();
}

void Player::onLostSight(Character * otherCharacter)
{
    refreshStealthIndicator();
}

void Player::onWeatherChanged(WEATHER oldWeather, WEATHER newWeather)
{
    refreshStealthIndicator();
}

void Player::refreshStealthIndicator()
{
    if (m_status == STATUS::Normal &&
        getAwarenessManager()->getSpottedCount(this) == 0 &&
        getWeatherManager()->getCurrentWeather() != WEATHER::Foggy)
    {
        getEyeIcon()->close();
    }
    else
    {
        getEyeIcon()->open();
    }
}
```

Here, all five implementations of the condition checks are collapsed into a single method, refreshStealthIndicator. That method is called whenever there's a change in the conditions that method checks. There's still a little bit of nonlocalized complexity, because the connection between the conditions you check and the callbacks that detect changes to those conditions isn't obvious, but there's way less of this than before.

And this implementation is linear with the number of conditions. If a new condition is added, you can add a new check to refreshStealthIndicator, write a bit of initialization code, and check for changes in the condition in one or two places. If you had 10 conditions, you'd have 10 times as much code.

That's much better than the earlier examples that didn't localize the complexity. In computer science terms, the code had *quadratic complexity*: every time you added a new condition, you added a new place to check all the conditions and a new check in each of the existing implementations of the logic. As a direct result, the number of lines of code implementing your design increased by the square of the number of conditions in that design. That's not good! You'll quickly run into a wall if your code's complexity grows quadratically.

Localized Complexity, Simple Interactions

The thing you want to avoid at all costs is complicated interactions between different parts of your system. You can accept some complicated details, *as long as the complexity is localized*. A component with a simple interface and simple interactions but some complicated internal details won't sink your project. A component with a complicated interface *and* complicated interactions might be your death knell, even if the internal details are simple.

A system built of components with simple interactions tends to have linear complexity. Each component makes the system a little bit more complicated, but the complexity stays manageable.

If the interactions between components are complicated, things get out of control fast.

If adding a new feature entails writing code in a lot of places, that's a bad sign. At best, it means the new feature is a misfit with your existing code—and if every feature you add requires code in lots of places, then you've probably failed to localize complexity. That's going to end in tears.

Is It Twice as Good?

Every project eventually hits the natural limits of its architecture—you hit some problem that just doesn't fit the way things work. Maybe you need to add a feature that can't be expressed in your paradigm. Say you've got a filtering mechanism that lets you specify a set of criteria that all need to be met, and you run into a case where you need to OR some criteria instead of ANDing them.

Or the shape of the data has changed. You built the system to solve problems of some size, and over time it starts to be applied to problems of a different size or shape, and you're running into existential performance problems.

It could be that things are just getting tangled. Your paradigm provides ways to tweak the core behavior of the system in special cases, which is one of the reasons it's lasted as long as it has. But now the extension mechanism is used in *every single case*, not just special ones. Every use of the system is a hopscotch through different exceptional cases, and it's hard for people to figure out *whether* something new works, much less *how* it works.

Maybe some bit of code is old enough that it just doesn't fit with the rest of your codebase. You've got a bit of C code in your fairly forward-thinking C++ project, and you recoil at all of its hand-rolled pointer structures. It represents an older, alien way of thinking, and everyone wants to rewrite it in a more modern paradigm.

This sort of thing is natural and inevitable, and shouldn't cause you to panic. It's not even really a problem. It's just how things go.

If you think you can forestall this—that hitting the natural limits of your architecture is a sign of poor initial design, and that a better design would have avoided the problem—then remember the example of Rule 4, that generalization takes three examples. Your initial design may well have been poor. But the most likely result of trying to predict the future would have been a similarly poor but more complicated design that would have hit its limits even earlier.

You won't hit architectural limits on every single part of your project, either. Some parts will happily tick along for years without any rework. That's not an accident—if you make good choices in your initial design, the problems you're solving stay pretty much the same, you and your teammates are diligent about keeping things tidy, and whatever exceptional cases you run into are localized and easily handled, then things can trundle along with no changes indefinitely.

That's why futureproofing is so dangerous. Some of the time it's not necessary, and the rest of the time it doesn't work.

Three Paths Forward: Ignore, Tweak, or Refactor

Anyhow, you've run into a natural limit of some sort. That doesn't mean you're forced to tear up the code and start again from scratch.

You could just live with the natural limit, for instance. Don't allow OR clauses in your filtering, or buy bigger hardware to deal with your performance problems, or live with some extra complexity and old-fashioned code.

Small tweaks and exceptional cases might also work. Maybe your filtering is really an AND-of-ORs, like most websites, and you can handle the one extra OR in your special case by combining two categories in your UI. Maybe most of your performance issue springs from recalculating some bit of data, and a little bit of caching will mostly fix the problem. Maybe every use of the system runs through the exceptional mechanism, but most of those exceptions are all the same thing, and you can just fold that case into your core code path and get rid of a bunch of exceptional cases. Maybe the only really old-fashioned thing is the use of a set of half-baked macro-driven functions to deal with allocating C arrays, and it's not too hard to just convert them to std::vector.

Or maybe you really *do* need to make some major changes. Your architecture was designed to address the problem as you understood it when work started. The problem has changed, though—or maybe your understanding of the problem is deeper now. Your current architecture just can't solve the problem as you now understand it, and you see a better approach.

So how do you decide which of these three basic approaches to take? Do you ignore the issue, tweak things to address it, or do a bigger refactoring?

Gradual Evolution Versus Continual Reinvention

There's a natural tendency in programmers to handle this question poorly—to make big changes for the wrong reason at the wrong time and end up causing more problems than they solve.

More specifically, there are two subspecies of programmers. Type One programmers think incrementally. They look at each new problem in terms of the existing solution; they always solve problems by tweaking the current design. Type Two programmers think of the problem and solution together; they're attracted to fixing all the issues with a system, not just the issue at hand, and jump at the chance to start over with a new design.

Either tendency taken to extremes is a disaster. If all fixes are incremental, you end up trapped, pushing off requests for improvements to the project, slowly buried under the weight of years of tweaks and exceptional cases. If no fixes are incremental, if all changes are ground-up reworks, then you thrash in place. You're continually throwing out the things you've learned about the last architecture. Every new architecture brings a new set of problems and you never make progress.

As in most things, the best results come from striking a balance. Choosing the right approach—ignore, tweak, or refactor—can be tricky, but knowing your tendencies and the tendencies of your coworkers can help you make better decisions. If your response to uncertainty is to make the decision that is comfortable for you, then you risk choosing the same alternative every time. If you're a Type One programmer, the comfortable decision is incremental, and all problems are solved by tweaking or ignoring. If you're a Type Two programmer, the comfortable decision is to rework everything, so that's what happens every time. That's not good; you need to balance the two.

Some red flags that Type One thinking might be getting out of control:

- Describing the issue at hand in terms of the current architecture. That might be as simple as using internal terms instead of describing the issue in its own problem space. Sometimes it's hard for Type One coders to even think about the problem except in terms of the existing architecture, and this shows up in the language they use.

- Using words like *impossible* to describe the issue. That's almost certainly not true—at worst, the issue is difficult to solve without major changes to the system architecture.

- Deploying the project schedule as a conversation-stopper. This is not to imply that schedule concerns aren't valid—they obviously are! But if the first and only argument you make against a big change is that it won't fit in the schedule, then you might be stuck in Type One thinking.

- It's been years since the last major change was made to the system, despite many incremental changes to it.

Some warning signs that Type Two thinking is taking over:

- The best reason you've got for reworking the system is "we really need to clean up that bit of code."

- The decision to rework a system is driven by one particular case, like a single feature that's hard to implement, or a dataset that creates poor performance.

- The argument for reworking things is driven by performance or resource issues, but nobody has actually profiled the system to find the bottleneck.

- You present arguments for reworking the system in terms of the solution, not the issue at hand. Any proposals that aren't grounded in the problem are pretty suspect.

- Some bright, shiny object—a new language, a new library, some new language construct—is central to the proposed reworking.

You might have recognized some of your own thought patterns in there! I certainly do—I'm Type Two at heart and have to keep that mind when I'm making decisions. Luckily there are lots of Type Ones on my team who I can rely on to provide some decision-making balance.

It's also common to get mixed signals, with Type One and Type Two warning signs popping up for the same problem. For example, maybe you're considering a big change for a system that hasn't seen fundamental rework for years, but the impetus for the suggested change appears to be excitement about deploying a cool new database technology. That's a Type One signal (the system's architecture has been static for a long time) and a Type Two signal (Squee! A new database!) mixed together.

Recognizing these patterns can help your decision-making process, but they won't make the decision for you. You might see some conservative Type One patterns in your logic, but that doesn't mean an incremental solution is wrong! Nor does the presence of Type Two signals mean that reworking your system is inappropriate. You need something more to help you make the big decision about whether to embark on major rework or keep making incremental changes.

A Simple Rule of Thumb

Here's my simple rule of thumb for making a big change: *is it twice as good?*

If you're confident that after your changes, the reworked system will be twice as good as the system you've got now, then the reward is big enough to justify the disruption and the new problems that the rework will inevitably introduce. If not—if the new system isn't going to be twice as good as the current one—then it's better to address the issue incrementally.

Sometimes the answer is obvious. You absolutely need to do something, and your current architecture absolutely can't do it. Say you need to rework your server code to support new legally mandated privacy restrictions. Those restrictions require a "right to be forgotten," implying functionality that your current architecture fundamentally can't support because it intermixes data histories in a way that precludes removing an individual's old data.

Will a new system be twice as good? In this case, you need to do something that the reworked system will support and the current system can't support. In some sense, the reworked system is infinitely better than the old one. Since "infinitely" is comfortably larger than "twice," the decision is clear, and you set forth on your rework.

More commonly the answer isn't as obvious, and you need to do some measurement (if possible) and estimation (if measurement isn't possible) to decide whether the new answer is twice as good as the old one.

For instance, when Sucker Punch started work on *Ghost of Tsushima*, we realized that the way we physically modeled the ground was going to struggle with the size of the new game. Our previous games had all represented the ground as a surface composed of hand-built triangles, but the new game covered 40 or so times as much ground. The actual ground of the island of Tsushima was created using a collection of height maps, each a 512×512 bitmap representing a uniform grid of heights covering a 200-meter square.

The incremental solution was to convert the height maps to triangles and feed them through our normal physics pipeline. This worked fine, but it was really bulky—there were half a million triangles, and even after some light optimization we were spending many megabytes of storage keeping track of all of them.

We had an alternative—we could rework the physics engine to support height maps directly, but this implied a lot of work. It meant handling the height maps' interaction with all of the other basic physics primitive types, figuring out how to encode the extra information our physics engine needed about surface types into the height map, adding height map support to all of our debugging tools, and so on. Getting everything working would end up taking about three programmer-months of work.

Applying the rule of thumb, then—would the reworked system be twice as good? On a few axes, absolutely! We already had the height maps for use by our rendering engine, and we could infer everything else we needed. Instead of the 20+ megabytes we'd needed to physically model each 200-meter-by-200-meter square of the game, we would need only a few hundred bytes to integrate a height map.[1]

Similarly, basic physics operations (like testing a short line segment) only needed to query a cell or two in the height map, instead of hopping through dozens of layers of the binary spatial partitioning tree we use to represent more free-form geometry. This would be much more than twice as fast.

So, the rule of thumb said that this rework made sense—the new system would be twice as good on important metrics, and we decided this would be worth the cost of implementing and dealing with the revised workflows and new bugs.

Dealing with Fuzzy Benefits

It's not always easy to quantify the benefits of reworking stuff, but that's not a good excuse for side-stepping the "twice as good" rule. If you're focused on soft improvements—like a change that will make your programmers happier, or a rebuilt authoring pipeline that will let your designers create slicker UX—then figure out how to quantify them.

If you don't, you're setting yourself up to make the most comfortable decision—the one that fits your natural tendency. If you make the comfortable decision too often, you'll get yourself in trouble.

Let's say the goal of some change is merely to make the programmers on the team happier, like the earlier example of replacing some old-fashioned code. So

---

1 For a complex set of reasons, we eventually ended up making a separate copy of the height map used by rendering, then converting it to floating point as part of the copy, at a total cost of about 1 megabyte for each 200-meter-by-200-meter square.

why will your programmers be happier? Will they be more productive because they're not struggling with the bugs that reliably pop from the current tangled mess? If so, how much more productive? Twice as productive?

Or let's say you're deciding whether to rebuild your UX authoring pipeline. How much slicker will the new UX be? Why and how will it be better for your product's users, and how can you predict that improvement? Will users spend more time enjoying your product, which is what we aim for with games? Or, if you work on more traditional software, will your users be able to get their tasks done more quickly and effectively?

Rework Is a Good Opportunity to Fix Small Problems

One last thought before we get back to a chapter with actual source code.

Once you've decided to rework a system, you might as well tidy up all the little things that are wrong with it. You wouldn't embark on major rework just to fix some bit of old-fashioned code—the benefit isn't worth the problems you'd introduce. But if you've already decided to tear up that bit of code, you're already going to absorb the cost of changing things, and you're going to be testing your changes thoroughly anyhow—so you might as well solve some smaller problems along the way, like replacing that bit with more modern code.

This is a pretty productive pattern. Note the little problems in your code that you can't fix right away. Then, when you're doing major work in an area, sweep up all those little problems at the same time.

That doesn't say you shouldn't look for incremental improvements. Use incremental changes to make those improvements. Maybe, over time, you'll collect enough small ideas about ways the system could improve that you can justify major rework. That's pretty common, actually, especially if you start to see patterns. If you see a half-dozen small issues with the current system that could all be addressed by the same bit of rework, then maybe you've found the tipping point where the cumulative value makes the rework worth the effort. Collectively, the improvement would be major and justifies major rework.

"Twice as good" is a convenient way to say that major changes require major improvements. Don't tear up something to replace it with something marginally better; that's a bad strategy. Tear something up to replace it with something *much* better. Twice as good.

Big Teams Need Strong Conventions

The most basic idea in this book is that programming is complicated, and that your productivity as an individual and as a team is gated on that complexity. The more complicated you make things—or let things become—the less successful you'll be. The simpler you keep things, the more successful you'll be—so keep things simple!

That advice holds true no matter what sort of project you're working on, but it's truer for some projects than others.

There are projects that are small enough and simple enough that unnecessary complexity won't really matter. If you're writing a hundred lines of code by yourself in an afternoon and you're going to throw away the code when you're done, then you can write that code just about any way you'd like and get away with it.

Once you're on a team, even if it's a two-person team, that's less true. You might try to draw lines between "my code" and "your code," with each of you deciding how code gets written on your side of the line...but this won't work very well. Unless your two halves are extraordinarily cleanly separated and remain that way through the life of the project, you'll be popping back and forth across the boundary routinely. Even defining the interface between the two halves gets problematic—for example, who decides how things in the interface are named, when half of the interface is on each side of the line?

There's no good way to extend this my-side-your-side pattern to larger teams, but that doesn't stop people from trying. For some programmers, there's a strong appeal to making all the decisions about "your" code. It's easy to argue that programming is a creative act, and that constraints make for less creativity. It's easy to argue that different parts of the projects have different needs, and so should be treated differently. It's easy to get attached to the smallest parts of your programming style, only to find yourself in a heated argument about where a curly brace goes.

All of these arguments are wrong. Not entirely wrong, but whatever small kernel of truth exists in each of them is outweighed by the reality of working on a large team on a large project. Differences in coding style add complexity, which makes everyone's jobs harder.

Formatting Conventions

Every bit of code embodies some style and philosophy. Working your way through some bit of code that uses a foreign style or philosophy is slower and more error-prone. It's like reading a foreign language you only mostly understand; everything is a struggle.

If you're used to code that looks like this:

```
/// \struct TREE
/// \brief Binary tree of integers
/// \var TREE::l
/// Left subtree
/// \var TREE::r
/// Right subtree
/// \var TREE::n
/// Data

/// \fn sum(Tree * t)
/// \brief Return sum of all integers in the tree
/// \param t Root of tree (or subtree) to sum
/// \returns Sum of integers in tree

struct TREE { typedef TREE self; self * l; self * r; int n; };
int sum(TREE * t) { return (!t) ? 0 : t->n + sum(t->l) + sum(t->r); }
```

...then code like this is going to be harder to read, and vice versa:

```
// Integer tree node

struct STree
{
    STree *     m_leftTree;
    STree *     m_rightTree;
    int         m_data;
};
```

```
// Return sum of all integers in tree

int sumTree(STree * tree)
{
    if (!tree)
        return 0;

    return tree->m_data +
            sumTree(tree->m_leftTree) +
            sumTree(tree->m_rightTree);
}
```

I'm not making a value judgment here—in some sense, this is the same code; the only differences are naming and formatting. I'm used to programming in something like the second style, so the first style seems strange to me. Reading it requires some mental translation. If you're used to the first style, you'd have the opposite reaction.

The problem here isn't the coding style, it's *mixing* those styles. If you mix styles—again, adding complexity—you're going to struggle when moving between them. Trying to maintain different styles for different sections of your code is a bad idea.

Language Usage Conventions

The same is true for use of language features. If you're used to "basic" C++ code like the previous example, then more "modern" C++ like this is going to be hard to read:

```
int sumTree(const Tree * tree)
{
    int sum = 0;
    visitInOrder(tree, [&sum](const Tree * tree) { sum += tree->m_data; });
    return sum;
}
```

If you're used to older versions of C++, you might not even recognize this as legitimate code! There's a lambda definition in there (it's the part starting with [&sum]), and lambdas weren't added until C++ 11.

Again, I'm not making a value statement here. Lambdas can be useful, and I understand why C++'s implementation works the way it does. If lambdas are a standard part of your team's workflow, and you all have a solid shared understanding of how and where to use them, then there's nothing wrong with the preceding code. If you're the lone lambda champion on the team, then the same code is a disaster. The problem here isn't the use of language features per se—it's mixing different expectations about which language features to use. If you're used to one set of language features, then adjusting to a different set saps your energy. That's especially true when those transitions are unexpected, leaving you unsure of which set of conventions is in force for some bit of code you're looking at.

Problem-Solving Conventions

Programmers don't run into a lot of problems that have only one solution, so we all develop our own instincts about how to solve a particular problem when writing code. That creates problems when your instincts don't match up with those of your teammates—you'll solve the same problem in different ways. At best, that increases cognitive load as you look at each other's code. More likely, it results in reinventing the wheel: you all end up solving the same problem multiple times in multiple ways, because you don't recognize that it has already been solved.

Take error handling. There are lots of ways of handling errors: some introduced by the language and its libraries, others extrapolated by teams to meet their own particular needs. Even if you limit yourself to the built-in parts of C++, you'll find at least three distinct error-handling models, each featured at some point in the 50-year evolution of the language.

Even the definition of *error* itself is up for grabs! You could reasonably decide that usage mistakes are errors—after all, this is what the operating system and most libraries do. You could just as easily decide that errors should be reserved for unavoidable problems, like a missing file, not entirely avoidable usage mistakes.

At Sucker Punch, for instance, we deal with usage errors as asserts, not as errors. That's our convention. Given the many choices about how to handle errors, we chose one, and we all stick to it.

Sticking to one convention is a challenge, not least because every library or other dependency drags you into its error-handling model. At a minimum, you need to deal with the errors the library returns—and then decide how to propagate them. If you're dealing with really old-school C-style file handling, that leads to some unpleasant code:

```
string getFileAsString(string fileName)
{
    errno = 0;
    string s;
```

```
FILE * file = fopen(fileName.c_str(), "r");
if (file)
{
    while (true)
    {
        int c = getc(file);
        if (c == EOF)
        {
            if (ferror(file))
                s.clear();

            break;
        }

        s += c;
    }

    fclose(file);
}

return s;
}
```

In this 1980s-style code, errors are returned with a combination of global state and special return values. The details aren't that important—but the relative lack of conventions here is notable. Every function has a slightly different idea of how to return errors—fopen returns nullptr on error, getc returns EOF but sets a global flag, and so on. Using this model means memorizing a bunch of arbitrary details.

Moving errors onto the objects themselves improves things slightly—and new, stronger conventions can be introduced:

```
bool tryGetFileAsString(string fileName, string * result)
{
    ifstream file;
    file.open(fileName.c_str(), ifstream::in);
    if (!file.good())
    {
        log(
            "failed to open file %s: %s",
            fileName.c_str(),
            strerror(errno));

        return false;
    }

    string s;
    while (true)
```

```
    {
        char c = file.get();
        if (c == EOF)
        {
            if (file.bad())
            {
                log(
                    "error reading file %s: %s",
                    fileName.c_str(),
                    strerror(errno));

                return false;
            }

            break;
        }

        s += c;
    }

    *result = s;
    return true;
}
```

The convention here is that functions with names starting with try might fail. They return true on success and false on failure, and any details about the failure are reported to a system error log. If you see a try-named function, you know exactly what to expect. That's the power of conventions—they're a shortcut to understanding, much preferable to reading through the code to figure out the details for yourself. As in this code, any library that doesn't use the convention forces some conversion work, but that's work only one coder has to do—the rest of the team can enjoy a consistent error-handling convention.

I've worked on projects that defined a richer error type, instead of returning a simple bool for success or failure:

```
struct Result
{
    Result(ErrorCode errorCode);
    Result(const char * format, …);

    operator bool () const
        { return m_errorCode == ErrorCode::None; }

    ErrorCode m_errorCode;
    string m_error;
};
```

This kind of error reporting lets code propagate errors around while still allowing detailed, contextual error information. This is a useful model for projects that deal with lots of errors, especially when combined with a naming convention like try:

```
Result tryGetFileAsString(string fileName, string * result)
{
    result->clear();

    ifstream file;
    file.open(fileName.c_str(), ifstream::in);
    if (!file.good())
    {
        return Result(
                    "failed to open file %s: %s",
                    fileName.c_str(),
                    strerror(errno));
    }

    string s;
    while (true)
    {
        int c = file.get();
        if (c == EOF)
            break;

        if (file.bad())
            return Result(
                        "error reading file %s: %s",
                        fileName.c_str(),
                        strerror(errno));

        s += c;
    }

    *result = s;
    return ErrorCode::None;
}
```

Or you could use exceptions, the third basic error-handling model of the C++ libraries:

```
string getFileAsString(string fileName)
{
    ifstream file;
    file.exceptions(ifstream::failbit | ifstream::badbit);
    file.open(fileName.c_str(), ifstream::in);

    string s;
```

```
file.exceptions(ifstream::badbit);
while (true)
{
    int c = file.get();
    if (c == EOF)
        break;

    s += c;
}

return s;
}
```

For better or worse, this function hides the actual exceptions, which are thrown from `file.open` or `file.get`. The advantage is that the normal flow of operation isn't cluttered with error-handling stuff; the disadvantage is that the complexity of how errors are detected and handled is hidden and scattered over multiple functions.[1]

All four of these styles are viable, as are many others. You could choose any of them as your convention—well, you're not going to use the first style, because that would be silly. But any of the other three could make sense, depending on your project.

Here's what doesn't make sense—mixing different error-handling conventions in the same project. Inconsistent conventions will leave everyone on the team slightly confused at all times, and confused programmers write bugs.

I hid an example of this in the two `try`-named function conventions. Both conventions pass back the "actual" return value of the function through a pointer. But in the first convention, the function leaves the actual return value unchanged if it fails; in the second convention, it's cleared in error cases.

You can make a solid argument for either option—but you can't mix them in the same project, because that's an obvious disaster. The same is true with mixing exceptions in amongst error codes, which is destined to end in tears.

You might also be able to argue that your program should have no error handling. That's right, no error handling! That's actually the approach we take for most of our game code—we don't define errors, so there's no error handling.

---

1 Given the other Rules in this book—most importantly Rule 10, "Localize Complexity"—it will not surprise you to hear that C++ exceptions are not used at Sucker Punch, and it's for this very reason. We do have a few `try` statements in the codebase, but only when forced to by external libraries in our toolchain.

Usage errors are handled with asserts. Catastrophic problems like running out of memory just halt the game. Edge cases trigger default behaviors rather than returning errors.

It's true that we're forced to deal with errors at the edges of our code—our networking code needs to handle packets getting dropped, for instance. But Sucker Punch programmers can go for months and months without generating or handling a single error.

Effective Teams Think Alike

Your goal as a team—not as individuals, but as a team—should be to think as one. The ideal situation would be for everyone on the team to be so in sync that each of you would write exactly the same code when presented with a particular problem. And by "exactly," I mean *exactly*: same algorithm, same formatting, same names for everything.

We all know that it's easier to read and work with your own code than it is to work with other people's code. Any bit of code embeds countless assumptions about how code should be written. When you're reading your own code, all of those assumptions feel natural, so you don't notice them. When you read other people's code, you trip over every single one of the assumptions you don't share.

If the naming conventions don't match your expectations, you hit a snag. Sure, you can figure it out, but it takes time and energy. If the curly braces are in the wrong place, or the code uses unfamiliar language features or does common things using more than one convention, like the constructor example earlier, same thing.

The solution is obvious. If you want to work smoothly and harmoniously as a team, align your assumptions! Use the same conventions! Stop being dumb!

The conventions themselves—where the curly brace goes and so on—rarely matter. You can have a principled discussion about curly brace placement, but there are lots of good answers to where they go. It doesn't matter which style you choose, as long as you all choose the same style and use it consistently.

Here's how we deal with this at Sucker Punch. We have a set of coding standards that set out pretty strict rules for everything we can think of, including:

- How to name everything.

- How to format code. If you're smart, your formatting conventions will exactly match the output from one of the many code-formatting tools, which makes following the convention easy—just run the formatting tool.[2]

- How to use language features, including which to use and which to avoid.

- Conventions for all the common problems we solve. We have a very standardized way to write a state machine, for instance, because our game code has lots of state machines.

- Where to draw file boundaries, and how code should be ordered and grouped within those files.

- How to represent constants in the code. It's not enough to say that you're going to use a `#define` or a `const` instead of embedding magic numbers in your code—what should your `const` be named? Where should you define it? Near the use, at the top of the source file with the other constants, or maybe in a project-wide header file?

Everyone follows these conventions, which are gently enforced during our code review process. It's an adjustment for many of our new coders to work within strict standards like these, but it doesn't take long for the benefits of strict adherence to the coding standards to become obvious.

At the beginning of every project, we let anyone on the coding team propose any change they'd like to the coding standards. We debate each proposed change, then vote. If a proposal wins a majority of the vote, it goes into effect for the new project. During the last round of voting, for instance, we approved the use of `auto` in certain circumstances, which (depending on your own proclivities) may seem horribly strict or entirely too permissive.[3]

Once we've made all the changes to our standard, we divvy up our fairly large codebase and sweep through it like a swarm of hungry locusts, converting everything to match the new standard. This isn't cheap, but it takes less than a week, and at the end we've got squeaky-clean compliance with our team conventions.

---

2 We are, alas, not this smart. Our formatting conventions are...idiosyncratic.

3 Hence conventions.

Remember our goal: that any Sucker Punch coder, faced with a particular problem, will write exactly the same solution as any other Sucker Punch coder. The closer we get to that, the closer we are to the perfect situation—where working with anyone else's code is as easy as working with your own. If I'm looking at some bit of Sucker Punch code and I can't tell who wrote it—or even whether I wrote it myself—then I know we're getting close to that goal, and we've set ourselves up for stress-free programming.[4]

---

4 OK, OK, not actually stress-free. But a lot less stressful.

Find the Pebble That Started the Avalanche

If I tell you that coding is really debugging, you'll probably shake your head ruefully and mutter something along the lines of "Ain't it the truth, buddy. Ain't it the truth."

Well, not really—nobody talks like that. But you'd certainly agree with the premise. When you're turning an idea into a fully working implementation, you'll inevitably spend a lot more time in the "getting it to work" phase than in the "typing it in" phase. Barring extreme circumstances—a simple idea and a run of incredible luck, say—you'll spend more time debugging than coding. This is so obvious it's rarely even stated.

Here's the twist.

You know that coding is actually debugging, but how does that affect the way you approach coding projects? You know that coding is actually debugging—so what are you going to do about it?

One obvious answer is to write code with fewer bugs. That's what the rest of this book is about, so let's set it aside for now. This Rule is about something different: writing code that's easy to debug.

The Lifecycle of a Bug

Let's take a step back and think about what debugging actually is. There are four basic stages in the lifecycle of a bug:

1. The bug is detected—you discover the problem.

2. Next it's diagnosed—you investigate and uncover what's causing the errant behavior.

3. Then you fix it, changing your implementation to eliminate the errant behavior.

4. Finally, you test to make sure that the bug has actually been fixed and that your fix didn't cause new problems, then you commit the fix.

The diagnosis phase is often the longest and most frustrating. That's because most bugs arrive with no details. Typically you've got a description of the symptom—the program crashed, or the OK button on a dialog is always disabled, or a list of all your users swaps the first and last names for a quarter of the entries. If you're lucky, the bug report will have some context, such as what the user was doing when the program crashed.

What you're missing is *why* the symptom occurred. What led to the symptom? What exactly went wrong? Diagnosis is the process of answering these questions. Until you know what went wrong, you can't fix the problem.

The thing you've got going for you is that computers are deterministic. If the computer is presented with exactly the same situation, it will generate exactly the same result. If you don't see the same result, then you didn't reproduce the situation exactly.

Bugs would be easy to diagnose if you could time travel back to right before things started going wrong. Then your job would be easy—just step through the code looking for trouble. If you accidentally step past the problem, or if you didn't start early enough, no worries: fire up your time machine and pop a little further backward in time.

Of course, you can't actually time travel—or, if you can, you'll have higher priorities for your time travel powers than fixing bugs in your code. Instead, you need to *fake* the ability to time travel, getting the code back into exactly the situation that will cause the problem, then break into the debugger right before things go sideways.

There's often a gap between things starting to go sideways and the bug's symptom showing up, so knowing when to break into the debugger is a bit of a magic trick. If you're really lucky, the actual underlying problem and the symptom are one and the same:

```
void showObjectDetails(const Character * character)
{
    trace(
        "character %s [%s] %s",
        (character) ? character->name() : "",
        character,
```

```
    (character->sourceFile()) ? character->sourceFile() : "");
}
```

A crash here with a null object is easy to diagnose. The symptom (the crash) is in the same statement as the actual problem (we're checking whether character is null, implying that null objects are supported, but then dereferencing character with no null check two lines later). With no gap between symptom and problem, diagnosis is easy.

Or, at some slightly smaller value of "lucky," the symptom and problem are neighbors:

```
int calculateHighestCharacterPriority()
{
    Character * bestCharacter = nullptr;

    for (Character * character : g_allCharacters)
    {
        if (!bestCharacter ||
            character->priority() > bestCharacter->priority())
        {
            bestCharacter = character;
        }
    }

    return bestCharacter->priority();
}
```

Another null pointer crash, this time if calculateHighestCharacterPriority is called when no characters exist. The symptom here (crashing with best Character still null) is separated by a few lines from the problem (the logic of the preceding loop doesn't handle an empty characters list).

Here we get the first inkling of the actual process of diagnosing a bug. Earlier we said that if we could time travel back to the point where things started going wrong, it would be easy to diagnose the bug. That's true, and that's sort of what we're doing during diagnosis, but it's rare to be able to jump all the way back to the original cause, the point where things started going wrong, all in one step.

It's more typical for things to fall apart bit by bit instead of all at once. Instead of jumping straight back in time to the point where things go wrong, you're working backward bit by bit. You identify something that looks wrong, then work backward to identify when it started looking wrong. That often leads to something else that looks wrong, another process of working backward, then more rounds of the same until you land on the pebble whose tumble started the whole avalanche that led to your eventual symptom. That's what diagnosing a bug is.

I understand if this effort to decompose the process of debugging doesn't seem useful. You started with an idea of what debugging is like. You're a programmer, and coding is debugging, so you've debugged code. Why all this effort to describe a process that's obvious?

Well, our goal is to make debugging easier, and we can't do that without a crisp definition of what debugging is.

If we define debugging as the process of stepping backward in time, reconstructing the cascade of things going wrong that eventually lead to the symptom we've detected, then we make debugging easier by making it easier to step backward in time. Eventually, we work backward to the pebble that started the avalanche, which is where we'd like to fix things. The easier it is to work backward, the more likely we are to follow the chain of causation to its source.

That's the thing about avalanches. We don't have to work all the way backward to the original pebble. We can just fix the symptom, and not worry about diagnosing our way backward to the cause of that symptom. Faced with the crash in our second example, we could just add a null pointer check to stomp on the symptom, the crash when called with no characters:

```
int calculateHighestCharacterPriority()
{
    Character * bestCharacter = nullptr;

    for (Character * character : g_allCharacters)
    {
        if (!bestCharacter ||
            character->priority() > bestCharacter->priority())
        {
            bestCharacter = character;
        }
    }

    return (bestCharacter) ? bestCharacter->priority() : 0;
}
```

When working backward is hard, there's a strong temptation to do exactly this—to fix the symptom rather than tracing back to its cause. The temptation is strong because in some sense it works. This code was crashing, and now it's not. Your work is done.

If we'd done just a little bit more tracing backward, we'd probably realize that a better fix would be getting rid of the bestCharacter pointer:

```
int calculateHighestCharacterPriority()
{
    int highestPriority = 0;

    for (Character * character : g_allCharacters)
    {
        highestPriority = max(
                          highestPriority,
                          character->priority());
    }

    return highestPriority;
}
```

Most bugs aren't as simple as this example. Patching the symptom without tracing backward to the original problem leaves that original problem still lying in wait, poised to start an avalanche.

In this example, the pebble is a pointer that's null, but only in a special case. We wrote code that missed the special case once. We're likely to miss that special case again. Better to get rid of the pebble by eliminating the pointer entirely.

The temptation to deal with the symptom rather than its cause exists at every step along the way of your exploration up the causal chain. As you slowly work your way backward in time from symptom to cause, and to the cause of that cause, and then the cause of that cause, at any point you can stomp on a problem and declare victory. This is a victory of sorts—the eventual symptom that prompted your debugging disappears.

But declaring victory midway through the avalanche means that the pebble is still there. At some point it will cause another avalanche, whether you're the coder who gets buried or someone else is. The easier we make it to take steps backward in time, the easier it is to resist the temptation to fix symptoms instead of tracing back to their root causes. That makes it easier to fix pebbles instead of patching avalanches.[1]

---

1 So how do you know when you've found the pebble and not just another symptom? Well, if you're not sure why or when the purported pebble occurs, then you probably haven't found the pebble and should keep investigating. But don't obsess about it—every step uphill toward the actual pebble is helpful.

Minimizing State

Given this definition of debugging, we can spot the opportunities for improvement:

Pushing symptoms closer to causes makes tracing upstream easier.
If the cause is nearby in the source code, or if it happened more recently, then discovering the connection gets easier.

Reducing the length of the causal chain shortens the debugging process.
A symptom that has a single cause is easier to fix than a symptom with a long cascade of symptoms leading to causes leading to other causes ad nauseum.

Making it easier to hop backward in time helps trace each link.
If it's easy to reproduce the state that led to the cause of each symptom, it will be easy to explore the causal chain.

The easiest target here is the last one listed. Reproducing state is hard if there's lots of state. If we reduce the amount of state we need to reproduce, we'll have an easier time hopping backward up the causal chain.

It's easy to debug a problem in a pure function—a function that has no side effects and depends only on its inputs. If the function returns an incorrect value for some set of inputs, just call it again with the same inputs and it will return the same output. Repeat as needed.

Say we're calculating Fibonacci numbers, and we've got a bug. Calculating Fibonacci numbers is a problem that is only ever solved in programming tests and whiteboard interviews, but hang with me. Here's the code.[2] The bug report is that getFibonacci returns the wrong value:

```
int getFibonacci(int n)
{
    static vector<int> values = { 0, 1, 1, 2, 3, 5, 8, 13, 23, 34, 55 };
    for (int i = values.size(); i <= n; ++i)
    {
        values.push_back(values[i - 2] + values[i - 1]);
    }
    return values[n];
}
```

---

2 This is not a good way to calculate Fibonacci numbers. Don't use it on a programming test.

This is a pure function, so reproducing the problem is easy. The only state it relies on is its argument, so every time we call getFibonacci(8) we'll get the same incorrect result, 23 instead of 21. Once we're stepping into the function, it's pretty obvious what's wrong—we're priming the values array with the wrong value. Diagnosis complete.

That's our first takeaway, then. If you build your code with pure functions, you'll have an easier time reproducing state and an easier time debugging problems.

Let's look at a more complicated scenario. Imagine we've got a Character method that returns a "threat" value based on that character's current weapon, armor, health level, status effects, and so on. We could write code to maintain that threat value as state in the character:

```
struct Character
{
    void setArmor(Armor * armor)
    {
        m_threat -= m_armor->getThreat();
        m threat += armor->getThreat();
        m_armor = armor;
    }

    void setWeapon(Weapon * weapon)
    {
        m_threat -= weapon->getThreat();
        m_threat += weapon->getThreat();
        m_weapon = weapon;
    }

    void setHitPoint(float hitPoints)
    {
        m_threat -= getThreatFromHitPoints(m_hitPoints);
        m_threat += getThreatFromHitPoints(hitPoints);
        m_hitPoints = hitPoints;
    }

    int getThreat() const
    {
        return m_threat;
    }

protected:

    int m_threat;
    Armor * m_armor;
    Weapon * m_weapon;
```

```
    float m_hitPoints;
};
```

There's a bug in this code, reported as something like "player doesn't appear threatened by an enemy with a +1 Sword of Grievous Wounding." Luckily this bug is easy to reproduce manually. If you walk up to the enemy holding the magic sword, the player character still plays his unconcerned animation instead of looking ready for action.

The preceding code isn't where that symptom shows up, of course. The actual symptom in this case is the player character playing an inappropriate animation, looking unconcerned when they should be looking threatened. We've already traced a few steps upstream in the causal chain before we hit our example code, but when we do we find that m_threat doesn't have the right value.

So now we need to figure out why it doesn't have the right value! We've got to do the magic trick of jumping backward in time, reproducing the state that led to m_threat being set to the wrong value.

And that's tricky in this case. The code isn't "nearby," like it was in the prior simple examples. Nor is it "recent." At some point in the past, we set m_threat to the wrong value, but we're not sure when.

That's the problem with stateful code. You don't detect problems until long after things have gone sideways, and this delay between cause and symptom makes diagnosing the problem difficult. In this case, we know that m_threat has the wrong value, but we're not sure why or when that incorrect value was set.

If you follow the advice about audit functions in Rule 2, then diagnosing the problem is cake. Add a call to the audit function whenever you're updating the character's state:

```
struct Character
{
    void setWeapon(Weapon * weapon)
    {
        m_threat -= weapon->getThreat();
        m_threat += weapon->getThreat();
        m_weapon = weapon;
        audit();
    }

    void audit() const
    {
        int expectedThreat = m_armor->getThreat() +
                             m_weapon->getThreat() +
                             getThreatFromHitPoints(m_hitPoints);
```

```
        assert(m_threat == expectedThreat);
    }
};
```

If we do this, then the audit function asserts at the end of setWeapon. Face palm; we meant to subtract the threat from the old weapon before adding the threat from the new weapon. It's no wonder the player character was so blasé.

Without the help of an audit function, diagnosing the problem is decidedly not cake. You probably end up placing breakpoints on all the lines where m_threat is set, then running the code and verifying the state each time you hit one of those breakpoints. Tedious, and in this case easily avoided—you shouldn't have been maintaining m_threat as a bit of state. Don't add state unless it's absolutely necessary.

Contrast with a similar bug in stateless code:

```
struct Character
{
    void setArmor(Armor * armor)
    {
        m_armor = armor;
    }

    void setWeapon(Weapon * weapon)
    {
        m_weapon = weapon;
    }

    void setHitPoint(float hitPoints)
    {
        m_hitPoints = hitPoints;
    }

    int getThreat() const
    {
        return m_armor->getThreat() -
            m_weapon->getThreat() +
            getThreatFromHitPoints(m_hitPoints);
    }

protected:

    Armor * m_armor;
    Weapon * m_weapon;
    float m_hitPoints;
};
```

With the stateless code, we have a clear plan of action when we discover `Character::getThreat` is returning the wrong value. Walk up to the enemy with the magic sword, then set a breakpoint on `getThreat`. Diagnosis is easy—there's an errant minus sign where a plus sign was clearly intended. Reducing the amount of state made diagnosis much easier.

We haven't eliminated state entirely from `Character`. The state that remains—the character's armor, weapon, and current hit points—is sort of the point of the `Character` object. It's irreducible.

That's true for a lot of video game code, where we're modeling real-world objects with virtual analogs, and those objects have state. Like an object's position and velocity, or the player's current hit points, or what magic gems are slotted into the player's magic sword. That's all state, and it's not easily eliminated.

But where you can get rid of state, do. State makes debugging harder, and coding is debugging. Where possible, build behavior out of pure functions. It's easier to get the details correct, and when things go wrong problems are a lot easier to diagnose.

Dealing with Unavoidable State

When state is unavoidable it makes diagnosing problems more complicated. Imagine you're diagnosing a problem—characters sometimes react inappropriately to arrow impacts. They're expected to stumble backward,[3] but sometimes they stumble forward instead.

Hmm. There's a suggestive word in that bug description..."sometimes" tells you that the problem is probably related to the state of the interacting objects—my guess would be the problem is inside the character, which probably has the most state, though the arrow is also a possibility. Diagnosing the problem is going to require reproducing that state.

That might be easy! If the bug is showing up 100% of the time in one of your unit tests, you're home free. The unit test is creating the state that leads to the incorrect behavior, which makes diagnosis straightforward. Set a breakpoint that fires when the ill-fated arrow hits the character and start debugging—you might need to explore up the causal stream to find the pebble that started the avalanche, but the hard part of each step backward in time is reproducing state, and the unit test is taking care of that for you.

---

3 This is movie logic. Arrows don't have that much energy. They're not going to knock anything bigger than a squirrel backward. But it's what everyone playing video games expects, so there you go.

Or maybe you're slightly less lucky. You don't have an automated test, but given a few tries you can reproduce the problem manually, and you can detect the problem when it occurs.

In the Sucker Punch engine there's an object that maps every damage record to an appropriate reaction—that's where the code decides what a character does when an arrow thunks into them. We can detect the problem in the mapping code—we just need to add code that makes sure the impact velocity of the arrow and the character stumble direction point in the same direction:

```
void DamageArbiter::getDamageReaction(
    const Damage * damage,
    Reaction * reaction) const
{
    // All the actual logic for mapping damage to reactions goes here.
    //  There's a single function that does this in the Sucker Punch
    //  engine. That function is nearly 3000 lines long and is not the
    //  purest embodiment of the Rules, though to be fair it's solving
    //  a very complicated problem.

    if (damage->isArrow())
    {
        assert(reaction->isStumble());
        Vector arrowVelocity = damage->impactVelocity();
        Vector stumbleDirection = reaction->stumbleDirection();
        assert(dotProduct(arrowVelocity, stumbleDirection) > 0.0f);
    }
}
```

When this assert fires, you're in good shape to diagnose the problem.

The getDamageReaction function is relatively pure—it returns the same Reaction every time for any bit of Damage, and it doesn't have side effects, but it also makes decisions based on the state of arbitrary objects in the world. That sounds like a disaster—do we have to reproduce the state of every single object in the world in order to reproduce the problem?

That's why it's important that we detect the problem early, before we return from getDamageReaction. That lets us diagnose the problem. The function has no side effects, so the state of all the objects in the world hasn't changed. If we call getDamageReaction again immediately, we should get the same result.

In the olden days I'd insert code to handle this. When the problem is detected, break into the debugger to let me start single-stepping, then call the pure function recursively:

```
void DamageArbiter::getDamageReaction(
    const Damage * damage,
    Reaction * reaction) const
{
    // All the actual logic for mapping damage to reactions goes here.
    //  There's a single function that does this in the Sucker Punch
    //  engine. That function is nearly 3000 lines long and is not the
    //  purest embodiment of the Rules, though to be fair it's solving
    //  a very complicated problem.

    if (damage->isArrow())
    {
        assert(reaction->isStumble());
        Vector arrowVelocity = damage->impactVelocity();
        Vector stumbleDirection = reaction->stumbleDirection();
        if (dotProduct(arrowVelocity, stumbleDirection) <= 0.0f)
        {
            assert(false);

            static bool s_debugProblem = CHRISZ;
            if (s_debugProblem)
            {
                getDamageReaction(damage, reaction);
            }
        }
    }
}
```

These days, I can be more improvisatory. The IDE we use at Sucker Punch lets me set the next line to execute whenever I'm stopped on a line in the debugger. This is not without some danger, since randomly jumping around in the code can create its own problems, but given some care it works well. If I realize I've hit a problem, especially in a pure function, I can pop backward in the code to identify the cause of the problem. This ability transforms diagnosis. A single step backward in time that was difficult to execute has become easy. If the underlying cause of the problem is local—recent, and nearby in the code—then it's easy to find.

Eliminating state doesn't have to be an all-or-nothing thing. Making some bit of code completely stateless will make it easier to diagnose problems, even if nearby code still maintains state. Every little bit of state you eliminate helps.

Dealing with Unavoidable Delay

In the examples we've looked at so far, we could detect the symptom mechanically. If we crashed, then the problem sort of detected itself. If our code is self-policing through asserts, then it detects its own problems. In cases like our arrow example, we noticed the problem through manual testing, but could translate the problem into an assert in the code.

Detecting symptoms like this isn't always possible, and this complicates diagnosis. Sometimes the symptom isn't immediately apparent.

Here's a Sucker Punch example—debugging problems in our animation code. The movement of characters in our games is driven by animations created by our animation team. Each animation describes where each part of the character's body moves as a function of time. Say, at 1.5 seconds into the animation, the left hand goes exactly here and is oriented exactly like this; at 1.53 seconds into the animation, it's moved slightly up and rotated forward a tiny bit. And so on, for each of the six hundred or so parts of the character body we manage, every sixtieth of a second as long as the animation lasts.

Each animation on its own is a pure function. It doesn't rely on any external state, or have any side effects. All it cares about is its sole input variable, the exact time within the animation's timeline we're evaluating. If we repeatedly evaluate the animation with the same input variable, we'll repeatedly get the same body position.

It's not quite that simple, though. When we switch from one animation to another—when a character who is running decides to jump, say—then we don't just cut over to the new animation. That would cause the character's body to pop into a new position, which looks bad. Instead, we smoothly transition from the old animation to the new one.

Smoothing makes things more complicated because it relies on the character's current body position as well as the position in the animation timeline. For us to reproduce a problem in smoothing, we need the position and orientation of all six hundred or so parts of the character's body we manage as well as that single timeline value for the animation.

Wait, it gets worse! While our brains are really good at detecting glitches in animations, it takes a while for us to realize we've seen a problem, and we're reevaluating the animation sixty times a second. By the time we realize that something looked wrong, we've reevaluated the animation a dozen times, and whatever state caused the animation glitch is long lost.

There's a solution, though it's an expensive one. Animation smoothing relies on a lot of state, but at least it's state we can identify. If we captured all of that state every time we evaluated the animation, then we could reevaluate the animation smoothing using that state to diagnose problems.

And in fact that's what we do. Because glitch-free animation is an absolute requirement, we've invested in debugging animations. We capture all the character state that affects animation every frame, and have a debugging tool that lets us scroll back and forth over recent evaluations of the animation. When we see a glitch, we can pause the game, fire up the animation debugging tool, scroll backward in time to the glitch, then break into the debugger to start tracing from symptom to cause up the causal chain.

With this tool we automated the hard part of debugging—reproducing the state that led to the problem. If you've got code that relies on state, but that state can be scoped, then capturing the state makes debugging a lot easier.

Think of this technique as creating an executable logfile—a logfile that doesn't just describe what happened, but contains all the data necessary to cause that same thing to happen again. If you've built your system out of pure functions, then building an executable logfile is completely plausible. You just capture all of the inputs and provide a way to play them back.

This isn't easy to do, but for crucially important and hard-to-debug problems like animation quality at Sucker Punch, it's worth the effort.

Code Comes in
Four Flavors

Here's an incredibly oversimplified but still useful model for thinking about code. Imagine that there are two kinds of programming problems to be solved—Easy and Hard.

You've already got an idea of what an Easy problem is, but let me give you some generic examples: Finding the largest and smallest values in an array of numbers. Inserting a node into a sorted binary tree. Removing odd values from an array.

Hard problems are also easy to identify: memory allocation, for instance—implementing the C standard library's malloc and free. Parsing a scripting language. Writing a linear-constraints problem solver.

Now, Easy and Hard, as I've defined them here, are really only two points on a spectrum, and they aren't even the extreme points. Some problems are trivial, even easier than the Easy examples—summing two numbers, say. And there are problems much harder than the Hard examples, like creating a journaling filesystem from scratch.

But they're two useful points. Between Easy and Hard lie most of the problems programmers solve every day. For what it's worth, I've written solutions to all of these examples—except building a journaling filesystem from scratch, although that sounds like fun.

It seems obvious that you're going to need to write more code to solve a Hard problem than to solve an Easy one, and that the code you'll write will be more complicated. This is often the case. Solutions to Hard problems are usually more difficult to write, and end up longer and more complicated than solutions to Easy problems.

That leads to another oversimplified model. This time, imagine that there are two kinds of solutions to problems: Simple and Complicated. Simple solutions are short and easy to understand. Complicated solutions are long and difficult to understand. Again, these are just two points on a spectrum. There are obviously Moderately Complicated or Simple-ish solutions, too, but it's useful to think about the Simple and Complicated points on that spectrum.

You're a programmer, so at this point you've figured out how we get to four flavors of code (Table 14-1), per the Rule title.

Table 14-1. *Simple and Complicated solutions to Easy and Hard problems*

	Easy problem	Hard problem
Simple solution	Expected	Aspirational
Complicated solution	Really, really bad	Accepted

It's obvious that there are Simple solutions to Easy problems, and that there are Complicated solutions to Hard problems. From personal experience, we can all attest that it's distressingly easy to write Complicated solutions to Easy problems. And, in some cases, it's possible to write Simple solutions to Hard problems.

Per Rule 1, we'd like to find solutions that are as simple as possible, so it's clear where this Rule is headed! But let's look at some examples.

Easy Problem, Simple Solution

Let's start with an example of an Easy problem—finding the largest and smallest values in an array. Here is a Simple solution to this Easy problem:

```
struct Bounds
{
    Bounds(int minValue, int maxValue)
    : m_minValue(minValue), m_maxValue(maxValue)
        { ; }

    int m_minValue;
    int m_maxValue;
};

Bounds findBounds(const vector<int> & values)
{
    int minValue = INT_MAX;
    int maxValue = INT_MIN;

    for (int value : values)
```

```
    {
        minValue = min(minValue, value);
        maxValue = max(maxValue, value);
    }

    return Bounds(minValue, maxValue);
}
```

The algorithm is simple—it just loops through the values, tracking the largest and smallest values it finds. There's some very minor subtlety about how to get started—I'm using a fairly standard trick to make sure the first element sets both minValue and maxValue. Other than that, the code is easy to follow and understand. It's appropriately simple.

Easy Problem, Three Complicated Solutions

It's entirely possible to take exactly the same algorithm and make the code much more complicated. We've all seen code that buries a simple algorithm under multiple layers of abstractions, like this:

```
enum EmptyTag
{
    kEmpty
};

template <typename T> T MinValue() { return 0; }
template <typename T> T MaxValue() { return 0; }

template <> int MinValue<int>() { return INT_MIN; }
template <> int MaxValue<int>() { return INT_MAX; }

template <class T>
struct Bounds
{
    Bounds(const T & value)
    : m_minValue(value), m_maxValue(value)
        { ; }
    Bounds(const T & minValue, const T & maxValue)
    : m_minValue(minValue), m_maxValue(maxValue)
        { ; }
    Bounds(EmptyTag)
    : m_minValue(MaxValue<T>()), m_maxValue(MinValue<T>())
        { ; }

    Bounds & operator |= (const T & value)
    {
        m_minValue = min(m_minValue, value);
        m_maxValue = max(m_maxValue, value);
```

```cpp
        return *this;
    }

    T m_minValue;
    T m_maxValue;
};

template <class T>
struct Range
{
    Range(const T::iterator & begin, const T:: & end)
    : m_begin(begin), m_end(end)
        { ; }

    const T & begin() const
    { return m_begin; }

    const T & end() const
    { return m_end; }

    T m_begin;
    T m_end;
};

template <class T>
Range<typename vector<T>::iterator> getVectorRange(
    const vector<T> & values,
    int beginIndex,
    int endIndex)
{
    return Range<vector<T>::const_iterator>(
                values.begin() + beginIndex,
                values.begin() + endIndex);
}

template <class T, class I>
T iterateAndMerge(const T & init, const I & iterable)
{
    T merge(init);

    for (const auto & value : iterable)
    {
        merge |= value;
    }

    return merge;
}

void findBounds(const vector<int> & values, Bounds<int> * bounds)
{
```

```
    *bounds = iterateAndMerge(
                Bounds<int>(kEmpty),
                getVectorRange(values, 0, values.size()));
}
```

This is exactly the same algorithm, though there's a lot to dig through to convince yourself of that. The code is well-meaning, at least. There's nothing egregious here—we're not exploiting any particularly weird quirks of C++, with template specialization being as fancy as things get. The names are all descriptive. You can imagine the justification for each line, with a little squinting.

And yet...it's four times as much code, and it's a lot harder to follow and understand than the simple example we started with. It's Complicated code, at least relative to the problem we're solving. Our previous example was appropriately Simple; this example is inappropriately Complicated.

That's only one way to overcomplicate the solution, obviously. We've also all seen code that oversteps the problem it attempts to solve:

```
struct Bounds
{
    Bounds(int minValue, int maxValue)
    : m_minValue(minValue), m_maxValue(maxValue)
        { ; }

    int m_minValue;
    int m_maxValue;
};

template <class COMPARE>
int findNth(const vector<int> & values, int n)
{
    priority_queue<int, vector<int>, COMPARE> queue;
    COMPARE compare;

    for (int value : values)
    {
        if (queue.size() < n)
        {
            queue.push(value);
        }
        else if (compare(value, queue.top()))
        {
            queue.pop();
            queue.push(value);
        }
    }

    return queue.top();
```

```
}

void findBounds(const vector<int> & values, Bounds * bounds)
{
    bounds->m_minValue = findNth<less<int>>(values, 1);
    bounds->m_maxValue = findNth<greater<int>>(values, 1);
}
```

Here we've chosen to solve a more general problem, finding the Nth largest (or smallest) number in an array, and then finding the min and max values as a special case. This sort of overly general approach is almost always misguided. Yes, there's not that much extra code, and it's more fun to write something clever like this than a simpler solution, but it's a lot harder to read.[1]

Finally, it's possible to overcomplicate things by getting the algorithm wrong. That's hard to do in this case, since the simple solution is pretty obvious, but we've all seen code that misses the easy algorithm:

```
struct Bounds
{
    Bounds(int minValue, int maxValue)
    : m_minValue(minValue), m_maxValue(maxValue)
        { ; }

    int m_minValue;
    int m_maxValue;
};

int findExtreme(const vector<int> & values, int sign)
{
    for (int index = 0; index < values.size(); ++index)
    {
        for (int otherIndex = 0;; ++otherIndex)
        {
            if (otherIndex >= values.size())
                return values[index];

            if (sign * values[index] < sign * values[otherIndex])
                break;
        }
    }

    assert(false);
    return 0;
```

---

1 Its performance is atrocious, too, but having told you not to worry about optimization in Rule 5, I feel duty-bound to demote the performance concern to a footnote. In my defense, the simplest solution here is the fastest, and that is not uncommon.

```
}
void findBounds(const vector<int> & values, Bounds * bounds)
{
    bounds->m_minValue = findExtreme(values, -1);
    bounds->m_maxValue = findExtreme(values, +1);
}
```

So, in all, these are three pretty commonplace ways to make things more complicated than they need to be: using too much abstraction, adding too much generality, and choosing the wrong algorithm.

The Cost of Complexity

There's a real cost to extra complexity. It takes longer to write complicated code than simple code, and *much* longer to debug it. Anyone reading the code has to fight their way through the complexity to understand what's going on. Our Simple solution has none of these problems—it's easy to get it right the first time, and it's easy to glance at it and understand both how it works and that it's correct.

In fact, this single issue—do you solve Easy problems with Simple solutions?—is the best discriminator between mediocre programmers and good ones. When we interview candidates at Sucker Punch, we look for two things: can the candidate solve Hard problems, and do they write Simple solutions for Easy problems? Unless the answer is yes to both of these questions, we're not interested.

Someone writing Complicated solutions to Easy problems isn't just making their own job harder, they're making it harder for everyone else on the team. Not only do their solutions take more time to create and introduce more bugs into the codebase, those solutions are more difficult and frustrating for everyone else to work with. We can't afford that.

The Four (But Really Three) Kinds of Programmers

Just like there are four flavors of code—Easy and Hard problems, Simple and Complicated solutions—there are four kinds of programmers. Given an Easy problem, do you write a Simple answer or a Complicated solution? And given a Hard problem, is your solution Simple or Complicated?

Now it turns out that there really *aren't* coders who write Simple solutions to Hard problems but Complicated solutions to Easy ones. That leaves us with three kinds of programmers, as Table 14-2 makes clear.

Table 14-2. Three kinds of programmers

Kind of programmer	Easy problem	Hard problem
Mediocre	Complicated	Complicated
Good	Simple	Complicated
Great	Simple	Simple

The difference between mediocre programmers and good ones is that good programmers write Simple answers to Easy problems. The difference between good programmers and great ones is that even as the problem gets Harder, the great programmer still finds a Simple solution.

At some point, problems get Hard enough that there are no Simple solutions to be found. The best measure of a programmer, then, is how far along this spectrum they can go before their solutions start getting Complicated. The farther along the spectrum they make it and the Harder the problems they can solve with Simple solutions, the better they are as a programmer.

In fact, you can look at this another way. The core skill of a great programmer is that they recognize when a problem that seems Hard is actually Easy, if considered from the right perspective.

Hard Problem, Somewhat Complicated Solutions That Don't Work

Consider the problem of checking whether any permutation of a particular set of letters (let's say "abc") appears in a string. That is, given a "permute string" that represents a set of letters, does some ordering of those letters appear consecutively in another "search string"? For the permute string abc, the function should return true if the search string is cabbage or abacus, but false if the search string is scramble or brackish.

It's not obvious how to solve this, right? The most obvious thing to do would be to generate all the permutations of the set of letters, then check whether any of them appear in the string. Generating permutations recursively is pretty simple. Grab each character from the permute string in turn, prepending it to all the permutations of the remaining characters in the search string. Here's a first attempt at this:

```
vector<string> generatePermutations(const string & permute)
{
    vector<string> permutations;

    if (permute.length() == 1)
    {
```

```
        permutations.push_back(permute);
    }
    else
    {
        for (int index = 0; index < permute.length(); ++index)
        {
            string single = permute.substr(index, 1);
            string rest = permute.substr(0, index) +
                            permute.substr(
                                index + 1,
                                permute.length() - index - 1);

            for (string permutation : generatePermutations(rest))
            {
                permutations.push_back(single + permutation);
            }
        }
    }

    return permutations;
}

bool findPermutation(const string & permute, const string & search)
{
    vector<string> permutations = generatePermutations(permute);
    for (const string & permutation : permutations)
    {
        if (search.find(permutation) != string::npos)
            return true;
    }

    return false;
}
```

The logic here is pretty simple, and things seem to work...until the permute string gets a teensy bit long. At that point things explode. The number of permutations is factorial in the length of the string, so our `findPermutation` function quickly becomes unusable. Give it a list of four characters to permute, as in our example, and it's happy as a clam. Give it a dozen and it disappears into a recursive hole, never to return.[2]

---

2 Well, not "never." With 4 letters, `generatePermutations` is so fast it's hard to measure on my PC. With 8 letters, it takes about a hundredth of a second. With 12 letters, I had to wait 42 seconds, during which my PC's fan kicked on full blast in a desperate attempt to stop me from melting something.

A naive reaction to this explosion would be to realize that I'm doing extra work. If any of the characters in the list are duplicated, then I'll have duplicate entries in the list of permutations. Maybe eliminating duplicates from the list of permutations would help:

```cpp
vector<string> generatePermutations(const string & permute)
{
    vector<string> permutations;

    if (permute.length() == 1)
    {
        permutations.push_back(permute);
    }
    else
    {
        for (int index = 0; index < permute.length(); ++index)
        {
            string single = permute.substr(index, 1);
            string rest = permute.substr(0, index) +
                    permute.substr(
                        index + 1,
                        permute.length() - index - 1);

            for (string permutation : generatePermutations(rest))
            {
                permutations.push_back(single + permutation);
            }
        }
    }

    sort(
        permutations.begin(),
        permutations.end());
    permutations.erase(
        unique(permutations.begin(), permutations.end()),
        permutations.end());

    return permutations;
}
```

Yeah, not so much. I didn't add that much code, which is great, and the code I added is simple, but I didn't really address the core problem. It's not possible to optimize your way out of a factorial mess. Unless all of our sets of characters to permute are small or are mostly duplicated letters, this code is still unworkable.

Hard Problem, Somewhat Complicated Solution

A better change is to let go of the idea that we're going to generate *all* the permutations. That approach is doomed.

Instead, we need to invert the way we're thinking about the problem. Let's check each substring of the search string. If we can match each character in the permute string to a single character in that substring, then we've found a permutation:

```cpp
bool findPermutation(const string & permute, const string & search)
{
    int permuteLength = permute.length();
    int searchLength = search.length();

    vector<bool> found(permuteLength, false);

    for (int lastIndex = permuteLength;
         lastIndex < searchLength;
         ++lastIndex)
    {
        bool foundPermutation = true;

        for (int searchIndex = lastIndex - permuteLength;
             searchIndex < lastIndex;
             ++searchIndex)
        {
            bool foundMatch = false;

            for (int permuteIndex = 0;
                 permuteIndex < permuteLength;
                 ++permuteIndex)
            {
                if (search[searchIndex] == permute[permuteIndex] &&
                    !found[permuteIndex])
                {
                    foundMatch = true;
                    found[permuteIndex] = true;
                    break;
                }
            }

            if (!foundMatch)
            {
                foundPermutation = false;
                break;
            }
        }
    }
```

```
        if (foundPermutation)
            return true;

        fill(found.begin(), found.end(), false);
    }

    return false;
}
```

This works, though the logic of the nested loops is a little tangled. You might get twinges of performance anxiety seeing the three nested loops—our first attempt at this function failed because of performance, after all—but in practice the N^3-ness of this approach isn't an issue. Unless the permute string is a thousand characters long, performance won't be the problem here.

If there's an issue here, it's the complexity of the logic. This is a Simple example, sized to fit this book, so the problem we're solving isn't actually *that* Hard. You might hope that we could find a Simple solution to it, and the preceding solution doesn't quite qualify. It's the sort of solution a Good programmer would write—completely functional, but more complicated than it needs to be.

Actually, a more typical solution from a Good programmer would include a spasm of premature optimization to avoid the three nested loops. They might keep running counts, for instance, then hash the set of counts to roughly linearize the function:

```
#define LARGE_PRIME 104729

bool findPermutation(const string & permute, const string & search)
{
    int permuteCounts[UCHAR_MAX] = {};
    int currentCounts[UCHAR_MAX] = {};

    int permuteHash = 0;
    int currentHash = 0;

    for (unsigned char character : permute)
    {
        ++permuteCounts[character];
        permuteHash += character * (character + LARGE_PRIME);
    }

    int permuteLength = permute.length();
    int searchLength = search.length();

    if (searchLength < permuteLength)
        return false;
```

```
    for (int searchIndex = 0; searchIndex < permuteLength; ++searchIndex)
    {
        unsigned char character = search[searchIndex];

        ++currentCounts[character];
        currentHash += character * (character + LARGE_PRIME);
    }

    for (int searchIndex = permuteLength;; ++searchIndex)
    {
        if (currentHash == permuteHash)
        {
            bool match = true;

            for (char character : permute)
            {
                if (permuteCounts[character] != currentCounts[character])
                    match = false;
            }

            if (match)
                return true;
        }

        if (searchIndex >= searchLength)
            break;

        unsigned char removeCharacter = search[searchIndex - permuteLength];
        unsigned char addCharacter = search[searchIndex];

        --currentCounts[removeCharacter];
        currentHash -= removeCharacter * (removeCharacter + LARGE_PRIME);

        ++currentCounts[addCharacter];
        currentHash += addCharacter * (addCharacter + LARGE_PRIME);
    }

    return false;
}
```

Again, this is functional, just overly Complicated. Under some conditions, it will have better performance than the last solution...but that doesn't matter. The last solution had perfectly reasonable performance and is easier to understand.

Hard Problem, Simple Solution

But is there a simpler solution, one that's easy to read and understand? What separates Great programmers from Good programmers is finding those sorts of solutions.

In this case, the algorithm we're using is fine—checking each substring of the search string to see whether it's a permutation of the permute string—it's our *expression* of that algorithm that's getting tangled. But there's a simpler way to think about checking for a match.

If we standardize the order of the letters in the permute string, then similarly standardize the order of each substring we compare it to, we can just compare the two standardized strings:

```
bool findPermutation(const string & permute, const string & search)
{
    int permuteLength = permute.length();

    string sortedPermute = permute;
    sort(sortedPermute.begin(), sortedPermute.end());

    for (int index = permuteLength; index < search.length(); ++index)
    {
        string sortedSubstring = search.substr(
                                index - permuteLength,
                                permuteLength);
        sort(sortedSubstring.begin(), sortedSubstring.end());

        if (sortedPermute == sortedSubstring)
            return true;
    }

    return false;
}
```

We haven't changed the fundamental algorithm here, but expressing it this way makes it much easier to understand. It's Simple where the last example was Complicated. A Great programmer finds simple and clear solutions like this one—and realizes that simplicity and clarity are almost always the important issues. The Greatest programmer isn't the one who can write the most complicated code: it's the one who finds the simplest answers to the most complicated problems.

Pull the Weeds

When my daughters were young, we had a Nintendo GameCube. It turns out that one side effect of having a dad who makes video games for a living is that your house is fully equipped with every single video game console. My children did not realize until much later that not everyone's house was like this.

Our favorite game was *Animal Crossing*, a game in which the three of us shared a small village filled with anthropomorphized animals. You could do all kinds of things in the village—dig for fossils, design new clothes, decorate your house, gather seashells, go fishing, make friends with the animals who lived in the town, or just kick back and listen to KK Slider play his guitar.

One of the things you sort of needed to do in *Animal Crossing* was pull weeds. Every night, a few weeds would pop up in your village, whether you'd played the game that day or not. Pulling weeds was easy—run over to the weed, push a button, and pop! The weed's out of the ground. But you needed to keep up. The weeds kept growing whether you pulled them or not. The weeds even grew on days you didn't play the game! If you stopped pulling weeds, the weeds took over.

They're still making *Animal Crossing* games 20 years later. Tens of millions of people have played some iteration of the game, and every single one has had the same experience—you come back to the tidy little village you've worked so hard on after a few weeks away, and it's completely overgrown with weeds. Twenty years later, I can still feel the pain.

Your project is like that village. You've got to pull the weeds—the little bits of annoyance that continually sprout in any codebase. Every day, whether you're working on the project or not, whether you're pulling weeds or not, more weeds are growing. If you don't pull the weeds, they'll choke the project.

So what are the weeds in this metaphor? They're small problems that are easy to fix, but also easy to ignore. Think of the weeds in *Animal Crossing*—

pulling them is as easy as pushing a button. Pulling a weed doesn't have side effects. It doesn't cause problems elsewhere. All that changes is that you have one less weed.

Here's a weedy bit of code:

```
// @brief Remove duplicate integers from a vector
//
// @param values Integer vector to compress

template <class T>
void compressVector(
    vector<T> & values,
    bool (* is_equal)(const T &, const T &))
{
    if (values.size() == 0)
        return;

    int iDst = 1;

    for (int iSrc = 1, c = values.size(); iSrc < c; ++iSrc) {
        // Check for unqiue values
        if (!is_equal(values[iDst - 1], values[iSrc]))
        {
            values[iDst++] = values[iSrc];
        }
    }

    values.resize(iDst);
}
```

There are a couple of obvious problems with the comments in this code. The header comment doesn't match the function, to begin with. It looks like this started as a function that compressed duplicate values from a vector of integers, and whoever adapted it into a template forgot to update the comment. On top of that, the comment itself is too vague—we're not removing all duplicate values, we're removing *adjacent* duplicates. Unless the array is sorted, those aren't the same thing. To complete the trifecta, there's a spelling mistake in the second comment. With those problems fixed:

```
// @brief Compress sequences of equal values in a vector
//
// For any sequence of values in the vector considered equal, keep only
// the first value in that sequence, removing the duplicates.
//
// @param values Vector to compress
// @param is_equal Comparison function to use
```

```
template <class T>
void compressVector(
    vector<T> & values,
    bool (* is_equal)(const T &, const T &))
{
    if (values.size() == 0)
        return;

    int iDst = 1;

    for (int iSrc = 1, c = values.size(); iSrc < c; ++iSrc) {
        // Check for unique values
        if (!is_equal(values[iDst - 1], values[iSrc]))
        {
            values[iDst++] = values[iSrc];
        }
    }

    values.resize(iDst);
}
```

Fixing these problems is pulling weeds. It's easy to do. Repairing the comments won't cause problems elsewhere. And I've made the code better—fixing the ambiguity of the comment is likely to save somebody a bug at some point.

I could do more, though. There are some naming and formatting issues sprinkled in, too. The i and c variables aren't following standard conventions—this project uses index and count, not one-letter conventions. The is_equal argument ought to be isEqual to match the project's function naming style. The curly braces aren't consistent, and this project's conventions frown on packing multiple arguments into the for statement. The conventions also expect blank lines after comments, which the second comment doesn't have.

All easy to fix:

```
// @brief Compress sequences of equal values in a vector
//
// For any sequence of values in the vector considered equal, keep only
// the first value in that sequence, removing the duplicates.
//
// @param values Vector to compress
// @param isEqual Comparison function to use

template <class T>
void compressVector(
    vector<T> & values,
    bool (* isEqual)(const T &, const T &))
{
    int count = values.size();
```

```
if (count == 0)
    return;

// Copy values that aren't equal to their predecessor

int destIndex = 1;
for (int sourceIndex = 1; sourceIndex < count; ++sourceIndex)
{
    if (!isEqual(values[destIndex - 1], values[sourceIndex]))
    {
        values[destIndex++] = values[sourceIndex];
    }
}

values.resize(destIndex);
}
```

This round of changes was also safe, though not as safe as the comment changes made in the first round. It's possible to introduce a bug with these sorts of changes—mistyping a `sourceIndex` when you meant `destIndex`, say. Unlikely, but possible.

Weed Identification

It's safety that defines whether an issue you spot is a weed or not. If you can fix it safely, then it's a weed that should be pulled. Fixing a spelling problem in a comment is absolutely safe. For a more substantive mistake in a comment, like the ambiguity we cleaned up in our first round of changes, fixing the problem is also safe...as long as you're actually right about what the function does!

You can fix naming issues safely, too. Doing a search + replace over a section of your source code will work, and the compiler will probably catch any mistakes you make, at least for compiled languages like C++.

In the second round of changes, I moved some variables around when I renamed them. That was safe-ish, but less safe than the other changes. Still a weed, probably, but getting less weedy.

There's a spectrum here, obviously! None of the changes I've made so far are functional—the compiler will generate the same code, more or less. We've improved its readability and consistency without affecting its functionality.

You can imagine more substantive changes that still don't affect the code's functionality—like changing the name of a class member, which requires matching changes in many source files, or writing a new expected-usage comment for a class. As long as the functionality of the code isn't affected, it's a weed. Changes that shouldn't change functionality as long as you get the details right, like moving or renaming a variable, are probably still weeds, but a little more caution is called for.

When you *are* intentionally changing functionality, it's not a weed anymore: it's a bug, and different rules apply. You pull weeds automatically; fixing bugs isn't as automatic, because doing so often introduces new problems. By definition, fixing a weed doesn't introduce new problems.

Pulling weeds is easy, and a weed-free codebase is much more pleasant to work in...so why do most projects have so many weeds?

How Code Gets Weedy

Well, it's easy to pull a weed, but it's just as easy to ignore it. We all have more tasks than time. And the cost of pulling the weed is immediate, though small, while its benefits are diffused and delayed. It's tempting to avert your eyes.

Furthermore, what looks like a weed to one coder may look like a flower to another.[1] You may be confused by a comment and suspect that it's incorrect, but not be confident enough in your understanding of the code to change it. You could take a more thorough look at the code or ask someone who's more familiar with it to double-check your suspicion, but (see previous paragraph) you've got a long to-do list, and fixing this random comment is not on it.

Or you may see some formatting issues in a chunk of code written by a new member of the team. You could fix them yourself, but it's easy to reason that fixing them yourself won't teach the new team member the right formatting. Better to let their next code review identify the mistake.

Even though weeds are easy to pull, it's almost as easy to leave them be. The factors that make you reluctant to pull them—needing to focus on important issues, being unsure of whether the weed is actually a weed or not—they're all real.

But weeds breed more weeds. You may have a crisply defined set of naming and formatting conventions, but if your project is full of weedy bits of nonconforming code, then no one will know what to trust. Do they trust the conventions, or the code? I know what happens in this case: they shrug and copy whichever they're more comfortable with.

---

1 Per the gardener's maxim, "A weed is just a plant in the wrong place." Which reminds me of the time I decided to surprise my wife by weeding her vegetable garden for her. The surprise in that case was that I pulled out all of the asparagus she'd recently planted. If my goal was to never be asked to weed anything ever again...mission accomplished.

The comment that confused you? It's going to confuse the next person who sees it, too. And you'd be surprised and how often the process of fixing a comment—verifying that the function does what you think, checking that the code around it is making the correct assumptions, talking about the new comment in a code review—turns up a "real" bug in the code.

Look, pulling weeds is by definition quick. This isn't something that needs to be scheduled. If something is going to take appreciable time, it isn't a weed.

Our focus at Sucker Punch on weeds works because we all agree what a weed is. We have strong and strict team conventions, per Rule 12. A lot of weed pulling fixes something that doesn't match the conventions. That strengthens the conventions themselves—not least because the change will get reviewed, and in the review the two of you will look at the noncompliant and compliant versions, pre- and post-weed pull, and agree that it was a weed that needed pulling. If as a code reviewer you think the reviewee is wasting time on unimportant issues, the problem is that you don't agree on what's important. Fix *that*.

In the end, it's simple. If you know something is a weed, pull it. If you suspect something is a weed, it's worth a small bit of effort to verify that and pull the weed.[2]

This places a counterintuitive imperative on your best, most senior team members. They're the ones who will be best at spotting weeds. The person who wrote your project conventions is best positioned to spot deviations from those conventions, after all. They're also likely to be one of the more senior people on the team. Does it make sense for them to spend a little bit of time fixing little problems?

Absolutely! Clearing the project of weeds makes everyone's job easier. It makes the important stuff more visible.

---

2 Just be sure it's not asparagus.

Work Backward from Your Result, Not Forward from Your Code

Forgive me for the following brief descent into metaphor.

Programming is about bridging gaps. You've got some problem you want to solve, and you've got some pile of code and tech to work with. In between, there's a gap. You'll build a bridge across it by extending the code you have and recombining bits and pieces of it in new ways, solving a bit of the problem at a time until you're done.

Sometimes you only have a small gap to cross. The code you have on hand nearly solves the problem, or just needs to be called in the right way. It barely even takes programming to build the bridge: you're just invoking your code with the right parameters set.

Sometimes the gap is huge. It's not at all clear how your code can solve the problem. Sometimes it's not entirely clear exactly what problem needs to be solved! That's particularly likely when you're working on a video game, where it's hard to predict what's going to be fun before you have it working. At Sucker Punch it's depressingly common to solve a tricky problem only to discover there was no point in solving it because the result isn't fun to play.

Every gap has two sides. You're standing on one side, looking across the gap at the other. The question here is—are you standing on the side that holds your existing pile of code, or are you standing on the other side, with the problem?

In other words, putting the bridge metaphor aside, are you thinking about the problem in terms of your existing code? Or are you thinking about your code in terms of the problem?

Probably the former, right? You know your existing code very well, whereas the problem may be entirely new. It might be described in completely different language than you'd use for your tech, for example. At Sucker Punch, we might describe a feature in terms of the emotions it generates in the player—say, that using an ability in the game should make the player feel "heavy" or "solid." It's not clear how that translates into loops and data structures!

If you're programming in a more traditional space, you still have to deal with problems defined in domain-specific ways: a reference to legal auditing requirements on the data you're updating, say, or some bit of business-school doublespeak about actionable measurables.

It's natural to try to understand the problem in terms of the tech you have on hand. In the Sucker Punch example, I might think about our "heavy-feeling" player ability in terms of the animation system, our sound and visual effects system, the tech we have for doing haptic feedback, and so on. I think about how I might put together these different bits of tech to make the ability feel heavy.

For those more traditional examples, I might think about how we can adapt our journaling system to handle a set of auditing requirements, or about how we can use our UX tech to pop together something to let our sales staff identify and track leads (which, it turns out, is what the new operations exec meant by "actionable measurables").

An Example

Let's say I'm building a system that has lots of parameters that need adjusting in different production environments. Some of the parameters are simple—a max number of worker threads we should fire up, or the path of a logfile. Others are more complicated, like a list of bits of plug-in logic along with parameters for each of the plug-ins. Depending on the environment, I might have hundreds of individual parameters to adjust.

Sounds like a config file is in order. As it turns out, I've got some JSON handling code on hand that seems like a good fit. The types and predictable structure of the parameters fit cleanly, it's easy to edit and debug the text-based format, and JSON is extensible enough to make me feel confident that new parameters will be easy to incorporate. Seems perfect!

Here's what the interface to my JSON code looks like:

```
namespace Json
{
    class Value;
    class Stream;

    struct Object
    {
        unordered_map<string, Value> m_values;
    };

    struct Array
    {
        vector<Value> m_values;
    };

    class Value
    {
    public:

        Value() :
            m_type(Type::Null),
            m_str(),
            m_number(0.0),
            m_object(),
            m_array()
            { ; }

        bool isString() const;
        bool isNumber() const;
        bool isObject() const;
        bool isArray() const;
        bool isTrue() const;
        bool isFalse() const;
        bool isNull() const;

        operator const string & () const;
        operator double () const;
        operator const Object & () const;
        operator const Array & () const;

        void format(int indent) const;

        static bool tryReadValue(Stream * stream, Value * value);
    };
};
```

Using JSON with this interface is straightforward—parse some JSON with `Json::Value::tryReadValue` to get a `Value`, then check its type before using the appropriate accessor. If a mismatched accessor is called—trying to convert an array to an object, say—the code asserts and returns a default value.[1]

In this simplified example, one of the configurable parameters we support is a list of blocked servers. Here's an excerpt from that part of the JSON config file:

```
{
    "security" : {
        "blocked_servers" : [
            "www.espn.com",
            "www.theathletic.com",
            "www.xkcd.com",
            "www.penny-arcade.com",
            "www.cad-comic.com",
            "www.brothers-brick.com"
        ]
    }
}
```

Apparently whoever configured things decided I shouldn't waste time at work, since that's a good chunk of my list of Chrome bookmarks. Things are looking good, though: that's pretty easy JSON to read and write.

Implementing a function to check the list of blocked servers is easy, if I'm willing to handle a little unpredictability in the config file. It's just a JSON file getting edited in a text editor, after all, so I can't count on it being set up exactly like I expect. Whoever is editing the file will make mistakes—misspelled option names, deprecated config options, specifying a number where a string is expected or a single string when we expect an array.

The JSON parser I'm using will take care of verifying the correctness of the JSON I pass it, so at least that's not a worry. And some unpredictability is part of the design, like making the `security` and `blocked_servers` keys optional. If they're omitted, then there aren't any blocked servers. I need to make sure the code is robust against other forms of unpredictability, though, like someone sticking a number in the list of blocked servers.

---

1 The eagle-eyed among you have likely spotted by now that this isn't a fully compliant JSON handler. Its object handling implies unique keys by using `unordered_map`, even though duplicate keys are explicitly allowed in JSON. Moving along.

Writing robust code for this file is straightforward, though a bit wordy:

```
bool isServerBlocked(string server)
{
    if (!g_config.isObject())
    {
        log("expected object for config");
        return false;
    }

    const Object & configObject = g_config;
    const auto & findSecurity = configObject.m_values.find("security");
    if (findSecurity == configObject.m_values.end())
        return false;

    if (!findSecurity->second.isObject())
    {
        log("expected object for config.security");
        return false;
    }

    const Object & securityObject = findSecurity->second;
    const auto & find = securityObject.m_values.find("blocked_servers");
    if (find == securityObject.m_values.end())
        return false;

    if (!find->second.isArray())
    {
        log("expected string array for config.security.blocked_servers");
        return false;
    }

    const Array & blockedServersArray = find->second;
    for (const Value & value : blockedServersArray.m_values)
    {
        if (!value.isString())
        {
            log("expect string array for config.security.blocked_servers");
            continue;
        }

        const string & blockedServer = value;
        if (blockedServer == server)
            return true;
    }

    return false;
}
```

So...victory, right? I took my existing JSON library and quickly adapted it to handle a config file. The code I wrote to walk through the parsed JSON data is a little bit bulky, but it's easy enough to write and read. The JSON code is known to be robust, so it makes sense to leverage it to solve this problem.

I've worked forward from the technology to solve the problem and, with not a whole lot of effort, ended up with something that worked OK. Anyone who's used the JSON library will have no problems working with the config file.

An Annoyance Appears

After a while, though, my team is likely to get a little annoyed with the amount of code required to delve down into the configuration info. It's easy code to read and write, but after you've written the same basic code a half dozen times—check that you've got an object, look for the key, handle a missing key, repeat as needed—you'll be ready to generalize.

I've already taken a step toward this with the errors I'm logging. They name a list of keys by separating the keys with periods, which is safe as long as the keys themselves don't have periods in them. I can accept that limitation on key names for my config file, leading to a simple function that walks through nested Objects (assuming I've got string splitting and joining functions to call):

```
const Value * evaluateKeyPath(const Value & rootValue, string keyPath)
{
    vector<string> keys = splitString(keyPath, ".");

    const Value * currentValue = &rootValue;
    for (unsigned int keyIndex = 0; keyIndex < keys.size(); ++keyIndex)
    {
        if (!currentValue->isObject())
        {
            log(
                "expected %s to be an object",
                joinString(&keys[0], &keys[keyIndex + 1], ".").c_str());
            return nullptr;
        }

        const Object & object = *currentValue;
        const auto & findKey = object.m_values.find(keys[keyIndex]);
        if (findKey == object.m_values.end())
            return nullptr;

        currentValue = &findKey->second;
    }
```

```
        return currentValue;
    }
```

That eliminates some of the bulk of isServerBlocked, roughly halving the amount of code required:

```
bool isServerBlocked(string server)
{
    const Value * value = evaluateKeyPath(
                            g_config,
                            "security.blocked_servers");
    if (!value)
        return false;

    if (!value->isArray())
    {
        log("expected string array for security.blocked_servers");
        return false;
    }

    const Array & blockedServersArray = *value;
    for (const Value & value : blockedServersArray.m_values)
    {
        if (!value.isString())
        {
            log("expected string array for security.blocked_servers");
            continue;
        }

        const string & blockedServer = value;
        if (blockedServer == server)
            return true;
    }

    return false;
}
```

I could simplify things further if I introduce a version of evaluateKeyPath that verifies it is returning an array:

```
bool isServerBlocked(string server)
{
    const Array * array = evaluateKeyPathToArray(
                            g_config,
                            "security.blocked_servers");
    if (!array)
        return false;

    for (const Value & value : array->m_values)
```

```
    {
        if (!value.isString())
        {
            log("expected string array for security.blocked_servers");
            continue;
        }

        const string & blockedServer = value;
        if (blockedServer == server)
            return true;
    }

    return false;
}
```

This all represents real progress—this version of isServerBlocked is half the size of my first attempt. With hundreds of options to handle, that's a big deal. That's just math.

But despite the improvement, it *still* feels like we're writing a lot of boilerplate code. What's going wrong?

Choosing a Side of the Gap

In all of these examples—the initial decision to use the JSON library, then my successive refinements—I'm starting from the technology and working forward. Our team has a JSON library that we all understand well, and I'm figuring out how to apply it to our config file problem. Once I've got that bit of tech working, I look to improve it incrementally.

In our bridge metaphor, I'm standing with my technology, looking across a gap at the problem I'm trying to solve. This is a common pattern—to think about the problem in terms of the solution you plan to apply.

Here's the problem with this approach, though. Through the lens of a JSON file, your config problem starts to adopt the shape of JSON. If you have a list of similar things, you think of them as a JSON array. You invent short names for each config option, because it's obvious that they're keys in a JSON object. You group related config options into objects, because that's a natural way to organize a big JSON file. If one of your config options is an enumerated option that says whether to run code locally or remotely, you think of it as a string instead, because that's one of the JSON types.

That's not inevitable. If you'd chosen a different format, you'd think about the problem differently. At Sucker Punch, one of our config files is written in a binary format, not as text. We didn't think about a hierarchy for the config options, because the serialization tech we use didn't suggest that. We're writing both integers and floating-point values directly, not converting everything to floating point as JSON does, because that's more natural. In short, the tech you're using strongly influences how you think about the problem you're trying to solve.

What if I broke this tendency and thought about the config file problem *without worrying about how I'm going to solve it*? How would I think about things if I were standing on the other side of the gap, the side with the problem, working backward from the problem instead of forward from the technology?

Working Backward Instead

Here's another way to frame that. If reading and writing the config file just magically happened, what would be the most convenient implementation of isServerBlocked?

Seems like it would be easiest to just have a global structure that holds all of the config options.[2] Then the list of blocked servers can just be a set of strings in that structure. Something like this:

```
struct Config
{
    set<string> m_blockedServers;
};
const Config g_config;

bool isServerBlocked(string serverURL)
{
    return (g_config.m_blockedServers.count(serverURL) > 0);
}
```

Hmm. That's a lot simpler than even the simplest version of isServer Blocked I built on top of our JSON tech. It's a lot easier to write and easier to read, with way fewer things to trip up on. It has much better performance, too, though that's probably not important in this context.

---

2 If the idea of a global object freaks you out, my apologies. This particular example—config options that are read at boot time then never changed, and hundreds of config option checks scattered through the project—is a great example of why global objects can be a good thing.

Actually, simplicity is only the start. If you really think about the config file problem, it doesn't take long to see some other issues with my JSON implementation. Some examples:

- My JSON code complains when some supported section of *config.json* doesn't have the expected structure—say, if a key's value has the wrong type or a required key is missing. Unsupported and unrecognized options are silently ignored. As long as the config file is legal JSON, it can contain all sorts of apparent config options that aren't actually hooked up to anything. That's not great—common mistakes like misspelling a config option name will be hard to discover.

- Our team will only discover problems with an option in our implementation when we try to use it. Here, `isServerBlocked` will log the issues it recognizes, but only when we call it to see whether a server is blocked. If the function isn't called, then any error in that section of the config file will go undetected. And if the function is called a lot, we could be spamming our log with a bunch of duplicate config-file formatting reports.

- At some point, our team is probably going to need to document the config file. When we do, we're starting from scratch. The expected structure of the config file is defined by all of the bits of code that use it, and they're scattered all over our codebase. Figuring out what config options are allowed is going to take some detective work.

These issues sound familiar...and that's because we've stumbled through a side door into the ongoing holy war between early-bound and late-bound solutions. As a programmer, you've probably at least dabbled in late-bound languages—Python, or Lua, or JavaScript—and tried early-bound languages like C or Java.

To simplify things to the breaking point: in late-bound solutions, you find out about problems late. With early-bound solutions, you discover at least some of your problems much earlier. In early-bound languages, you discover some of your bugs (but rarely all, unfortunately) when you compile. With late-bound languages, all the bugs appear when your code runs.

The solutions I built on top of our JSON library were late-bound. Any problems with the `security.blocked_servers` key aren't discovered until `isServerBlocked` is called. Contrast that with the solution based on a global config struct, which was early-bound. When I initialized that `Config` struct—

presumably loading it from some sort of config file—I ironed out any problems I found, making it much easier to implement isServerBlocked.

Maybe I haven't actually improved things, then—it sounds like I just moved the problem around. Sure, this implementation of isServerBlocked is much simpler, but is that because I've left out the parsing and validation code that must live somewhere? Having to write parsing code for the hundreds of options in our config file doesn't sound like fun.

There's nothing stopping me from combining the two approaches—using our JSON library to read the config file, but using a Config struct when I'm accessing config options in the code. I just need to write a function to unpack the data our JSON parser reads into the Config struct. With the right set of helper functions, that's not hard:

```
void unpackStringArray(
    const Value & value,
    const char * keyPath,
    set<string> * strings)
{
    const Array * array = evaluateKeyPathToArray(value, keyPath);
    if (array)
    {
        for (const Value & valueString : array->m_values)
        {
            if (!valueString.isString())
            {
                log("expected %s to be an array of strings", keyPath);
            }

            strings->emplace(valueString);
        }
    }
}

void unpackConfig(const Value & value, Config * config)
{
    unpackStringArray(
        value,
        "security.blocked_servers",
        &config->m_blockedServers);
}
```

There are hundreds of config file options, but most of them are pretty simple—simple types, or lists of simple types, accessed through a simple hierarchical namespace. I can handle just about everything with a dozen or so "unpack" functions. I'll have to write a bit of code if I'm dealing with a list of structured data—in JSON terms, an `Array` of `Objects`—but it's not tricky code.

Structuring things this way solves some of the problems I touched on earlier. I discover problems in the config file earlier, since they're all reported when the config file is unpacked. I don't spam our log with multiple reports of the same problem. If the config file has required options, then I can write my code to expect that they're present—and if they're missing, our `unpackConfig` file can report an error and fail at startup time.

I haven't solved all of my problems, though. I noted earlier the need to document the config file format somehow, and haven't made any progress against that. I'm also not doing anything to detect attempts to set unrecognized config options.

With the implementation I have now, the supported structure of this config file is defined by the code that unpacks it, so maybe there's a way to infer the structure from the unpacking calls I make. Since I'm unpacking the entire config file, for instance, I might infer that anything in the JSON file that doesn't get unpacked is unsupported. If I track which bits of JSON have been successfully unpacked, then any bits of the JSON file that weren't unpacked can be reported as unrecognized options.

Similarly, I know the name and type of every option in the config file, since I'm unpacking the whole thing. From the names and types, I can build minimal documentation listing the supported options and types. Better minimal documentation than none, after all—and this minimal documentation has the huge plus of being reliably accurate, since it's derived directly from the code!

It's possible to do both these things—but it's not simple. I wrote code to detect and report unrecognized options. It's not terribly long, but it was too long to fit in this chapter. And besides, it felt like I was marching forward from the solution I'd built, not backward from the problem space.

And Now for Something Completely Different

Here's a wild idea—if the problem is that I'm having a hard time inferring the structure of the config file from the code I've written, why not flip things around? Define the structure, then infer the code from that.

A word of warning first—this is a pretty long example! I wanted a "nothing up my sleeve" example of what working backward from your result can look like, and the code in this example is surprisingly tight given how functional it is.

Alone among the examples in this book, this one is usable as is. So bear with me for the next few pages!

For this simple example, I might define the structure of the config file like this, using a global structure to manage all of the config options:

```
struct Config
{
    Config() :
        m_security()
        { ; }

    struct Security
    {
        Security() :
            m_blockedServers()
            { ; }

        set<string> m_blockedServers;
    };

    Security m_security;
};
Config g_config;

StructType<Config::Security> g_securityType(
    Field<Config::Security>(
        "blocked_servers",
        new SetType<string>(new StringType),
        &Config::Security::m_blockedServers));

StructType<Config> g_configType(
    Field<Config>("security", &g_securityType, &Config::m_security));
```

It should be pretty obvious what the intent is here, even though the code is a bit of a C++ template rodeo. Each of the objects in the JSON file is described with a global variable using the StructType template. Here the "security" object is described by g_securityType; the "server.blockedServers" config file option is described as part of g_securityType. The config file as a whole is described by g_configType.

These descriptors define the translation from JSON objects to C++ structs. I need to know four bits of information to do this translation—the JSON keys and types for the object fields, and the C++ types and member pointers for the matching C++ structs. It's a little bit tricky to do this sort of metaprogramming in C++, but it's feasible.

The hard part is shuffling the C++ type information around to keep things type safe. To do that, I define a template class that couples a C++ type with a matching JSON type:

```
struct UnsafeType
{
protected:

    template <typename T> friend struct StructType;
    virtual bool tryUnpack (const Value & value, void * data) const = 0;
};

template <class T>
struct SafeType : public UnsafeType
{
    virtual bool tryUnpack(const Value & value, T * data) const = 0;

protected:

    virtual bool tryUnpack(const Value & value, void * data) const override
        { return tryUnpack(value, static_cast<T *>(data));  }
};
```

The SafeType abstract struct provides *type-safe unpacking* for a particular C++ type—it ensures that we're unpacking strings into string variables, integers into integer variables, and so on. For the most part, I'll use SafeType to unpack things. When I get around to handling structs, though, the code will be a little bit simpler (thanks to the type-unsafe unpacking interface introduced by Unsafe Type), but still type safe (thanks to some template trickery).

Here are SafeType definitions for some C++ types:

```
struct BoolType : public SafeType<bool>
{
    bool tryUnpack(const Value & value, void * data) const override;
};

struct IntegerType : public SafeType<int>
{
    bool tryUnpack(const Value & value, void * data) const override;
};

struct DoubleType : public SafeType<double>
{
    bool tryUnpack(const Value & value, void * data) const override;
};

struct StringType : public SafeType<string>
```

```
{
    bool tryUnpack(const Value & value, void * data) const override;
};
bool BoolType::tryUnpack(const Value & value, bool * data) const
{
    if (value.isTrue())
    {
        *data = true;
        return true;
    }
    else if (value.isFalse())
    {
        *data = false;
        return true;
    }
    else
    {
        log("expected true or false");
        return false;
    }
}

bool IntegerType::tryUnpack(const Value & value, int * data) const
{
    if (!value.isNumber())
    {
        log("expected number");
        return false;
    }

    double number = value;
    if (number != int(number))
    {
        log("expected integer");
        return false;
    }

    *data = int(number);
    return true;
}

bool DoubleType::tryUnpack(const Value & value, double * data) const
{
    if (!value.isNumber())
    {
        log("expected number");
        return false;
    }

    *data = value;
```

```
        return true;
    }

    bool StringType::tryUnpack(const Value & value, string * data) const
    {
        if (!value.isString())
        {
            log("expected string");
            return false;
        }

        *data = static_cast<const string &>(value);
        return true;
    }
```

This is the same sort of code as in earlier instantiations of our Config example. Here it's packaged as a type class, but the purpose is the same—check the types of the JSON values, then convert them into native values. That lets me handle the common cases, like config values that are known to be integers. Numeric values in JSON are floating point, so the IntegerType code checks that the floating-point value is actually an integer.

Moving beyond the simple types, let's look at lists of strings, like the blocked servers list in the config file example. I used a C++ set to represent that list, so I need to create a SetType:

```
    template <class T>
    struct SetType : public SafeType<set<T>>
    {
        SetType(SafeType<T> * elementType);
        bool tryUnpack(const Value & value, set<T> * data) const override;

        SafeType<T> * m_elementType;
    };

    template <class T>
    SetType<T>::SetType(SafeType<T> * elementType) :
        m_elementType(elementType)
    {
    }

    template <class T>
    bool SetType<T>::tryUnpack(const Value & value, set<T> * data) const
    {
        if (!value.isArray())
        {
            log("expected array");
            return false;
```

```
}

const Array & array = value;
for (const Value & arrayValue : array.m_values)
{
    T t;
    if (!m_elementType->tryUnpack(arrayValue, &t))
        return false;

    data->emplace(t);
}

    return true;
}
```

With hundreds of config file options, I'm likely to have some lists, too. I'll leave the VectorType that wraps vector as a proof for the reader—it's nearly identical to SetType. The only difference is that it calls the vector's push_back() method, where SetType calls the set's emplace() method.

The last thing to handle is mapping JSON objects to C++ structs—or, more precisely, mapping JSON key/value pairs into members of C++ structs or objects. I define a type-safe Field struct to be used by StructType:

```
template <class S>
struct Field
{
    template <class T>
    Field(const char * name, SafeType<T> * type, T S:: * member);

    const char * m_name;
    const UnsafeType * m_type;
    int S::* m_member;
};

template <class S>
template <class T>
Field<S>::Field(const char * name, SafeType<T> * type, T S::* member) :
    m_name(name),
    m_type(type),
    m_member(reinterpret_cast<int S::*>(member))
    { ; }
```

I'm handling type safety a bit differently in the Field struct. Type safety is imposed by the constructor. I require that the SafeType and member pointer have matching types. I can then safely use the type-unsafe UnsafeType and integer pointer-to-member values in the Field struct, since I know they actually have matching types.

StructType is surprisingly straightforward. Given all the other template wackiness going on here, I'm going to use a *variadic template* (a template that takes a variable number of arguments) in the constructor. In for a dime, in for a dollar:

```
template <class T>
struct StructType : public SafeType<T>
{
    template <class... TT>
    StructType(TT... fields);

    bool tryUnpack(const Value & value, T * data) const override;

protected:

    vector<Field<T>> m_fields;
};

template <class T>
template <class... TT>
StructType<T>::StructType(TT... fields) :
    m_fields()
{
    m_fields.insert(m_fields.end(), { fields... });
}
```

The tryUnpack method is pretty simple—loop through the fields of the JSON object, matching each of them to a field from our StructType. Building the looping this way makes it easy to report unrecognized options in the config file, knocking off one of my lingering problems:

```
template <class T>
bool StructType<T>::tryUnpack(const Value & value, T * data) const
{
    if (!value.isObject())
    {
        log("expected object");
        return false;
    }

    const Object & object = value;
    for (const auto & objectValue : object.m_values)
    {
        const Field<T> * match = nullptr;
```

```
        for (const Field<T> & field : m_fields)
        {
            if (field.m_name == objectValue.first)
            {
                match = &field;
                break;
            }
        }

        if (!match)
        {
            log("unrecognized option %s", objectValue.first.c_str());
            return false;
        }

        int T::* member = match->m_member;
        int * fieldData = &(data->*member);

        if (!match->m_type->tryUnpack(objectValue.second, fieldData))
            return false;
    }

    return true;
}
```

Once I've got a `Value` from the JSON library, I just call `tryUnpack` on the `StructType` I built for the config file:

```
bool tryStartup()
{
    FILE * file;
    if (fopen_s(&file, "config.json", "r"))
        return false;

    Stream stream(file);
    Value value;
    if (!Value::tryReadValue(&stream, &value))
        return false;

    if (!g_configType.tryUnpack(value, &g_config))
        return false;

    return true;
}
```

Things are looking good at this point! I've got solid, type-safe parsing of the config file and didn't have to write a lot of code to get it—all of the type and unpacking logic is less than 300 lines of C++. That's a huge example for a book, but a tiny part of most coding projects. With hundreds of config options in this example, that cost amortizes out pretty quickly. My description of the config file schema isn't self-documenting yet, but that's easy to add—tack a description string onto each `Field`, then write a simple recursive descent through the type hierarchy to generate the documentation.

Working Forward and Working Backward

This chapter explored two paths for parsing a config file. In the first path, we started with the format of the config file. We realized we could represent all of our options in JSON, recognized that we had a JSON parser ready to go, then just marched forward. And this absolutely worked—it was easy to parse the config file and easy enough to extract options from it.

In the second path we pivoted to look at the problem from another perspective: that of the programmers implementing the hundreds of config options supported, not the programmer parsing the config file. I chose a solution in the first path that was convenient to implement, but inconvenient to use. In the second path we worked backward from our desired solution, rather than forward from our tech, and ended up with a simpler and better solution.[3]

---

3 If you're interested in doing something like this, you might also take a look at generated-code solutions like protocol buffers (*https://oreil.ly/qvptL*) or C++ reflection magic like clReflect (*https://oreil.ly/pOnLe*).

Sometimes the Bigger Problem Is Easier to Solve

"Pick the most boring approach to every problem you encounter; if you can think of an exciting approach to solving a problem, it's probably a bad idea."

If this is how you'd paraphrase most of the advice in this book, I wouldn't blame you. A lot of these Rules can be a bit of a buzzkill. They point to some interesting or clever technique you might use to solve a problem, then immediately inform you that it would be a bad idea to use that technique. And it's true that the simple, boring approach is *almost* always the best approach. But only almost!

On some very special occasions, the clouds majestically part and you're bathed in the warmth of a single ray of sunlight spearing down from the heavens to illuminate you at your keyboard.[1] And in this brief, glorious moment, you realize that it would be simpler and easier to solve a more general version of whatever specific problem you're working on.

Revel in these occasions, because they don't come very often. When they do come, be ready to take advantage. Write the simple code, solve the general problem, and glory in the moment.

Jumping to Conclusions

Here's an example. In one of the early Sucker Punch games, the player bounds through levels as the master raccoon thief Sly Cooper. Sly is very agile, leaping into the air, then landing on tiny outcroppings or alighting on thin tightropes

---

1 You'll forgive the metaphor. I've lived in Seattle for 35 years; I've earned a cloud metaphor.

strung between buildings. The controls are simple—press the X button to jump, bend Sly's midair trajectory (in a physically impossible but entirely believable way) using one of the controller's sticks, then press the O button to land on things like spires or tightropes.

Of course, there was code to make this all happen![2] The trickiest bit of that code handled choosing the place where Sly lands when the player presses the O button. The player knows where they want to land when they press O, and the game needs to guess the player's intent somehow. When the guess is correct, the player doesn't even notice the magic; when the guess isn't, the player is very, very frustrated.

Guessing the landing spot the player has in mind is much easier said than done. Imagine that the player is steering Sly toward a tightrope and there are no other possible landing spots nearby. The code needs to decide *where* on the tightrope the player is trying to land. What's the algorithm for choosing this point?

The simple answers don't work very well. Steering for the point on the tightrope closest to Sly's current location doesn't work very well—if you're jumping along the tightrope, you'd get sucked backward to the point you were over when you pressed the button. To avoid that particular problem, the code could project Sly's current trajectory forward, then land on the point on the tightrope closest to that trajectory. That's a better solution, but it still broke badly in common cases. And in fact these seemingly simple answers weren't at all easy to implement, given that the tightrope was actually a cubic curve, not a straight line.

Cue a long sequence of increasingly desperate prototypes, each trying some new hacky heuristic to solve the problem of landing on a tightrope. This went on for weeks. Painful, painful weeks.[3]

Until, one day, the metaphoric clouds opened and a metaphoric beam of light hit me at the keyboard as I struggled with yet another doomed prototype. The problem was that I was thinking small, and I needed to think big.

I'd been looking for an analytic solution, trying (and repeatedly failing) to find a single magic function that would spit out the best position given the inputs—Sly's position and velocity, the player's input on the controller, and the

---

2 This algorithm is covered by US Patent 7,147,560. Sorry, software patents were in vogue at that point. Fear not; the patent expires on December 12, 2023, at which point you're entirely free to create your own raccoon-agility-centered platformer using the exact algorithm presented here.

3 Personally suffered through by your author, who wrote the code in question.

geometry of the tightrope. I didn't want to calculate the best landing point on the tightrope, I now realized—what I *really* wanted was to write a function that would evaluate the appropriateness of every single point on the tightrope, then choose the best one.

Well, not exactly. I didn't actually need to evaluate the function for each individual point on the tightrope—I only needed to find the point that was *most* appropriate. I needed to minimize a cost function (measuring appropriateness) over a domain (a parameter identifying the points along the tightrope).

In short, I had an optimization problem. If I solved the bigger problem of finding a local optimum for a function that mapped floats to floats, then wrote a cost function for Sly landing on a point, I could find the point with the lowest cost. If the cost function matched what the player had in mind, then the game would choose the right point on the tightrope.

The golden section optimization algorithm (*https://oreil.ly/oocWS*) is pretty bulletproof and not hard to implement:[4]

```
float optimizeViaGoldenSection(
    const ObjectiveFunction & objectiveFunction,
    float initialGuess,
    float step,
    float tolerance)
{
    // Track a domain + range pair for the objective function

    struct Sample
    {
        Sample(float x, const ObjectiveFunction & objectiveFunction) :
            m_x(x),
            m_y(objectiveFunction.evaluate(x))
            { ; }
        Sample(
            const Sample & a,
            const Sample & b,
            float r,
            const ObjectiveFunction & objectiveFunction) :
            m_x(a.m_x + (b.m_x - a.m_x) * r),
            m_y(objectiveFunction.evaluate(m_x))
            { ; }
```

---

4 The algorithm isn't complicated—you could sort it out from the code that follows without giving yourself a headache—but if you've got better ways to spend the next 10 minutes, take a look at the Wikipedia explanation. As it turned out, the golden section optimizer helped solve multiple problems, and we call it from a couple of dozen places in the Sucker Punch codebase.

```
        float m_x;
        float m_y;
};

// Get an initial triplet of samples around the initial guess

Sample a(initialGuess - step, objectiveFunction);
Sample mid(initialGuess, objectiveFunction);
Sample b(initialGuess + step, objectiveFunction);

// Make sure the "a" side has a smaller range value than the "b"
//   side. If we haven't lucked into an initial range bracketing a
//   minimum, we'll travel toward "a" until we find one.

if (a.m_y > b.m_y)
{
    swap(a, b);
}

// Find a point where the "mid" range value is smaller than the
//   "a" and "b" range values. That guarantees a local minimum
//   somewhere between a and b.

while (a.m_y < mid.m_y)
{
    b = mid;
    mid = a;
    a = Sample(b, mid, 2.61034f, objectiveFunction);
}

// Loop until we've got a tight enough bracket on the domain

while (abs(a.m_x - b.m_x) > tolerance)
{
    // Makes sure the "a" side brackets a bigger domain than the
    //   "b" side, so that the golden section is taken out of the
    //   bigger side.

    if (abs(mid.m_x - a.m_x) < abs(mid.m_x - b.m_x))
        swap(a, b);

    // Test a point between the "mid" sample (our best guess so
    //   far) and the "a" sample. If it's better than the mid
    //   sample, it becomes the new mid sample and the old mid
    //   sample is the new "b" side. Otherwise, the new sample
    //   becomes the new "a" side.

    Sample test(mid, a, 0.381966f, objectiveFunction);

    if (test.m_y < mid.m_y)
    {
```

```
            b = mid;
            mid = test;
        }
        else
        {
            a = test;
        }
    }

    // Return the best domain value we found

    return mid.m_x;
}
```

Once the general-purpose golden section algorithm implementation was tight, I could implement an objective function for falling to the tightrope. Tightropes were modeled as Bezier curves (*https://oreil.ly/YWuzT*), one of many ways to represent a cubic curve. To simplify the actual code just a bit, the objective function is the time it takes to fall to the landing point (meaning that points the player can land on earlier are preferred) times the maximum acceleration needed to land on that point. The context required to calculate this, like Sly's current position and velocity, is part of the object that implements the objective function:

```
struct BezierCostFunction : public ObjectiveFunction
{
    BezierCostFunction(
        const Bezier & bezier,
        const Point & currentPosition,
        const Vector & currentVelocity,
        float gravity) :
        m_bezier(bezier),
        m_currentPosition(currentPosition),
        m_currentVelocity(currentVelocity),
        m_gravity(gravity)
    {
    }

    float evaluate(float u) const override;

    Bezier m_bezier;
    Point m_currentPosition;
    Vector m_currentVelocity;
    float m_gravity;
};
```

The evaluate method isn't very complicated:

```
float BezierCostFunction::evaluate(float u) const
{
    // Get point along curve

    Point point = m_bezier.evaluate(u);

    // Calculate how much time it will take to fall to the height
    //   of that point

    QuadraticSolution result;
    result = solveQuadratic(
                0.5f * m_gravity,
                m_currentVelocity.m_z,
                m_currentPosition.m_z - point.m_z);

    float t = result.m_solutions[1];

    // Assume we scrub off all horizontal velocity before landing

    Vector finalVelocity =
        {
            0.0f,
            0.0f,
            m_currentVelocity.m_z + t * m_gravity
        };

    // Get immediate and final accelerations...since we're
    //   following a cubic curve one of these will be the maximum
    //   acceleration

    Vector a0 = (6.0f / (t * t)) * (point - m_currentPosition) +
                -4.0f / t * m_currentVelocity +
                -2.0f / t * finalVelocity;

    Vector a1 = (-6.0f / (t * t)) * (point - m_currentPosition) +
                2.0f / t * m_currentVelocity +
                4.0f / t * finalVelocity;

    // Ignore acceleration in Z, since we know that's gravity

    a0.m_z = 0.0f;
    a1.m_z = 0.0f;

    // Calculate cost function

    return t * max(a0.getLength(), a1.getLength());
}
```

Running the golden section optimizer on this function produced a landing point that felt more or less natural. It did require some tuning, and I've left the edge cases out of the evaluate implementation,[5] but even the first results were better than the long string of failed prototypes this solution replaced. After tuning, it felt completely predictable and natural—and in practice, players trained themselves to match the cost function, and the game guessed what they had in mind nearly all the time.[6]

As a rule, it's almost always better to solve the specific problem you do understand rather than trying to solve a general problem you don't understand. Generalization takes three examples, per Rule 4. But that truth isn't *quite* universal—sometimes the general problem is easier to solve than the specific one. In this case, the specific problem of choosing a spot for Sly to land on the tightrope was hard to solve, at least analytically, while the general problem was relatively easy to solve.

Finding a Clear Path Forward

Time for another example drawn from the annals of Sucker Punch history...this one a bit more recent. In *Ghost of Tsushima*, the player can make a short, explosive dash, usually to avoid incoming attacks. They deflect a stick on the controller to choose a direction, then press a button to dash. Poof! Our samurai hero, Jin Sakai, dodges in that direction and danger is averted. Or at least that's what it feels like for players.

Jin doesn't always dash in *exactly* the direction the player has chosen. If the player is fighting enemies in a forest, say, it's no fun if Jin dashes straight into a tree—even if, strictly speaking, that's the direction the player has chosen. Nobody wants to be a clumsy samurai! Instead, the code chooses a direction to dash that avoids all the trees, while staying close to the direction the player has chosen. The player is none the wiser—they feel graceful instead of clumsy, and everyone's happy.

---

5 The edge cases aren't that bad—and were easy enough to handle by adding penalties onto the cost function. If the evaluate function tries to evaluate a point off the end of the curve, a penalty is added. Careful construction of the penalty helps point the optimizer back toward the valid range of the curve. Similarly, if Sly doesn't jump high enough to reach a point, this adds a separate penalty.

6 If you try using an optimizer like this to solve problems, remember that it will find a minimum, but maybe not the minimum you want. Your cost function needs to be constructed carefully, as does your initial guess.

The Sucker Punch engine has code to do this sort of pathing through the game environment—roughly speaking, to try to reach the far end of a search area while skirting areas the player can't move through. To oversimplify the code: it checks the line segments starting from an initial point to the end of the search area, wraps around any obstructions we encounter, then straightens out kinks in the resulting path as best it can. To undersimplify the code, it's A* over a discovered graph.[7]

Using this pathing code as is was a great start toward natural-feeling-but-graceful dashes, but it wasn't good enough to ship. Jin dodged gracefully through trees, but blundered clumsily into other characters, whether they were enemies or allies. The obvious fix was to adjust the pathing checks to include characters as well as trees. That was not something the existing pathing code knew how to do! It worked against the fixed obstacles in the environment, like trees and buildings, but it knew nothing about temporary obstacles, like an enemy character charging at the player.

It didn't seem too hard to add that support, though, so that's what I did. Remember that at a simple level, the pathing code checks for the intersection of a path with obstructions. If the path runs into an obstruction, the pathing code builds a new path that wraps around that obstruction. So adding support for characters meant two things: checking for intersections between the path and characters, and wrapping paths around characters. Neither was too hard, though it was all new code because characters were represented as circles. And a bonus problem was added—I needed to worry about the intersections between the space carved out for characters with environmental obstacles, and the inter-sections between characters themselves. All of these intersections were plausible endpoints to the path.

Ugh. This worked, but it meant a lot of new code to handle a lot of new cases. This made the complicated pathing code even more complicated, all to handle the special case of player dashes. Then I discovered that the simple circular obstacle I was carving out for characters didn't work very well for moving

---

7 The A* algorithm (*https://oreil.ly/XOban*) isn't that complicated, but nevertheless it's too much to explain here. By *discovered graph*, I mean that the theoretical search space consists of links between any pair of points in the world. We discover which pairs of points are accessible from each other as we go, by clipping the line between them against all the obstacles in the world.

characters, so I switched to lozenge-shaped obstacles instead[8]—and things got worse. The extra complexity I was adding felt unjustified.

Cue the metaphoric parting of clouds and beam of light. I was adding code in the wrong place! The pathing code already supported the arbitrary geometry of the environment, after all. Trees are circular obstacles, just like a character standing still. If I could just pretend people were temporary trees, the pathing code could just avoid them, without all the extra complexity I'd added.

Once I pivoted to this point of view, a clear path forward presented itself. The underlying representations of trees and buildings and fences and all the other fixed parts of the environment were just a really big grid, with each cell marked as passable or impassable. I could introduce temporary obstructions via a simple interface—all I needed was an extra check for whether a particular cell in the grid was blocked:

```
struct GridPoint
{
    int m_x;
    int m_y;
};

struct PathExtension
{
    virtual bool isCellClear(const GridPoint & gridPoint) const = 0;
};
```

This extension interface could then be passed into the basic calls to the pathing code, like checking a line segment for obstructions or finding the best path forward in a given direction. Here's what the original calls looked like:

```
class PathManager
{
public:

    float clipEdge(
        const Point & start,
        const Point & end) const;
    vector<Point> findPath(
        const Point & startPoint,
        float heading,
```

---

8 Just as a circle is the set of points at some fixed distance from a point, a *lozenge* is the set of points at a fixed distance from a line segment. Paper clips and running tracks are lozenge-shaped—two half-circles connected by parallel lines.

```
        float idealDistance) const;
};
```

And here's the new version:

```
class PathManager
{
public:

    float clipEdge(
        const Point & start,
        const Point & end,
        const PathExtension * pathExtension = nullptr) const;
    vector<Point> findPath(
        const Point & startPoint,
        float heading,
        float idealDistance,
        const PathExtension * pathExtension = nullptr) const;
};
```

The internal details of clipEdge and findPath were barely affected. Wherever they had previously checked the giant pathing grid, I added an extra check to the PathExtension interface. That's less than a dozen lines of code, total, across these functions and a handful of other similar functions.

This account leaves out the work to implement the PathExtension interface, but that work was similarly simple:

```
struct AvoidLozenges : public PathExtension
{
    struct Lozenge
    {
        Point m_points[2];
        float m_radius;
    };

    bool isCellClear(const GridPoint & gridPoint) const override
    {
        Point point = getPointFromGridPoint(gridPoint);

        for (const Lozenge & lozenge : m_lozenges)
        {
            float distance = getDistanceToLineSegment(
                            point,
                            lozenge.m_points[0],
                            lozenge.m_points[1]);

            if (distance < lozenge.m_radius)
                return false;
```

```
    }

        return true;
    }

    vector<Lozenge> m_lozenges;
};
```

And that was that. A couple of dozen lines of simple code, instead of the thousand or so lines of nastiness I'd struggled with in my attempt to solve the problem directly.

The new `PathExtension` interface was much more general, obviously—it handled any sort of temporary obstruction you wanted to add to the grid, with no stipulation about shape or size or way the obstruction was represented. That's a step forward from the first attempt, which only added hardwired support for circles and then lozenges. But this extra generality is entirely beside the point!

The point isn't that this solution was more general—it's that it was simpler and easier to implement than the more specific, less general solution. In fact, as I write this, the Sucker Punch codebase has exactly one implementation of `PathExtension`—the one I've just presented. We haven't taken advantage of the extra generality, and that's perfectly OK.

Recognizing the Opportunity

Most of the time, the specific solution is easier to implement than the general solution. Solve the problem you understand. Don't try to solve a more general problem until you've got enough examples to be confident that the more general problem is worth solving.[9]

It's rare to bump into a problem like the examples in this Rule, where the general problem is simpler and easier to solve than the specific one. These two examples are separated by 18 years (!), and nearly all of the umpteen problems we solved in between were solved simply and directly.

While such general solutions are rare, they're important. These two examples, along with a handful of others, were important breakthroughs for Sucker Punch. Sometimes the breakthrough represented a new paradigm, as in the first example, which prompted us to solve many gameplay problems via a local optimizer; other times it was just a one-off solution to a hard problem, as in the second example. They all created better, more successful products.

---

9 Where "enough" is "at least three."

That leaves open an important question—what are the clues that a more general solution will create simpler code? How can you spot these opportunities in your code?

I did find one common factor as I looked over the quarter-century-long engineering history of Sucker Punch. In all the examples of the general solution being the simpler path, *a major change in perspective was necessary.* The general solution represented a completely different way of thinking about the problem, and this new perspective allowed a radically simpler solution.

In this Rule's examples, the change in perspective was technical—switching from an analytic approach to an optimization approach in the first example and adding the new feature in a completely different part of the code in the second example.

Sometimes, though, the change in perspective isn't technical at all. You might realize that your code targets the wrong user for a feature, for instance. We've often unlocked much simpler approaches by moving a feature historically used by the programming team to the production team instead, or vice versa.

But there's always a moment when you realize you've been thinking about the problem all wrong. And when that realization hits, there's a chance that the clouds will part and a beam of sunshine will hit and you'll get to experience the infinite joy of solving a single tough problem with a simple, general solution.

Let Your Code Tell Its Own Story

There's a lot of focus in this book about making your code easier to read, whether it's by being careful about hiding the behavior of your code behind extra abstractions, choosing good names for things, or choosing the simplest workable approach to a problem. Writing code that's easy to read makes everything else go more smoothly, since we all spend a lot more time reading and debugging code than we spent writing it in the first place. When you're debugging a bit of code, it's much easier to figure out what's going wrong when you have a quick way to understand what it's trying to accomplish.

That's especially true for a project you're working on as part of a team, but it's even true for a solo project. If you've got a nontrivial solo project going, one that you're spending weeks or months or even years on, you'll end up needing to refamiliarize yourself with code you wrote long before. Whatever thoughts you had in your head when you wrote that code will have faded away; all that's left will be the code itself. At this point, you're in pretty much the same place as a coworker on a group project: you need to sort out what the code is doing (or trying to do) by reading it.

Here's another way of thinking about this—Future You is a stranger.

Unless your project will get wrapped up and thrown away in a day or two, expect to come back to your code as a stranger. Do Future You a favor and make it easy to read.

Imagine walking someone through some bit of code you've written. If your team does code reviews (and it should; see Rule 6), then you're probably used to doing that. You talk about what this code is trying to accomplish, how it fits into the larger scope of the project, and why you made the decisions you did. You point out any bits of trickiness or cleverness (hopefully there aren't many), note any issues that haven't been taken care of yet, walk through how the pieces fit together, and probably narrate the control flow through the individual functions you've written.

In short, you're telling the story of your code. The better a job you do of telling that story, the more quickly and completely your audience will understand that code. And in a perfect world, the code would tell its own story, without your narration.

That's a pretty lofty target, especially if your code has to be a little bit complicated to solve its target problem. Nevertheless, code that tells its own story is what you should always be shooting for.

Don't Tell Stories That Aren't True

So—what does it mean for code to tell its own story? I've touched on some of the important concepts, like choosing good names (Rule 3), and making the intent of your code as simple and obvious as possible (Rule 1). After all, it's much easier to follow a simple story than it is to follow a complicated one!

I haven't really addressed formatting or commenting yet in this book—the code examples accompanying the Rules are largely comment-free. That's not a statement on my part—in this book I can write whole paragraphs of text explaining the code examples, so keeping them comment-free and compact makes sense. In real code, comments can be a huge help for code readability.

That doesn't mean all comments are good, though! It's entirely possible for comments to do more harm than good. Some comments are never true to begin with; others were true when the comment was written, but reality has since drifted away.

Here's an example:

```
void postToStagingServer(string url, Blob * payload)
{
    // Will always get a valid handle back due to Connect::Retry

    ConnectionHandle handle = connectToStagingServer(
                        url,
                        Connect::Retry | Connect::InternalServer);

    // Post data

    postBlob(handle, payload);
}
```

This seems pretty simple, but it's not—the first comment is wrong. When the code was written, the `Connect::Retry` flag guaranteed success. Things got more complicated when the (imaginary, in this case) team decided that there were no situations in which infinite retry (hanging until a successful connection was made) was a good strategy. The behavior of `Connect::Retry` changed, but this bit of code, which relied on the old behavior, didn't change to match.

So now there's a bug in `PostToStagingServer`, but one that doesn't show up very often, because `ConnectToStagingServer` almost always works. Pity the poor programmer who's trying to debug this, especially if `PostBlob` is written to be robust against the empty handle that `ConnectToStagingServer` returns in error cases. The poor programmer reads the code, sees the comment, accepts it, and moves on, missing the actual problem.

If not for that comment, the bug would have been found sooner, because it would have been obvious that an error was possible. It's this sort of situation that leads some programmers to argue that all comments are bad, insisting that the problems caused by out-of-date comments outweigh the benefits of accurate ones.

Remember that code that isn't running doesn't work, per Rule 8. If some bit of code isn't getting exercised frequently, it will stop working, and you won't know that it's stopped working because it isn't getting run.

In some sense, comments are code that never runs—the closest they come to running is when someone reads through and compares the comments to the actual code. That doesn't happen very often, and generally isn't very thorough when it does, so it shouldn't be a surprise that comments "stop working" as the functionality of the code they describe slowly drifts out of touch with the comment.

The easiest way to avoid this is to change the comment into an assert. Don't mention in a comment that one of the arguments to a function is expected to be non-null—assert that it is. Or in this case, don't claim that `ConnectToStaging Server` always returns a valid handle—assert that it does. You've told the same story, just in a much more effective way.

Make Sure There's a Point to the Story

Sometimes comments aren't wrong—they're just useless. We've all seen less-than-informative comments, often as an unintended result of some fixed commenting style that all code on your project must follow. Here's an example of code that adheres to a project-wide dictate that all functions must be documented with Doxygen.[1] The comment here follows the rule without actually passing along any information:

```
/**
 * @brief Post payload to staging server
 *
 * Attempt to post the given payload to the staging server at the
 * given address, returning @c true if the post is successful and
 * @c false if it fails for some reason.
 *
 * @param url URL to server
 * @param payload Data to post
 * @returns true on success
 */
bool tryPostToStagingServer(string url, Blob * payload);
```

Nothing in that comment is wrong—it's just not very useful. We can assume that the "try" at the beginning of the function name is a project convention that marks functions that return true on success. If that's the case, then all of the information in the comment is directly implied by the function declaration. The comment isn't adding anything new; it just restates the function name, then restates it, then restates it again.

If the comment accompanies the declaration of a function rather than its definition, as in this example, then the space taken up by fixed-format comments can quickly overwhelm the space devoted to actual function declarations. That's the cost of this commenting style—the comments make it hard to find the actual code. This is exacerbated by whatever awkwardness pops up in the comment itself as it fits itself to the format—those @cs in the comment aren't helping readability.[2]

There is a potential upside—the point of Doxygen isn't just the comments, it's also the documentation that's generated from them. That documentation isn't as useful as it once was, now that editors are much better at hyperlinking back and forth within projects, but it can still be useful if done thoughtfully.

---

1 Doxygen is a widely used tool that extracts strangely formatted comments from source code and generates project documentation from them. The idea is that documentation that's right next to the code is more likely to stay up-to-date. This is true, though in my experience only for small values of *more* and *likely*. I apologize for the formatting to non-C++ programmers. I wanted to use a real example, and all of these documentation-generating tools use strange formatting on purpose—because the tool looks for the strange formatting to mark the text it needs to process.

2 They mark terms that should be typeset in a fixed-width font, like Courier. Hence "c".

That's usually not the case, though. Programmers in a hurry write hurried comments, not thoughtful ones. They aim to meet mechanical standards before moving on, which produces comments that are correct but uninformative, like the one in this section. A list of uninformative entries for individual functions and types doesn't make for a useful introduction or reference to the code—you're not learning anything you wouldn't learn from reading through the code.

Telling Good Stories

So what makes a good comment?

The most obvious answer is that a good comment tells the reader something about the code that *isn't obvious*. A comment that recapitulates the obvious, like the prior example, is correct but not very useful. A good comment, one that helps the reader understand the code, might explain why the code is written the way it is, give the expected usage for a function, or mark some bit of logic that might need further work.

There's another important role that good comments fill—they punctuate the code. They tell you what parts of the code fit together and separate bits of code that represent separate thoughts. In this way, they act like spaces and punctuation in writing. Youcanreadsentencesthatdontincludespacingorpunctuation...but it's a lot easier to read sentences that do, right? The spaces break up the words. Punctuation breaks up sentences and clauses. Paragraphs break separate thoughts.

The same is true of code, with spacing and comments filling the roles that spacing and punctuation do in normal writing. Here's an example. (I'm exaggerating the point here by using a super-compact naming style for variables and compressing out more whitespace than you'd normally see.)

```cpp
bool findPermutation(const string & p, const string & s)
{
    int pl = p.length(), sl = s.length();
    if (sl < pl) return false;
    int pcs[CHAR_MAX] = {}, scs[CHAR_MAX] = {};
    for (unsigned char c : p)
    { ++pcs[c]; }
    int si = 0;
    for (; si < pl; ++si)
    { ++scs[static_cast<unsigned char>(s[si])]; }
    for (;; ++si)
    {
    for (int pi = 0;; ++pi)
    {
```

```
    if (pi >= pl) return true;
    unsigned char c = p[pi];
    if (pcs[c] != scs[c]) break;
    }
    if (si >= sl) break;
    --scs[static_cast<unsigned char>(s[si - pl])];
    ++scs[static_cast<unsigned char>(s[si])];
    }
    return false;
}
```

It's certainly possible to figure out what this function is doing—it has a descriptive name, at least, so you've got a head start. Adding more descriptive names, spacing to separate thoughts, and comments to explain those thoughts will make it much easier to read:

```
// Check whether any permutation of the permute string appears in the
//   search string

bool tryFindPermutation(const string & permute, const string & search)
{
    // If the search string is shorter than the permute string, then there's
    //   no way it can be a permutation. Exit now to simplify things.

    int permuteLength = permute.length();
    int searchLength = search.length();
    if (searchLength < permuteLength)
        return false;

    // Count how many times each letter shows up in the permute string.
    //   We'll compare these counts to running counts we'll keep in the
    //   search string.

    int permuteCounts[UCHAR_MAX] = {};
    for (unsigned char c : permute)
    {
        ++permuteCounts[c];
    }

    // Make the same counts for the first possible match in the
    //   search string

    int searchCounts[UCHAR_MAX] = {};
    int searchIndex = 0;

    for (; searchIndex < permuteLength; ++searchIndex)
    {
        unsigned char c = search[searchIndex];
        ++searchCounts[c];
```

```
}

// Loop over the possible matching substrings in the search string

for (;; ++searchIndex)
{
    // Check whether the current substring matches the permute string

    for (int permuteIndex = 0;; ++permuteIndex)
    {
        // If we didn't find any character count mismatches after we've
        //   checked all the characters in the permute string, then we've
        //   found a permutation. Return true to mark that success.

        if (permuteIndex >= permuteLength)
            return true;

        // If the count of this character in the permute string doesn't
        //   match the count in this substring of the search string, then
        //   the substring isn't a permutation. Move on to the next one.

        unsigned char c = permute[permuteIndex];
        if (permuteCounts[c] != searchCounts[c])
            break;
    }

    // Stop once we've checked all possible substrings in the
    //   search string

    if (searchIndex >= searchLength)
        break;

    // Update the running character counts to match the next
    //   possible match

    unsigned char drop = search[searchIndex - permuteLength];
    unsigned char add = search[searchIndex];

    --searchCounts[drop];
    ++searchCounts[add];
}

// If we make it here, then we're out of substrings and didn't find
//   any matching permutations, since we return immediately once
//   they're found.

return false;
}
```

Much easier to follow, right? Read the previous example and you're in for some tough sledding figuring what's going on. Read this example from top to bottom, and you understand exactly what it's doing and why.

The extra spacing breaks up the bits of logic, just like spaces break up words in a sentence. Indentation groups related thoughts. Choosing good names for variables is a shortcut to understand their purpose—good names are your first and most important bit of documentation. Comments provide context and explanation—they focus on the big picture, the "why" to the code's "what."

If you're used to explaining code or having it explained to you, then reading code written this way feels familiar. Good comments feel like reading a story.

You could also think of good code as a song. Songs have music and lyrics, with each playing complementary roles. Good code is the same way—the actual code and the comments have separate but related roles. They support each other. The lines of code are the functioning part; good naming and formatting make the function of each line clear. The comments support this with context, explaining how the lines fit together and what the purpose of each line is.

Your code editor probably color-codes things, with comments showing up in a different color than lines of code. Since most people's brains are pretty good at sorting colors, spacing and color-coding make it easy to focus on code or comments separately, while still keeping it easy to look at them together. That's just like reading sheet music: the music is shown as notes in a staff, while the lyrics are printed alongside, roughly aligned but separate. You can focus on the music or the lyrics when reading sheet music.

You'll be in great shape if you remember that good comments complement code instead of duplicating it. They pull the bare mechanics of the code into a story, making it much easier to understand the code. If you can read through the comments while ignoring the code and still feel like you understand what's going on, then you've done a top-notch job.

Rework in Parallel

Most of the time, for most of the work you do as a programmer, you'll only make brief departures from the main codebase. You'll investigate a problem, check out the files you need to fix the problem, test and review your changes, then commit them back into the main branch. You might complete the whole cycle in a day, though that's pretty quick if there's any testing to be done; more typically, you'll spend days with stuff checked out.

Eventually, though, you run into a task where this simple model falls apart. You're teaming up on something with another programmer, say. When you're working solo, the work in progress only exists on your machine, but that doesn't work when you're partnered with someone. The two of you need to maintain a shared version of the work in progress.

The standard answer to this is to create a new branch in your source code control system for the work the two of you have planned. This branch starts as a copy of the main branch, but quickly diverges from the main branch as you work. You probably look for occasional chances to integrate changes from the main branch into your branch to keep up with the work being done by the rest of the team, resolving any conflicts introduced by changes on the main branch. Eventually your work is complete; you integrate one last time from the main branch, do a final test, review your work, and check in.

Bumps in the Road

This approach works—that's why it's the standard answer—but it's not free of problems.

Integrating changes from the main branch can be hard, for instance. The rest of the team has no visibility into what you're doing on your branch, so it's easy for them to break your work in progress. This can be a minor annoyance, as when someone introduces a new call into the system you're reworking. It can be more troublesome, as when someone fixes a bug in the old system that has to be mirrored in your reworked version. Or it can be truly painful, like someone deciding to reorganize a source file, destroying all the diffs you've been relying on.

If you're reworking the old system in place, which is typically the case, then it's easy to lose sight of how the old system worked. You started with source code for the old system, which you could consult to understand its function—but every line you change makes it harder to see which behaviors were original and which have been added. The workarounds for this—like keeping a full copy of the original source to consult, or continually referring to diffs from the original source—are painful.

If you're part of a big team, then just keeping up with the churn from the rest of the team can be a challenge. Typically, the core of the work you're focused on is confined to a handful of source files, but calls to that core can be scattered across dozens of files. Every change to any of those dozens of files is a potential merge conflict. If you've got a big team of people checking in changes to the main branch, then the smaller team working on a branch can get saturated just integrating changes.

It's easy to get lost in a tangle of source-code control branches. The flexibility branching provides is tempting, and it's easy to get carried away. The simple branching I described for the standard approach—a single branch leaving the main branch and rejoining it later—is easy enough to track. If it gets more complicated than that—throwaway branches for testing new approaches to the problem, branches for personal backups, multiple main branches to manage release staging—you can get lost pretty quick.

We've followed this standard branch-and-change approach for a few big changes at Sucker Punch. The results were painful, so we've tried alternatives. We've had pretty good luck with a particular approach, a duplicate-and-switch model.

Build a Parallel System Instead

Here's the idea—instead of changing a system in place, we build a parallel system. The new system is checked in while work is still in progress, but is only enabled (via a runtime switch) for the small team working on it. Most of the team uses the old system, never touching the new code paths. When the new system is ready to go, we use the runtime switch to enable it for everyone. Once everyone is successfully using the new system, we excise the old one from the project.

There's a great aphorism from Kent Beck (*https://oreil.ly/8YWdU*) that applies:

For each desired change, make the change easy (warning: this may be hard), then make the easy change.

It's straightforward to apply this aphorism on small projects. The parallel system technique is a way to apply it to big changes on larger projects, where the preparatory work spans many bits of code committed from multiple coders. All the hard work of building the parallel system sets you up for the cut-over point, which is easy in comparison.

A Concrete Example

Let's look at a real-world example. It's going to take a few pages to set up the context, but we'll return to the idea of building a parallel system before too long.

At Sucker Punch we use a stack-based memory allocator in much of our code, instead of relying on the standard heap allocator in all cases. The basic idea of a stack allocator is to simplify allocation by not freeing allocated blocks—at least, not *individual* blocks. With the standard heap allocator, each allocated block must later be freed. A stack allocator works more like variables on the call stack— any block allocated in a function is automatically freed when the function exits. Stack-based allocation is easier to use because you don't have to worry about freeing blocks. It's also wicked fast, which is important in a lot of our game programming scenarios.

Scopes are defined with a "context" object. All stack allocations are associated with the current context. When a context goes out of scope, all blocks associated with that context are freed. The blocks have all been allocated sequentially, so this mass freeing is trivial, just as each allocation was. We're just pushing pointers around. Here's the allocator:

```
class StackAlloc
{
    friend class StackContext;

public:

    static void * alloc(int byteCount);

    template <class T>
    static T * alloc(int count)
        { return static_cast<T *>(alloc(sizeof(T) * count)); }
```

```
protected:

    struct Index
    {
        int m_chunkIndex;
        int m_byteIndex;
    };

    static Index s_index;
    static vector<char *> s_chunks;
};

StackAlloc::Index StackAlloc::s_index;
vector<char *> StackAlloc::s_chunks;

const int c_chunkSize = 1024 * 1024;

void * StackAlloc::alloc(int byteCount)
{
    assert(byteCount <= c_chunkSize);

    while (true)
    {
        int chunkIndex = s_index.m_chunkIndex;
        int byteIndex = s_index.m_byteIndex;

        if (chunkIndex >= s_chunks.size())
        {
            s_chunks.push_back(new char[c_chunkSize]);
        }

        if (s_index.m_byteIndex + byteCount <= c_chunkSize)
        {
            s_index.m_byteIndex += byteCount;
            return &s_chunks[chunkIndex][byteIndex];
        }

        s_index = { chunkIndex + 1, 0 };
    }
}
```

The stack allocator tracks a list of chunks of memory, where blocks may have been allocated from the chunks at the start of the list. If a requested allocation fits in the last chunk with allocated blocks, we add the new block to that chunk, right after the last allocated block in that chunk. If it doesn't, we add it at the beginning of the next chunk, allocating new chunks when necessary.

The context object is even more trivial. It just remembers the next place we'd allocate a block:

```
class StackContext
{
public:

    StackContext()
    : m_index(StackAlloc::s_index)
        { ; }
    ~StackContext()
        { StackAlloc::s_index = m_index; }

protected:

    StackAlloc::Index m_index;
};
```

This allocation model has a few advantages. It's much faster than a general heap allocator, since allocations are simple pointer math and releasing a context is almost free.[1] More importantly, it has great locality, since consecutively allocated blocks are right next to each other in memory. And since the blocks are freed automatically, there's no risk that you'll forget to free one.

There are plenty of disadvantages, too,[2] but there are two main use cases where stack-based allocation is a good fit. First, you often need to allocate some scratch space for a function's internal logic, and stack-based allocation is perfect for that. Second, if you're returning variable-sized data, then allocating space for that returned data via StackAlloc works really well.

Stack Allocation in Practice

The original Sucker Punch version of stack allocation looked roughly like the code in the previous section. Over time, however, we've mostly migrated to using stack-based vectors instead—a quick search of the codebase turns up a few hundred calls to raw stack-based allocation, but five thousand uses of stack-based vectors.

---

1 Yes, the first lesson of optimization is "don't optimize," as Rule 5 explains; believe me when I tell you that we have *plenty* of data about the importance of quick dynamic-memory allocation in our games.

2 Most importantly, the blocks only stay around as long as the context. If you want to hold onto some bit of data for longer than the context's lifetime, you're out of luck.

Here's a simplified version of the stack-based vector class, with method names chosen to match the standard C++ vector:

```cpp
template <class ELEMENT>
class StackVector
{
public:

    StackVector();
    ~StackVector();

    void reserve(int capacity);
    int size() const;
    void push_back(const ELEMENT & element);
    void pop_back();
    ELEMENT & back();
    ELEMENT & operator [](int index);

protected:

    int m_count;
    int m_capacity;
    ELEMENT * m_elements;
};
```

Creating the vector is trivial, since it starts with no elements. Destroying it is almost as simple. There's no memory to free, so all that's needed is to call the destructor for each of the elements in the vector:

```cpp
template <class ELEMENT>
StackVector<ELEMENT>::StackVector() :
    m_count(0),
    m_capacity(0),
    m_elements(nullptr)
{
}

template <class ELEMENT>
StackVector<ELEMENT>::~StackVector()
{
    for (int index = 0; index < m_count; ++index)
    {
        m_elements[index].~ELEMENT();
    }
}
```

The basic vector operations are straightforward. Note that if the vector needs to be resized, the old memory doesn't need to be freed. The elements need copying to the new storage, but that's it:

```cpp
template <class ELEMENT>
void StackVector<ELEMENT>::reserve(int capacity)
{
    if (capacity <= m_capacity)
        return;

    ELEMENT * newElements = StackAlloc::alloc<ELEMENT>(capacity);

    for (int index = 0; index < m_count; ++index)
    {
        newElements[index] = move(m_elements[index]);
    }

    m_capacity = capacity;
    m_elements = newElements;
}

template <class ELEMENT>
int StackVector<ELEMENT>::size() const
{
    return m_count;
}

template <class ELEMENT>
void StackVector<ELEMENT>::push_back(const ELEMENT & element)
{
    if (m_count >= m_capacity)
    {
        reserve(max(8, m_capacity * 2));
    }

    new (&m_elements[m_count++]) ELEMENT(element);
}

template <class ELEMENT>
void StackVector<ELEMENT>::pop_back()
{
    m_elements[--m_count].~ELEMENT();
}

template <class ELEMENT>
ELEMENT & StackVector<ELEMENT>::back()
{
    return m_elements[m_count - 1];
}
```

```
template <class ELEMENT>
ELEMENT & StackVector<ELEMENT>::operator [](int index)
{
    return m_elements[index];
}
```

Here's a simple usage example:

```
void getPrimeFactors(
    int number,
    StackVector<int> * factors)
{
    for (int factor = 2; factor * factor <= number; )
    {
        if (number % factor == 0)
        {
            factors->push_back(factor);
            number /= factor;
        }
        else
        {
            ++factor;
        }
    }

    factors->push_back(number);
}
```

So far, so good! It's just a vector with better performance in some well-defined circumstances, which is a pretty simple thing to get your head around. That's why stack vectors are used so widely in our codebase.

A Cloud on the Horizon

But there's a nagging problem. There are two main use cases for stack vectors—allocating scratch storage for a routine and returning values from a routine—and they don't mesh. Let me explain.

Imagine you'd like to write a function for a video game that returns enemies within five meters of the player. Imagine further that you've got a good starting point: a function that returns all nearby characters, whatever their emotional relationship to the player, along with their positions, all in a stack vector. It should be possible to call that code to get nearby characters, then filter out everyone except the enemies.

Here's the code you'd like to write:

```
void findNearbyEnemies(
    float maxDistance,
    StackVector<Character *> * enemies)
{
    StackContext context;
    StackVector<CharacterData> datas;
    findNearbyCharacters(maxDistance, &datas);

    for (const CharacterData & data : datas)
    {
        if (data.m_character->isEnemy())
        {
            enemies->push_back(data.m_character);
        }
    }
}
```

But this doesn't work, at least not with the simple stack allocator defined in the last section.

The problem is that two stack contexts are getting tangled up. You create a StackContext and StackVector for the character data returned by findNearby Characters, and this works great. But when you call enemies->push_back in the second half of the function, it will allocate memory from the stack context you created locally, rather than the stack context associated with the enemies array. The enemies array is probably defined in the calling function, inside a different stack context.

That's bad! You'd get unpredictable results if you used the returned array in the caller. In fact, when the real Sucker Punch stack vector class tries to allocate memory with a mismatched stack context, it asserts to catch exactly this kind of bug. It's possible to work around the stack context tangle, but I'm not going to show you the code because, frankly, it's a little embarrassing.

Making Stack Contexts a Little Smarter

There's a fairly straightforward way to fix this. The stack allocator defined earlier is global, like the standard heap allocator—when you allocate a block, it's associated with the stack context created most recently. That was the root cause of the tangled stack contexts we're trying to untangle. If it was possible to associate a block with a particular stack context, we could fix things.

That's not hard. The easiest way to do this is to move the `alloc` method to the `StackContext` object. If you're allocating from the current context, you'll allocate bytes from a shared stack. In the uncommon case that you're allocating from some context that's not current, you'll switch to a backup allocation strategy. You can do this without sacrificing the benefits of stack allocation if you're careful with the implementation.

First, here is the restructured `StackContext` class:

```
class StackContext
{
public:

    StackContext();
    ~StackContext();

    void * alloc(int byteCount);

    template <class T>
    T * alloc(int count)
        { return static_cast<T *>(alloc(sizeof(T) * count)); }

    static StackContext * currentContext();

protected:

    struct Index
    {
        int m_chunkIndex;
        int m_byteIndex;
    };

    static char * ensureChunk();
    static void recoverChunk(char * chunk);

    struct Sequence
    {
        Sequence() :
            m_index({ 0, 0 }), m_chunks()
            { ; }

        void * alloc(int byteCount);

        Index m_index;
        vector<char *> m_chunks;
    };

    Index m_initialIndex;
    Sequence m_extraSequence;
```

```
        static const int c_chunkSize = 1024 * 1024;

        static Sequence s_mainSequence;
        static vector<char *> s_unusedChunks;
        static vector<StackContext *> s_contexts;
};
```

New functions are created to create big chunks of memory as needed, reusing them when they're no longer needed:

```
char * StackContext::ensureChunk()
{
    char * chunk = nullptr;

    if (!s_unusedChunks.empty())
    {
        chunk = s_unusedChunks.back();
        s_unusedChunks.pop_back();
    }
    else
    {
        chunk = new char[c_chunkSize];
    }

    return chunk;
}

void StackContext::recoverChunk(char * chunk)
{
    s_unusedChunks.push_back(chunk);
}
```

The code to allocate a new block into the last chunk moves into a new Sequence object:

```
void * StackContext::Sequence::alloc(int byteCount)
{
    assert(byteCount <= c_chunkSize);

    while (true)
    {
        int chunkIndex = m_index.m_chunkIndex;
        int byteIndex = m_index.m_byteIndex;

        if (chunkIndex >= m_chunks.size())
        {
            m_chunks.push_back(new char[c_chunkSize]);
        }
```

```
        if (m_index.m_byteIndex + byteCount <= c_chunkSize)
        {
            m_index.m_byteIndex += byteCount;
            return &m_chunks[chunkIndex][byteIndex];
        }

        m_index = { chunkIndex + 1, 0 };
    }
}
```

The stack context methods that are left are simple. Track the current set of nested stack contexts. When an allocation is made from the topmost stack context (the typical case), it comes from a global sequence. When an allocation is made from any other stack context (the exceptional case), a sequence owned by that stack context is used instead:

```
StackContext::StackContext() :
    m_initialIndex(s_mainSequence.m_index),
    m_extraSequence()
{
    s_contexts.push_back(this);
}

StackContext::~StackContext()
{
    assert(s_contexts.back() == this);

    for (char * chunk : m_extraSequence.m_chunks)
    {
        recoverChunk(chunk);
    }

    s_mainSequence.m_index = m_initialIndex;
    s_contexts.pop_back();
}

void * StackContext::alloc(int byteCount)
{
    return (s_contexts.back() == this) ?
                s_mainSequence.alloc(byteCount) :
                m_extraSequence.alloc(byteCount);
}
```

In normal usage, the backup sequence in the stack context isn't used, so there's very little penalty for this new functionality. Allocation is still fast and easy.

The new stack context code forces a few simple changes to the StackVector class, which now needs to specify which stack context to allocate from. Leaving out the stuff that doesn't change:

```
template <class ELEMENT>
class StackVector
{
public:

    StackVector(StackContext * context);

protected:

    StackContext * m_context;
    int m_count;
    int m_capacity;
    ELEMENT * m_elements;
};

template <class ELEMENT>
StackVector<ELEMENT>::StackVector(StackContext * context) :
    m_context(context),
    m_count(0),
    m_capacity(0),
    m_elements(nullptr)
{
}

template <class ELEMENT>
void StackVector<ELEMENT>::reserve(int capacity)
{
    if (capacity <= m_capacity)
        return;

    ELEMENT * newElements = m_context->alloc<ELEMENT>(capacity);

    for (int index = 0; index < m_count; ++index)
    {
        newElements[index] = move(m_elements[index]);
    }

    m_capacity = capacity;
    m_elements = newElements;
}
```

With these new implementations, we're in good shape. We've kept the positive aspects of stack allocations—lightning-fast allocation and free operations, plus good locality—while fixing the annoying inability to mix and match local scratch space and variable-sized return values.

Migrating from Old Stack Contexts to New Ones

Now it's time to circle back to the main premise of the chapter, which you've likely forgotten in this blizzard of source code. You'll recall that we've got an old version of stack allocation and a new one, and they're not exactly the same.

So how do we get from Point A to Point B? The new stack allocator and stack array are conceptually the same as the old versions, but their interfaces have evolved a bit. The thousands of places in our source code where we've used the old model of StackContext and StackVector don't match the new interface exactly, so we can't just drop in the new implementation. There's a lot of existing source code that needs slight changes.

You should be a little nervous about introducing new problems with the switch to the new implementation. There are likely bugs lurking somewhere in those thousands of uses of the old model. Somebody somewhere is relying on the old system's behavior—allocating memory from the wrong stack context without realizing it, perhaps, and relying on the old behavior to keep their code working. That bit of code will break when we switch to a new model that actually supports out-of-order allocation.

An easy way to address these problems is by building parallel implementations and using a runtime flag to switch between them.

First, give the two classes different names so that they can coexist in the same codebase. In C++, wrap the StackAlloc and StackContext classes with two namespaces—say, OldStack and NewStack—so that the classes have names like NewStack::StackContext. (You could just as easily rename the classes to NewStackAlloc and OldStackAlloc.)

Second, create new StackAlloc and StackContext adapter classes. These adapter classes will delegate to either the old or the new versions of StackAlloc and StackContext, depending on a new global flag. The adapter classes support the union of the slightly different interfaces to the old and new classes.

This is pretty simple:

```cpp
bool g_useNewStackAlloc = false;

class StackAlloc
{
public:

    static void * alloc(int byteCount);
};

void * StackAlloc::alloc(int byteCount)
{
    return (g_useNewStackAlloc) ?
        NewStack::StackContext::currentContext()->alloc(byteCount) :
        OldStack::StackAlloc::alloc(byteCount);
}
```

The StackAlloc adapter just consults the runtime flag and calls the right allocator; simple. The StackContext adapter can be even simpler—since the old StackContext didn't have an alloc method, no code has been written to call it. Any new code calling alloc on the StackContext adapter is opting into using the new StackContext:

```cpp
class StackContext
{
public:

    StackContext() :
        m_oldContext(),
        m_newContext()
        { s_contexts.push_back(this); }
    ~StackContext()
        { s_contexts.pop_back(); }

    void * alloc(int byteCount);

    static StackContext * currentContext()
        { return (s_contexts.empty()) ? nullptr : s_contexts.back(); }

protected:

    OldStack::StackContext m_oldContext;
    NewStack::StackContext m_newContext;

    static vector<StackContext *> s_contexts;
};
```

```
vector<StackContext *> StackContext::s_contexts;

void * StackContext::alloc(int byteCount)
{
    return m_newContext.alloc(byteCount);
}
```

Your goal at this point is to minimize intervention in the old code path. As long as the global flag is false, the code is running through almost exactly the same logic as before the change. You'll create old-style StackContexts as before and StackAlloc works as before, so you shouldn't find any big issues while testing.

At this point, assuming testing works out, you could commit your work. You don't need to update StackVector first, since it will work as is. It's allocating stack memory like any other stack memory user, and you can switch between the old and new stack memory allocators using the runtime flag.

The ability to check in partial work to the main branch is a big advantage of the parallel rework technique. It's not so important here, with this small example—you could easily incorporate the next couple of steps into a single change list and skip the intermediate steps. With a more realistically sized example, though, being able to migrate to a new solution over a series of partial steps makes the process much easier to pull off.

Preparing to Migrate StackVector

The next step is to decide how to migrate the StackVector class. One obvious answer is to follow the model we used for StackContext, where a new shim StackVector class embeds both an old-style and a new-style StackVector, switching between the two of them based on the global flag. That leads to delegation methods like this:

```
template <class ELEMENT>
size_t StackVector<ELEMENT>::size() const
{
    if (g_useNewStackAlloc)
        return m_oldArray.size();
    else
        return m_newArray.size();
}
```

As a temporary measure, this isn't too bad. Creating the delegation functions is a little mind-numbing, but at least it's obvious what's going on to anyone who stumbles into this code during the migration to the new system.

The other option is to make the switch where the stack allocator is called. That works beautifully in this case—the StackVector class allocates stack memory in exactly one place. If that code can handle both allocating memory from a global stack (as in the original code) and from an explicit stack context (which we're migrating to) then you'll be in good shape:

```
template <class ELEMENT>
class StackVector
{
public:

    StackVector();
    StackVector(StackContext * context);

    void reserve(int capacity);

protected:

    bool m_isExplicitContext;
    StackContext * m_context;
    int m_count;
    int m_capacity;
    ELEMENT * m_elements;
};

template <class ELEMENT>
StackVector<ELEMENT>::StackVector()
: m_isExplicitContext(false),
    m_context(StackContext::currentContext()),
    m_count(0),
    m_capacity(0),
    m_elements(nullptr)
{
}

template <class ELEMENT>
StackVector<ELEMENT>::StackVector(StackContext * context)
: m_isExplicitContext(true),
    m_context(context),
    m_count(0),
    m_capacity(0),
    m_elements(nullptr)
{
}
```

```
template <class ELEMENT>
void StackVector<ELEMENT>::reserve(int capacity)
{
    if (capacity <= m_capacity)
        return;

    assert(
        m_isExplicitContext ||
        m_context == StackContext::currentContext());

    ELEMENT * newElements = (m_isExplicitContext) ?
        m_context->allocNew<ELEMENT>(capacity) :
        m_context->alloc<ELEMENT>(capacity);

    for (int index = 0; index < m_count; ++index)
    {
        newElements[index] = move(m_elements[index]);
    }

    m_elements = newElements;
}
```

Having two StackVector constructors lets you track which kind of allocation is appropriate. All your existing code will use the first constructor, at least to start with, since it takes the same arguments as the original version of the class. You'll eventually migrate to using the second constructor, but none of that code has been written yet. If the first constructor is used, then isExplicitContext won't be set, and reserve will run exactly as before.

Once again, you're at a safe point to commit changes. All existing uses of StackVector will go through the old stack allocation code path if the global flag is unset. Anyone setting the global flag runs through the new code path, as does any code that creates a stack array with the new explicit-context constructor.

Time to Migrate

Now you're set up to migrate!

At Sucker Punch, we'd do this in a few steps. First, some small number of first penguins[3] set the global flag that switches to the new stack allocation system.

---

3 In case you're not familiar with this expression, an explanation. Penguins nest on land, but hunt at sea. This means diving off ice floes into the ocean, not sure whether a hungry leopard seal is lurking underneath the waves. Penguins tend to gather in jostling mobs at the water's edge, all waiting for one penguin to be brave enough to dive in—or, more likely, to be jostled in; there is no honor among penguins. Anyhow, if that penguin doesn't get eaten, the rest of the penguins follow. Hence, "first penguin."

If they don't discover problems, we then recruit a larger set of people. When everything looks safe, we check in with the global flag set to true so that everyone uses the new system. If at any point during this rollout we detect a problem, it's simple to switch everyone back to the old system while we diagnose and fix the problem.

Once everyone is safely using the new system, we can start to tear out the adapters. The new StackContext class replaces the old one without trouble. We can tear out the small bit of wiring we added to the StackVector class, too, since everything goes through the new allocator now.

There's a policy decision to make about whether to require a context to be passed to each StackVector. It's a trade-off between the convenience of inferring the topmost stack context and the bugs that pop up when a stack context is accidentally deleted or misplaced. If we decide to require a context, then we can do that in parts—we don't have to update all five thousand (!) places where we create stack arrays at once.

It might seem crazy that we'd consider converting five thousand lines of code when there's a reasonable defaulting strategy that avoids the need for any conversion...but our focus is on the long term. If requiring the context would make us more efficient by avoiding a whole class of bugs, then it's probably worth the effort.

It's not that hard to convert the code. Just write a little bit of Python to find all the StackVectors, figure out what stack context was implied (which isn't that hard, because it's nearly always the last StackContext defined), update the constructor, and check out the changed file. The real cost isn't updating the code—it's figuring out how to test the change.

The compiler will catch almost all the problems, but for this case I'd also apply this chapter's strategy recursively. I'd add a special constructor for all the places where I've inferred a context, then assert at runtime that the constructor passed is topmost on the context stack. Once I verify that I haven't changed contexts, I'd switch to the normal constructor. If I've got a good code-coverage test, I'm in great shape.

All that's left at this point is the code that allocates stack memory directly. We've got two choices: continue to support a global stack allocation that implicitly uses the current stack context, or convert a few hundred lines of code to call alloc on the StackContext variable directly. In this case, I'd convert everything, gaining the robustness of the new allocation model.

Once the last bits of direct allocation are converted, you're done. All of the vestiges of the old stack allocation are gone—and you were able to do it bit by bit, in a series of commits, taking small, safe steps. With this approach, if you run into any bumps along the way, you can quickly back up to the old behavior, so the team as a whole isn't disrupted.

Recognizing When Parallel Rework Is a Good Strategy

This parallel rework strategy is very useful in the right circumstances, but it's not a panacea. You'll still run into the occasional need to fix bugs in two places. Coders who aren't running with the new version of the system will inadvertently break your work. These things will happen less often and be less disruptive than if you'd gone on off onto your own private branch in source control, but they will happen.

Parallel rework imposes some overhead, too. Just managing three separate names for the same concept—original, reworked, and adapter—is a hassle. You'll write more code overall, since you're likely to make copies of some of the bits of the original solution.

It may be that your new, reworked system is so fundamentally different from the original version that parallel rework doesn't make sense. If you can't define an adapter layer, something that switches dynamically between the old and new versions, then you can't apply the technique as I've described it here.

In a lot of cases, though, parallel rework provides a manageable way to make major changes to your codebase incrementally and safely. At Sucker Punch we don't use it for all changes, but for big rework it's our go-to strategy.

Do the Math

This isn't a very math-y book. Sure, numbers pop up in a few of the Rules (like Rule 4, "Generalization Takes Three Examples", and Rule 11, "Is It Twice as Good?"), but the Rules are more concepts than equations.

It's sort of surprising that there isn't more math in computer programming. Computers are just number processing machines, after all. Everything is reduced to numbers for processing—words are sequences of characters represented as numbers, bitmaps are pixels represented by colors represented by numbers, music is a pair of waveforms represented as a series of numbers. You'd think that some of that would leak through—that, as a programmer, you'd be figuring equations at some point. That doesn't happen very often, though.

Most of the decisions a programmer makes are squidgy. Deciding whether the clarity a lengthy comment would add is worth complicating the flow of logic, say. Choosing between `getPriority` or `calculatePriority` as the name for a function.[1] Identifying the right time to switch over to a new version of some system.

It's easy to fall into thinking that *all* decisions are squidgy, not just *most* decisions. Some decisions boil down to simple math, though, and you need to recognize them when they pop up. If you don't, if you forge ahead without doing the simple math, you may be in for a painful realization later on. You may discover that the approach you've followed was never going to work, and that you could have saved yourself a lot of time by just doing the math. This will make you sad; better to do the math up front.

---

1 It will not surprise you to learn that we have a convention for this at Sucker Punch: "get" implies that no (or very little) calculation is done, while "calculate" or something similar implies that work is involved to produce the value. It's a nice head start on understanding what a function does.

To Automate or Not to Automate

Here's a common scenario. You've got some process you've been doing by hand, and you're thinking about automating it. Is the automation work worth doing?

That's just a math problem! If you'll spend less time writing the code than you'll spend repeating the task by hand, then it's worth doing. If not, then it isn't.

This may seem obvious, and it is, but that doesn't mean the math gets done.

I've seen this math get skipped way more times than I've seen it done. Let me spin a typical counter-example—a programmer gets annoyed by some manual process, immediately dives into a two-day project to automate it, then congratulates themselves every time they run the resulting macro. Which they do maybe once a week, saving 15 seconds each time.

The two-day automation project may have been fun, but it wasn't justifiable, and doing the math before starting would have made this clear. Look, we're programmers because we like to program. We're going to have a bias toward solving problems by programming—but programming isn't the right solution to every problem.

Deciding whether to automate some task is an optimization problem—you're just optimizing the *work process* rather than the program execution. You apply the same steps as with any optimization, including the absolute need to measure the process before trying to optimize it.

Let's look at a concrete automation scenario. Imagine you're writing a book about programming. You're using Visual Studio to edit all of your coding examples, but you're using Word to write the book. The code examples are indented in the source file, but shouldn't be indented in the book.[2] Your manual process is simple and pretty fast:

1. Select a code block in your editor.

2. Unindent it.

3. Copy it to the clipboard.

4. Undo the unindentation.

5. Switch to Word.

---

2 Ahem. This is not a hard scenario for me to imagine.

6. Create a paragraph with the right style.

7. Paste the code example into the paragraph.

Is this worth automating? Will you save time overall by automating this operation? Time to do the math.

There are two sides to the math here: the cost side and the benefit side. The cost is how much work will be required to implement the automation. The benefit is how much time you'll save once the task is automated.

In this concrete scenario, some of the steps will still remain even after automation. You'll still switch to your code editor to select the code block, and you'll still switch back to Word to paste it in. When you're doing the math for the scenario you can ignore the steps that don't change, since you're only interested in the time difference pre- and post-automation. Everything else can be automated, and once automated will take effectively zero time.

You can't do the math without numbers. Where possible, use real numbers rather than estimates. That means measuring the things that can be measured—in this case, how long the manual process takes. So time it—let's say it takes 6 seconds.[3] You look at the chapters you've written and they average 8 code samples, so 8 code samples per chapter goes into the math. Your publishing contract calls for 20 or so chapters, so that's the number to use. You've also noted that it's common to revise code samples, and this means cutting and pasting them more than once. You think that on average each example is pasted 3 times; that's the one estimate in all of this.

That's enough to do the benefit side of the math:

6 seconds (per copy operation) ×
8 (code samples per chapter) ×
20 (chapters) ×
3 (revisions of each sample) = 48 minutes

OK, so that's the benefit side of things. On to the cost side.

How long will it take to automate the process? It's not easy to automate things in Visual Studio, at least as it comes out of the box, but Word is surprisingly automatable. If you've written Word macros before, and especially if you've

---

3 Because that's how long the manual process took when I timed it.

written code that manipulates the clipboard, then you've got the basics covered. There's just some text cleanup to do on top of the clipboard manipulation.

And that cleanup doesn't seem bad. Pull the contents of the clipboard into an array of strings, one per line of text. Detect the minimum amount of indentation in any string, then rebuild the array subtracting out that indentation. You'll probably need to think about how blank lines affect things, and also should consider that spaces and tabs look pretty much the same in the text editor but pretty different in Word. And after cleaning up the lines you have to reassemble them into a text block and insert it in the document, then bind your new macro to a hot key.

Let's say your estimate is an hour to get this all working correctly.[4]

An hour is more than 48 minutes, so the math tells us to not do the automation. But it seems close; maybe the estimates on the benefit side were a little off. Maybe it's an average of 4 revisions per sample instead of 3. That would be enough to push the math positive—if it's 4 revisions per sample instead of 3, the math says go ahead. And the fact is, it is really annoying to do the steps by hand, even if it's only taking 6 seconds a pop.

Hold on there, cowpoke. Which do you think is more likely—that you were a little too pessimistic on your estimate of the benefits, or a little too optimistic on how much time it was going to take to get the code working? You're a programmer, you know the answer to this question. You're much more likely to miss your estimate on coding time.

If the cost-benefit math for automation looks like a toss-up, then don't do it.

Look for Hard Limits

If you've got hard limits in your problem space or on your solution, then you should respect them from the start of your design process.

One of the nice things about creating games for video game consoles is that they present plenty of hard limits. Like the amount of memory in a console—that's fixed. The number of bytes you can pack on a Blu-ray disk is fixed. The size of a UDP networking packet is fixed. Each frame is a sixtieth of a second, full stop.

Our team will also invent hard limits to clarify our technical design process. Take available network bandwidth, for example. It varies from customer to customer, and it can be unpredictable, but we have pretty reliable numbers on

---

4 An optimistic estimate, in my opinion.

measured network bandwidth for customers around the world. We can invent a hard limit on network bandwidth that covers nearly all of our customers; if we stay within that invented hard limit, the game will run well for almost everyone.[5]

It may seem strange to rejoice in hard caps like this. Why would having hard limits be something to celebrate?

Take the hard limit on memory that we work with when doing console programming. This seems like a bad thing—wouldn't virtual memory make programming easier? The answer is yes, of course, but it's at the cost of turning a hard limit on memory into a softer limit. If you overflow available physical memory, virtual memory swaps pages out to disk, trading time for space. That's a problem for a video game. Updating the screen once every couple of seconds when virtual memory starts thrashing isn't acceptable; we have a hard limit of a sixtieth of a second for each frame. In the end it's simpler to accept a hard limit on memory.

So we identify the hard limits that exist, and invent hard limits out of softer limits to simplify our design decisions. That's true for the coding team, but even more so for all of the Sucker Punchers who aren't coders. Trade-offs and soft limits are really hard for people to wrap their heads around. Hard limits are easier—they turn some parts of the design process into simple math, and that's easy to do.[6]

Consider a network protocol design example. The basic networking design is fixed—you're writing a peer-to-peer game, so every connected machine is communicating directly with the other connected machines. Each machine is the "authority" for a subset of the characters in the game, and is responsible for broadcasting to the other machines the state of those characters. The hard limits you need to respect are 1 Mbps network bandwidth received and 256 Kbps bandwidth sent—if you stay within those bounds, nearly all players will get good performance. You need to support four connected players.

The design you're considering is for each machine to broadcast in UDP packets the position and orientation of each character it has authority over each frame, plus enough information to reconstruct the animations currently applied to that character. In combination, that's enough to position and pose the

---

5 Not everywhere, though. McMurdo Station in Antarctica shares 25 Mbps of bandwidth between a thousand people in the summer. That's less than our hard cap; sorry, scientists. Also it might make sense to cut back on the Netflix, scientists; sorry about that too. Keep up the good work, though.

6 Well, it's easy for the coders to do the math, at least. And easy for the coders to explain to anyone who doesn't want to do the math.

character on the other machines. If packets get dropped, it's not that big a deal, since you're sending information about each character 60 times a second.

This is just another math problem! You've got a hard limit on network bandwidth that has to be respected, so you need to figure out how much data your design would send each second. That means measuring wherever possible, and estimating where a measurement can't be made.

In the simplest possible version of this design, you'd use the native representation for the things you're going to network. Internally, character positions are a vector of three 32-bit floating point numbers, and the character orientation can be boiled down to a compass heading also represented in floating point. That covers position and orientation, leaving the information necessary to reconstruct animations in the remote machine.

Luckily, you've got a single-player version of the game that you can use for measurement, and you discover that on average each character blends together the effects of six animations. You'll need to send an animation count, plus enough data to reconstruct each of the active animations. That means identifying the animation—internally, you do that with a unique 8-byte identifier. You'll also need to capture where you are in the timeline for the animation, internally a 4-byte floating-point number, and any factor used to blend between the results of two animations, also represented in floating point.

The math for each character is clear now, in this simple version of the design. Your floating-point values are all stored in 4 bytes, and you use 4-byte integers for counts by default.

Position is 12 bytes, plus 4 bytes for orientation, plus 4 bytes for an animation count. Each animation is an 8-byte identifier, then two 4-byte floating-point values for the timeline and blend factor. That's $12 + 4 + 4 + 6 \times (8 + 4 + 4) = 116$ bytes per character, which doesn't seem too bad.

There's more math, though. You broadcast information about each character once per frame, so you need to multiply by 60 to calculate how many bytes per second of bandwidth you're using.

Your peer-to-peer architecture means that you send out three copies of the character's data each frame, too—one copy to each of the three peers. You also receive data from each of the three peers about the characters they have authority over. The worst case with this design is when a machine ends up with authority over all the characters—that machine then sends out three copies for all characters, and receives copies for none.

You've got one more fixed point—the number of characters you need to handle, which your game design team has decided is 30. Now you've got enough numbers to do the math:

30 (frames per second) ×
3 (copies to our peers) ×
30 (characters) ×
116 (bytes per character) ×
8 (bits per byte) = 2.5 Mbps

Uh oh. That's 10 times your available bandwidth on bits sent. Doing the math let you know that the simple design you had in mind couldn't work. Actually, the dangerous part is that the design will work fine on your internal 1G network, where it won't even cause a ripple in available bandwidth. You'll only discover the problem when you deploy to the field. Yikes.

It's a little bit tough to salvage this simple design.

There's lots of room to compress the data sent about each character, so that's a place to start. Maybe 16 bits is enough for each of the coordinates, given that multiplayer areas are small, and 8 bits should be enough detail for heading. Creating a table of all networkable animation names would mean that 10 bits would be enough to identify an animation, and each animation could write its own networked state, which is more compressible than the raw blend weights and time values you sent. Throwing all of these compression tricks at the problem, you squeeze the bytes per character down to 16 instead of 116.

The math still doesn't work out:

30 (frames per second) ×
3 (copies to our peers) ×
30 (characters) ×
16 (bytes per character) ×
8 (bits per byte) = 345 Kbps

Much closer, but still above the hard limit. Something's going to have to give—maybe the design team can be persuaded that 24 characters is enough. On the technical side, maybe you could get away with sending data about characters every other frame, rather than every frame. Either of these changes would get the design safely under the hard cap.[7]

Crucially, the math happens before implementation starts. The math told you that the initial design couldn't work. It's a lot easier to switch to the design where the math pencils out before all the code is written. Once all the multiplayer content is built, it's going to be a *lot* harder convincing the design team to reduce the maximum character count to 24!

It's important to note that doing the math is designed to identify solutions that *won't* work, not to necessarily verify that a solution *will* work. This simple network design could fall apart for any number of other reasons—but at least it won't fail due to basic math.

When the Math Changes

Let's go back to the first example, where you had to decide whether to automate a manual process to cut and paste code samples from Visual Studio into Word. The process focused on normalizing the indentation of the code samples, and the math told you that automation wasn't worth doing.

Imagine, then, that your first understanding of the problem was incomplete. Normalizing the indentation isn't enough. All of the tabs in the code samples need to be converted to spaces, too, because that's how the publisher lays out books.

Does the original math still apply? Not anymore—because the manual process you measured doesn't match the new requirement. You'll need to tweak the manual process—say, by finding a Visual Studio plug-in that converts tabs to spaces,[8] then adding an extra step to trigger this plug-in on the selection, then adding an extra undo step—then remeasure.

That tweak affects both halves of the math. The extra two steps—a tabs-to-spaces conversion, and an extra undo—will slow down the manual process. Maybe each run through the cut-and-paste process takes 10 seconds now instead of 6, and that increases the benefit side of the equation.

The tweak also affected the cost side of the manual process, too, because now you're spending time to find and install the right extension, then spending

---

7 Actually the easiest fix is to miss the ship date for your game by a few years and hope that your customers' internet connections get faster. You'd be surprised at how often this turns out to be the eventual fix for a performance problem.

8 Because the alternative of switching from using tabs to using spaces in your code is completely unacceptable, naturally. We all have our foibles.

time experimenting to understand exactly how it works. Your process depends mightily on how the new plug-in interacts with the undo stack, for instance. It's only fair to add this to the cost side of the math, since the time you spend finagling the extension could have been spent on your automation effort instead.

If you do the math again with these two adjustments and some new estimates, the balance changes, first for the manual process:

10 seconds (per copy operation) ×
8 (code samples per chapter) ×
20 (chapters) ×
3 (revisions of each sample) = 80 minutes

If you add in 45 minutes to research an appropriate tabs-to-spaces plug-in, including installation and experimentation, and bump up your estimate of automation to 90 minutes to include the extra work of doing tabs-to-spaces conversion, the math changes:

80 minutes + 45 minutes (manual process) > 90 minutes (automated process)

Now the math tells you to do the automation. You could still cut and paste code samples with a manual process, but the process will be slower and will take time to figure out. Better to just automate it.[9]

When the Math Problem Changes Back into a Word Problem

If you take this chapter to heart, you'll do a better job identifying problems that imply a little bit of math. Quantifiable constraints and measurable solutions are the cue—when you see both of them, you should do the math to help identify solutions that will never work.

But be wary that there aren't qualitative problems lurking in all of the quantitative analysis! Take task automation: it's not always as simple as just doing the math.

Your primary goal when automating a task is to reduce the total time spent... but that may not be your only goal. The manual process might be error-prone, for

---

9 I had an excellent time writing the resulting Word macro, by the way. Word macros are written in Visual Basic for Applications, and Basic was the first programming language I learned. Good times.

instance. Maybe you could quantify how often errors occur, and how much time they take to fix, but these are tough things to be crisp about.

Or maybe a manual task that should be completed daily is so annoying that it's only done weekly. It doesn't make sense to focus solely on the time spent on the task. If automation ensures that the task is done daily, then it might be worth doing, despite the amount of time saved being small.

And it's not unreasonable to consider team sanity as a soft goal. A manual task may not be all that time consuming, but if it's a constant irritant and it can be fixed relatively easily, it might be worth doing even if the math doesn't quite work out. Don't be afraid to spend a day now and then just to make everyone's lives more pleasant—especially when the math is a close call anyhow.

On the flip side, if you don't deeply understand a task, then be wary of automating it even if the numbers look good! In the preceding examples, I was automating one of my own tasks. I knew all of its ins and outs. If it had been someone else's job to cut and paste code examples into this book, things would have been a lot fuzzier. I wouldn't have been sure I knew what the right approach to automation was, much less that I'd got the math right.

Fundamentally, though, trust the numbers. If there's quick arithmetic you can do that verifies the basic sanity of the problem-solving approach you're considering, then do the math.

Sometimes You Just Need to Hammer the Nails

Programming is an inherently creative, intellectually challenging activity. That's a big part of why I love it, and you'd probably say the same. Every problem is different than the ones before, requiring a little bit of cleverness to solve—though, per the Rules in this book, hopefully not too much cleverness!

But not every problem has an elegant solution. Even the most exciting programming assignment has moments of drudgery: tasks that aren't interesting, that it's difficult to get excited about, that nobody wants to do. It's easy to work on the exciting stuff instead, putting off the drudgery and secretly hoping that someone else on your team will take it on instead.

With that setup, the moral of this chapter will come as no surprise—*don't skip the drudgery*. That unlovable task isn't going anywhere. There's no hidden army of code elves who'll do the work while you're sleeping. And half-completed tasks are a slow poison, working to kill your project.

The key is to know the danger signs. You're a clever person,[1] more than clever enough to rationalize away the necessity of the tasks you don't enjoy. That's especially true if you have a long backlog of more interesting tasks to get to.

Knowing the sorts of tasks that you personally tend to ignore is a key bit of self-knowledge. Your list may not match mine, or match your coworkers'—one programmer's drudgery is another programmer's day at the park, to coin a

---

1 You've made it to the last Rule in the book, which I'm taking as evidence of your wisdom and insight.

phrase. Once you can identify which tasks you tend to avoid, you can be more conscious of giving them the priority they deserve.

That said, this would be a pretty empty chapter without some examples! They were not hard to find, since I could draw both from the kinds of tasks I personally dread and from the tasks I've seen others avoid.

A New Argument

Imagine that you've got a function like this:

```
vector<Character *> findNearbyCharacters(
    const Point & point,
    float maxDistance);
```

The function returns all characters within some bounding sphere. Dozens and dozens of calls to this function are scattered throughout your codebase. You've found a handful of places where the basic behavior of this function isn't quite right. In these cases there are a handful of characters you'd like to exclude from the search, and you've decided to add a new argument to handle the exclusion:

```
vector<Character *> findNearbyCharacters(
    const Point & point,
    float maxDistance,
    vector<Character *> excludeCharacters);
```

Now you're faced with a choice—do you update all the places the old code was called, adding the new argument? Or do you avoid this work by specifying a default argument, like this:

```
vector<Character *> findNearbyCharacters(
    const Point & point,
    float maxDistance,
    vector<Character *> excludeCharacters = vector<Character *>())
{
    return vector<Character *>();
}
```

Or perhaps avoid the work by having two overloaded versions of the function?

```
vector<Character *> findNearbyCharacters(
    const Point & point,
    float maxDistance);
vector<Character *> findNearbyCharacters(
```

```
    const Point & point,
    float maxDistance,
    vector<Character *> excludeCharacters);
```

Overloading and default arguments let you skip the work of updating existing uses of findNearbyCharacters. That's good, right? You can get on with the stuff on your backlog.

Maybe, maybe not. Going through the places the old version of the function is called isn't just about converting them—it's also about looking at *how* those pieces of code are using the function. The chances are good that a few of them are excluding characters from the list—exactly what your new argument handles. These examples should be converted to use the new argument.

Imagine that soon thereafter, you run into the need for finer-grained filtering. Say that you want to find only nearby enemies that pose a threat, instead of all characters. You decide to add a simple filtering interface:

```
struct CharacterFilter
{
    virtual bool isCharacterAllowed(Character * character) const = 0;
};

vector<Character *> findNearbyCharacters(
    const Point & point,
    float maxDistance,
    CharacterFilter * filter);
```

Here's a filter that accepts threatening enemies, but rejects allies and incapacitated characters:

```
struct ThreatFilter : public CharacterFilter
{
    ThreatFilter(const Character * character) :
        m_character(character)
        { ; }

    bool isCharacterAllowed(Character * character) const override
    {
        return !character->isAlliedWith(m_character) &&
               !character->isIncapacitated();
    }

    const Character * m_character;
};
```

Now you have another set of decisions to make. Add another overloaded version of findNearbyCharacters? Or maybe *two* new overloaded versions: one with filtering and an excluded characters list, the other just with filtering? That would bring you up to three or four overloaded versions of the function. Seems complicated—three or four versions of the function to keep in sync? Confusion about where to set breakpoints? Things are starting to get out of hand.

It might be better to handle excluded characters with a filter instead. Implementing a CharacterFilter that checks a list of characters is trivial. That would keep the number of versions of the function under control, and you'll likely find a few more uses of findNearbyCharacters that would be simpler with a filter:

```
struct ExcludeFilter : public CharacterFilter
{
    ExcludeFilter(const vector<const Character *> & characters) :
        m_characters(characters)
        { ;  }

    bool isCharacterAllowed(Character * character) const override
    {
        return m_characters.end() == find(
                                        m_characters.begin(),
                                        m_characters.end(),
                                        character);
    }

    vector<const Character *> m_characters;
};
```

Converting to using filters everywhere implies some work. There are dozens of places where findNearbyCharacters is called. All of the calling code has to be inspected, and at least some of it will get converted to the new filter model. That sounds like drudgery to me. Faced with that amount of work, it's really tempting to live with three overloaded versions and just convert the code that has to be converted.

That's a mistake—or, at best, a reasonable decision made for the wrong reasons. You're trading off the short-term cost of inspecting and updating the existing code against the long-term benefit of a simpler, cleaner model for finding nearby characters.

As programmers, most of us have a tendency to tie-break in favor of short-term costs instead of long-term benefits, usually to our later chagrin. If you think you know what the right solution to a problem is, but you're reluctant to do it because of the amount of work involved, just cowgirl up[2] and do the work.

There's Never Just One Bug

Here's another example. You stumble onto a bug—some bit of code is calling another bit of code incorrectly. That's understandable, because the second bit of code has doubled down on its poor name choices by omitting any documentation:

```
void squashAdjacentDups(
    vector<Unit> & units,
    unsigned int (* hash)(const Unit &));
```

Seems pretty straightforward—it looks like the function squashes out adjacent duplicate values using the provided hash function. And that's *almost* what it does:

```
void squashAdjacentDups(
    vector<Unit> & units,
    int (* hash)(const Unit &))
{
    int nextIndex = 1;

    for (int index = 1; index < units.size(); ++index)
    {
        if (hash(units[index]) != hash(units[nextIndex - 1]))
        {
            units[nextIndex++] = units[index];
        }
    }

    while (units.size() > nextIndex)
    {
        units.pop_back();
    }
}
```

The problem is that the `hash` argument to `squashAdjacentDups` is expected to return a fully unique value, given how the code is written. That's not what a hash function does, though. Given two equivalent objects, the hash function returns the same hash value, but it also might return that hash value for another

---

2 Or cowboy up, if that's your style.

object that *isn't* equivalent. You always have to check for equivalency after the hash values are compared, which squash doesn't do.

The bug you've just fixed is a result of this quirk—the caller passed in a hash function, not a unique identifier function:

```
struct Unit
{
    int m_id;
    string m_firstName;
    string m_lastName;
    string m_userName;
};

unsigned int hashUnit(const Unit & unit)
{
    return combineHashes(
                hashString(unit.m_firstName),
                hashString(unit.m_lastName),
                hashString(unit.m_userName));
}
```

This almost always works, which is why the bug wasn't caught earlier...but once two adjacent Units hashed to the same value, things broke.

So should you fix the bug and move on? Nope, not until the drudgery is out of the way.

First of all, you have to rename the hash argument. Its current name is a lie, and that's going to cause more problems. Either use it like a real hash function, with a separate call to check actual equivalence, or rename the argument to reflect its actual usage.

Second, you should review all the other places where squashAdjacentDups is called. Odds are good that at least one of them is going to exhibit exactly the same bug you just fixed. In fact, there's a decent chance that *all* of the callers of squashAdjacentDups will exhibit the bug. You've done the work to diagnose a pretty subtle bug, so leverage your new understanding to find the other instances of that bug in the code.

Fixing the name takes very little time—it's easy to convince yourself to take that step. Reviewing all the other callers of squashAdjacentDups, on the other hand, is going to be a slog. But it will pay off—maybe not for you, but for someone on your team. Short-term pain, long-term benefit. Take your time, review the other callers, and fix the problems you find.

The Siren Call of Automation

Programmers have a predictable reaction to encountering some bit of drudgery: they want to automate it.

Automation can take many forms. Perhaps you could fiddle together a regular expression in your source editor to find all of the calls to findNearby Characters and insert a new argument. Or maybe it would be better to write some Python code to do this, since that would let you handle the exceptions more easily. For that matter, you've had to deal with this sort of argument-adding situation before—maybe what the project *really* needs is a generalized argument-adding utility app written in Python. That would be a good project; better get started on it!

Believe me, I get it. It's more fun to noodle on a regular expression until it flawlessly handles every variation of whatever bit of drudgery you're facing, or to write a bunch of clean-sheet Python code to do the same thing. It's certainly a lot more fun than making the same manual edit over and over again. But it isn't very smart. You'll spend less time just making the edits by hand; do the math, per Rule 20.

Maybe you can get a running start with regular expressions—hey, if there's an easy, no-fiddling-required regular expression that solves 80% of the drudgery, by all means do it! You can sweep up the other 20% of the drudgery by hand.

Keep in mind that tasks like the examples presented here feel repetitive, but rarely are they so repetitive that they're easily automated. There's judgment involved, even if it's as simple as breaking up a function call over multiple lines or adjusting a comment to match the new function signature.

Managing File Sizes

Code evolves over time—and despite the undeniable joys of deleting code, you'll end up adding more code to your project than you end up deleting. In the process of adding code, your source files get longer and longer, maybe to the point of being uncomfortably long.

That may be a natural product of your team's conventions. At Sucker Punch, by convention the source code for a particular class all resides in a single source file and a single header file. And, like a lot of teams, despite our best efforts we've ended up with a couple of kitchen-sink classes, like our main character class. It's a convenient spot in the class hierarchy to add features, so lots of features have been added, and lots of features mean lots of source code. I just checked, and the implementation file for our main character class is 19,000 lines long. Ouch.

Is this a problem? Yeah, at least a little bit. It's harder to work in a file that size. You have to use text search to find anything, as paging through the code gets you nowhere fast. It takes longer to compile than the other files, which throws off your build distribution. It's hard to tell which bits of code are related to which other bits when they're separated by thousands of lines.

So why hasn't it been fixed? Because reducing the number of lines would involve a lot of drudgery: copying and pasting code to a new file, refactoring chunks of behavior into separate classes to respect our "one source file per class" convention, reexamining the header files in the old and new files to make sure they're still appropriate, and resolving any dangling references after the files are moved. That work is zero fun, and we're all busy. We've collectively decided to whistle past the graveyard, avoiding the drudgery and ignoring the increasingly unwieldy size of the file, even though we'd all be happier with a shorter version of the file.

I should note that the Sucker Punch team is well-adjusted, with everyone on the team showing their commitment every day to a clean and functional codebase. For the first two examples, everyone on the team would have chosen the hard path, powering through the drudgery to update code to match the new argument set or looking for bugs similar to the one that had just been fixed. But we still have a 19,000-line source file that we're all faintly embarrassed about.

Look, it's hard to dive into the drudgery, even for a disciplined team. The first step is to recognize that you're avoiding a task because you don't want to do it. The second step is to take a step back to evaluate the long-term benefits of tackling it—it's entirely possible that the task is both unpleasant and not particularly valuable, in which case you certainly shouldn't do it! But if it's going to pay off in the long term, even though it's going to suck in the near term, then it's time for step three: hammer the nails.

There Are No Shortcuts

Imagine that you've got a big chunk of wood with a hundred nails sticking out of it. They make it impossible to use the chunk of wood for anything else. You could just ignore the nails. You could hope that someone else will hammer the nails for you. You could spend a lot of time tinkering with a nail-hammering machine that might work someday.

Or you could just take out your hammer and get to work. Sometimes you just need to hammer the nails.

Conclusion: Making the Rules Your Own

The Rules, as I've laid them out in this book, distill the lessons we've learned at Sucker Punch over the quarter-century of its existence. They're specific to our experience. They reflect the things that we think are important—our programming culture. And that programming culture reflects the specific constraints and characteristics of creating the sorts of video games that Sucker Punch makes.

You've read a lot of Rules at this point. I'd guess that you immediately saw how some of the Rules apply to the work you do, while others feel more loosely connected to your experience. That's not a surprise! If the programming work you do is radically different from the work we do, then some of our Rules may not make sense for you.

So what makes writing video games like ours different—and how does that affect the Rules?

- First of all, our projects are long. Our last game, *Ghost of Tsushima*, took about six years to create. And we weren't starting from scratch—most of the code in *Ghost* is an evolution (or just a direct copy) of code that ran in earlier Sucker Punch games. We place a premium on long-term code quality because we *have* to—the code we write today has a good chance of still running ten years from now.

- The coding team is big, with 30-odd full-time coders currently on staff. Depending on your own situation, that may seem tiny or huge. Personally, I'd define a "small" programming team as one where one person can know all the details of all the code. By that standard, Sucker Punch hasn't been small for a long time. At this point, nobody knows *all* the details of the codebase, and all of us have to sort things out in unfamiliar code. If our code isn't easy to read and understand, we'll be in deep trouble.

- Performance is important for video games, much more so than for most code. There are websites (*https://oreil.ly/eBohg*) that measure our performance to the millisecond! But that doesn't mean *all* of our code needs to run fast. We're like any project—our performance is determined by a small subset of our code. Some of our code needs to *run* quickly, but most of our code needs to be *created* quickly.

- We release our games infrequently. That's not true for *all* games—whatever games you're playing on your mobile phone are likely updated all the time—but it is for us. That makes it easier to sign up for big changes to the code. It also means we face less of a constant quality burden—it's important that our code keeps running reliably and correctly, because otherwise the 80% of Sucker Punch that isn't on the coding team is going to be really grumpy, but the changes we make aren't showing up in the customer experience until long after we check them in. We can tolerate a few temporary bugs in the code if it helps us create the game more quickly.

- Every game for us is a fresh sheet of paper. While we build on top of the work we'd done for our last game, we're not locked into it. We have no backward compatibility or continuity issues, and that makes it easier to for us to make major changes.

- Our approach to game development is iterative. Our successes come from trying lots of new ideas to see which one works, not from designing a game first on paper and then building it. Ideas we try that sort of work are tweaked and experimented with; ideas that don't work are immediately deleted. We prioritize creating and iterating on new code quickly...while still remembering that the code that does survive is likely to be around forever. That's a tough combination.

These characteristics have an obvious effect on the Rules. For example, the fact that we release games infrequently has a huge impact on how we approach big changes to the code—if we had a weekly release schedule, we'd need a very different approach.

Use Your Best Judgment

The Rules can send you in contradictory directions, too—maybe your team's conventions expect `get` and `set` functions to access an object's protected state, but that means writing a `set` function you know is never called. That's a conflict between following team conventions (Rule 12) and deleting code that isn't called (Rule 8). Use your best judgment in cases like this—I'd follow team conventions if the `set` function is simple, but that's just me.

You'll also need to use your best judgment to decide which Rules apply to your own work. Some of our Rules might be a poor fit if the characteristics of the work you do differ enough from our projects at Sucker Punch. If that's the case, then don't follow the Rule—this isn't a dogma, it's just a set of useful rules.

But...there's a chance that a Rule is true for you even if it's hard to accept. I accept plenty of things now that I would have rejected ten or fifteen years ago. Take Rule 10, "Localize Complexity". In the early years of Sucker Punch, I designed and built a lot of systems out of tangles of interacting objects. It took a long time—and a lot of failed architectures—to realize that my mistake was fundamental. Rule 10 grew out of those failures, and out of our more recent successes after localizing complexity.

Discuss Amongst Yourselves

This book was never intended to be a complete set of Rules, just a useful one. Use these Rules as a starting line, not a finish line. Develop your own set of Rules.

Obviously that will work best if you're on the same page with the rest of your team! Everyone on the team choosing their own set of Rules is a recipe for chaos and strife. That's probably not your goal.

Here's an idea—start a book club. Everyone on the team reads a Rule or two, then you all get together to discuss how the Rules you've just read apply to your own projects. Figure out how you'd amend the Rule to better match the work you do, if it isn't a good fit. Or decide to discard it entirely, if you all think that makes sense!

If you're like most technical teams, you don't spend a lot of time talking about coding philosophy. And when you do, it's probably in the context of some particular technical issue you need to sort out, which inevitably leads to the technical discussion and philosophical one getting all tangled up. That's not a recipe for progress. Better to separate the two discussions; you're more likely to end up in a happy place that way.

You'll be much more effective as a team if you've aligned your ideas of how to write code, and the quickest way to get there is to talk about those ideas. The Rules can be a good starting point for that sort of discussion. They can provide some structure to your discussion, a framework to come to some consensus about how to write code. And that's worthwhile—investing in developing a shared coding philosophy will pay off many times over.

Signing Off

So that's it! No more Rules!

This book has been fun to write; I hope it's been fun to read.

If you've got reactions or comments you'd like to share, see *The Rules of Programming* website (*https://oreil.ly/jTEGo*) for pointers. I promise your input won't be piped straight to dev/null. The website also points you at the source code examples used in the book.

Reading C++ for Python Programmers

The examples in this book are all presented in C++. That's the language I do most of my programming in, and it's the language I'm most proficient in. That said, I've written a reasonable amount of Python, too—it's the second-most used programming language at Sucker Punch. At the moment, we have about 2.8 million lines of C++ in our codebase and about 600,000 lines of Python.

If you're a Python programmer, you don't need to learn how to program in C++ in order to read the examples in this book. Code is code, basically—a loop is a loop, variables are variables, and functions are functions. There are some cosmetic differences, but the basic ideas in this book's C++ examples translate pretty directly to Python, even when that translation isn't immediately obvious!

This chapter is about explaining the translation. You won't be able to write C++ code after working your way through this appendix—that's at least a whole book's worth of content—but you should be much more capable of reading it.

Types

Nothing like an example to show how straightforward reading C++ can be for a Python programmer! Here's a simple function that calculates the sum of an array of numbers, first in Python:

```python
def calculateSum (numbers):

    sum = 0

    for number in numbers:
        sum += number

    return sum
```

And then in C++:

```cpp
int calculateSum(const vector<int> & numbers)
{
    int sum = 0;

    for (int number : numbers)
        sum += number;

    return sum;
}
```

It's the same code, right? There's some extra cruft in the C++ version, but the variables and the logic are the same.

As a Python programmer, you can pretty much ignore the curly braces and semicolons in this book's examples. In C++, the curly braces and semicolons define sections of code, like indentation does in Python. Here, though, I'm also indenting the C++ to show sections, because that makes it easier to read; the curly braces and semicolons aren't adding much value.[1]

The most confusing bit of C++ for an old-school Python programmer is the types—the int and const vector<int>& syntax. These type annotations tell the C++ compiler what kinds of values to expect for the annotated variables or arguments—in this case, an integer and a list of integers. The compiler needs to know the types before it can actually compile the code.

There are types in Python, too, of course, even if the language doesn't force you to worry about them. In Python the type details are usually sorted out when the code runs, not when it's compiled. You can always call isinstance() to find out what the actual type is for an expression.

There are advantages to knowing about the types earlier in C++, most importantly that it helps you find bugs earlier, but specifying types does mean writing a bit more code. Python lets you skip some steps that C++ requires, which makes it easier to just write a little bit of code in Python.

Here's how you can tell that both of these approaches are appealing: new versions of C++ let you skip the type annotations in lots of cases, and recent versions of Python let you add type annotations. Now you can write Python that looks more like C++:

---

1 That's why Guido ditched them.

```python
def calculateSum (numbers: Iterable[int]) -> int:

    sum:int = 0

    for number in numbers:
        sum += number

    return sum
```

And C++ that looks more like Python:

```cpp
auto calculateSum(const vector<int> & numbers)
{
    auto sum = 0;

    for (auto number : numbers)
        sum += number;

    return sum;
}
```

The examples in this book stick to "old-school" C++ and use explicit types. That's our policy at Sucker Punch—we think it makes the code easier to read—so I've continued the practice here.

Formatting and Comments

Sometimes the overall structure of the code is the same in C++ and Python, but the syntax you'll use to get there has more differences than in the first example. Here's a function that shows up in Rule 1—it merges two arrays into a single array by doing a riffle shuffle.[2] First, in Python:

```python
# Riffle shuffle two lists into a single list by randomly
#   choosing a number from one list or the other until both
#   lists are exhausted

def riffleShuffle (leftValues, rightValues):

    leftIndex = 0
    rightIndex = 0

    shuffledValues = []

    while leftIndex < len(leftValues) or \
            rightIndex < len(rightValues):
```

---

2 Like a deck of cards. Or poker chips, if you're trying to look like a professional poker player.

```python
        if rightIndex >= len(rightValues):
            nextValue = leftValues[leftIndex]
            leftIndex += 1
        elif leftIndex >= len(leftValues):
            nextValue = rightValues[rightIndex]
            rightIndex += 1
        elif random.randrange(0, 2) == 0:
            nextValue = leftValues[leftIndex]
            leftIndex += 1
        else:
            nextValue = rightValues[rightIndex]
            rightIndex += 1

        shuffledValues.append(nextValue)

    return shuffledValues
```

The algorithm is simple—choose a value from one list or the other until you've exhausted both lists, appending those values to a list of shuffled values. In C++ the same code looks like this:

```cpp
// Riffle shuffle two lists into a single list by randomly
//   choosing a number from one list or the other until both
//   lists are exhausted

vector<int> riffleShuffle(
    const vector<int> & leftValues,
    const vector<int> & rightValues)
{
    int leftIndex = 0;
    int rightIndex = 0;

    vector<int> shuffledValues;

    while (leftIndex < leftValues.size() ||
           rightIndex < rightValues.size())
    {
        int nextValue = 0;

        if (rightIndex >= rightValues.size())
        {
            nextValue = leftValues[leftIndex++];
        }
        else if (leftIndex >= leftValues.size())
        {
            nextValue = rightValues[rightIndex++];
        }
        else if (rand() % 2 == 0)
        {
```

```
        nextValue = leftValues[leftIndex++];
    }
    else
    {
        nextValue = rightValues[rightIndex++];
    }

    shuffledValues.push_back(nextValue);
    }

    return shuffledValues;
}
```

Again, the structure of the code is the same. The two languages have the same basic features, so it's easy to see how the various parts correspond to each other, but there are lots of small syntactic differences.

COMMENTS

First, comments—there are a few ways to comment C++ code, but the examples in this book use a double forward slash to mark comments:

```
// Riffle shuffle two lists into a single list by randomly
//   choosing a value from one list or the other until both
//   lists are exhausted
```

Compare to Python's hash comments:

```
# Riffle shuffle two lists into a single list by randomly
#   choosing a value from one list or the other until both
#   lists are exhausted
```

INDENTATION AND SPLIT LINES

Rules about splitting lines are different, too. In C++, all whitespace is considered equivalent. Spaces, tabs, and line breaks are interchangeable, so splitting the condition of the while loop across two lines requires no special syntax. You're just exchanging a space for a new line:

```
while (leftIndex < leftValues.size() ||
        rightIndex < rightValues.size())
```

Line breaks are important in Python, so the two-line condition requires an explicit line continuation with a backslash:

```
while leftIndex < len(leftValues) or \
        rightIndex < len(rightValues):
```

Indentation is more free-form in C++, too, and that can take getting used to for a Python programmer. The actual grouping is defined by curly braces or semicolons—there's no real meaning to the indentation. In this example, the two clauses are lined up in the same column, but that's just to make the code easier to read.

BOOLEAN OPERATIONS

Boolean operations are represented with symbols in C++. In this loop condition, C++ uses || where Python uses the much more straightforward or. In the same vein, C++ uses && for Python's and, and ! for Python's not.

Sometimes the two languages don't line up exactly. The C++ function rand returns a random integer; this example checks whether that random integer is even or odd to randomly choose a source vector. The % character here calculates a modulo value, in this case 0 if the random value is even and 1 if it's odd:

```
else if (rand() % 2 == 0)
```

In Python, the random module's randrange function is used to do the same thing:

```
elif random.randrange(0, 2) == 0:
```

LISTS

What Python calls "lists" are called "vectors" in C++. Python lists and C++ vectors work pretty much the same way, albeit with different names for everything. C++ uses the particularly lovely name push_back to append an item to the end of a vector:

```
shuffledValues.push_back(nextValue);
```

Python's append is much clearer:

```
shuffledValues.append(nextValue)
```

You also use a size method on a C++ vector to get its length, rather than calling a global len function like Python does.

INCREMENT OPERATORS

Finally—wow, there were a lot of little details packed into this example—C++ has a syntactic shortcut for incrementing or decrementing a variable. This expression retrieves the leftIndex'th value from leftValues, increments leftIndex, then puts the retrieved value into nextValue:

```
nextValue = leftValues[leftIndex++];
```

The same logic takes two lines in Python:

```
nextValue = leftValues[leftIndex]
leftIndex += 1
```

So, overall, lots of small differences, but everything in this C++ example has a pretty close analog in Python.

Classes

Both C++ and Python support classes, and the syntax for doing so isn't all that different. The ways the two languages actually *implement* classes are very different, but that's not important for the examples in this book. If you think of a C++ class as being like a Python class, where all of the instance attributes are set in __init__, you'll find the examples easy to follow.

Here's a Python class implementing a 3D vector concept:

```
class Vector:

    _vectorCount = 0

    def __init__(self):
        self.x = 0
        self.y = 0
        self.z = 0
        self._length = 0
        Vector._vectorCount = Vector._vectorCount + 1

    def __del__(self):
        Vector._vectorCount = Vector._vectorCount - 1

    def set(self, x, y, z):
        self.x = x
        self.y = y
        self.z = z
        self._calculateLength()

    def getLength(self):
        return self._length

    def getVectorCount():
        return Vector._vectorCount
```

```python
def _calculateLength(self):
    self._length = math.sqrt(self.x ** 2 + self.y ** 2 + self.z ** 2)
```

Any 3D vector class is going to track three coordinates: x, y, and z. This particular class also caches the length of the vector and counts the number of vectors that currently exist. There's no justification for the latter two features, by the way, other than illustrating a couple of syntactic differences between Python and C++.

Here's the C++ equivalent:

```cpp
class Vector
{
public:

    Vector() :
        m_x(0.0f),
        m_y(0.0f),
        m_z(0.0f),
        m_length(0.0f)
        { ++s_vectorCount; }
    ~Vector()
        { --s_vectorCount; }

    void set(float x, float y, float z);

    float getLength() const
    {
        return m_length;
    }

    static int getVectorCount()
    {
        return s_vectorCount;
    }

protected:

    void calculateLength();

    float m_x;
    float m_y;
    float m_z;
    float m_length;

    static int s_vectorCount;
};

void Vector::set(float x, float y, float z)
```

```
{
    m_x = x;
    m_y = y;
    m_z = z;
    calculateLength();
}

void Vector::calculateLength()
{
    m_length = sqrtf(m_x * m_x + m_y * m_y + m_z * m_z);
}
```

I've inadvertently demonstrated one of the benefits of Python here—Python is typically more concise than C++, with the Python version of this example clocking in at about half as many lines as the C++ version.

These two versions of the class have the same pieces, but those pieces are rearranged. Sometimes the rearrangement is obvious. In Python, the __init__ method is called when an object is created, and __del__ is called when the object is destroyed:

```
class Vector:

    def __init__(self):
        self.x = 0
        self.y = 0
        self.z = 0
        self._length = 0
        Vector._vectorCount = Vector._vectorCount + 1

    def __del__(self):
        Vector._vectorCount = Vector._vectorCount - 1
```

In C++, the class name itself is used for those two methods, with a pre-pended tilde (~) to mark the latter method. These two methods are called the *constructor* and *destructor* in C++ land. There's also special syntax to initialize the instance variables:

```
class Vector
{
public:

    Vector() :
        m_x(0.0f),
        m_y(0.0f),
        m_z(0.0f),
        m_length(0.0f)
        { ++s_vectorCount; }
```

```
~Vector()
    { --s_vectorCount; }
};
```

Slightly different syntax is used for accessing the class's variables. In Python, you need to be explicit about this with the self keyword:

```
class Vector:

    def getLength(self):
        return self._length
```

In C++, this is optional. You're allowed to use this, C++'s equivalent to self, but the class's variables are already in scope. The compiler can implicitly look up member variables for you:

```
class Vector
{
    float getLength() const
    {
        return m_length;
    }
};
```

If you see something in C++ that looks like a reference to a variable that hasn't been defined yet, it's probably a class variable.

Visibility

Python and C++ have different ways to manage the bits of internal logic that users of the class shouldn't touch. In Python, there's a convention to follow: start the name with an underscore. The Python example uses this for a class variable:

```
class Vector:

    _vectorCount = 0
```

There's also a method:

```
class Vector:

    def _calculateLength(self):
        self.length = math.sqrt(self.x ** 2 + self.y ** 2 + self.z ** 2)
```

C++ solves the same problem with syntax, not conventions. The public keyword at the top of the Vector class marks what follows as being visible and usable to anyone with an instance of the object. The `protected` keyword, a bit further down, hides what follows from any code outside the class. As a result, users of the class can call the `set` method, but can't call `calculateLength`. The `calculateLength` method can only be called from inside other `Vector` methods.

```
Class Vector
{
public:

    void set(float x, float y, float z);

protected:

    void calculateLength();
};
```

Declarations and Definitions

Next, let's look at splitting a function's declaration from its definition. In Python, all of a class's methods are defined in the class itself:

```
class Vector:

    def set(self, x, y, z):
        self.x = x
        self.y = y
        self.z = z
        self._calculateLength()

    def getLength(self):
        return self.length
```

Many of the examples in this book will do the same thing in C++:

```
class Vector
{
public:

    float getLength() const
    {
        return m_length;
    }
};
```

In other cases, though, the examples will split the declaration of the method. First the code establishes that a method with a given name and type signature exists:

```cpp
class Vector
{
public:

    void set(float x, float y, float z);
};
```

The function is then defined separately:

```cpp
void Vector::set(float x, float y, float z)
{
    m_x = x;
    m_y = y;
    m_z = z;
    calculateLength();
}
```

These two forms are typically compiled differently in C++, with methods defined inside the class compiled *inline*, meaning that a separate copy of the function is generated and inserted wherever it's called, while a single copy exists for functions with a separate definition. That's not important for the examples in this book, though, so don't worry about the distinction.

The last thing to point out in this example is how C++ deals with class attributes. In Python, class attributes are defined with statements in the class, and instance attributes are added in an __init__ method:

```python
class Vector:

    _vectorCount = 0

    def __init__(self):
        self.x = 0
        self.y = 0
        self.z = 0
        self._length = 0
```

In C++, both class and instance attributes (or "members," in C++-speak) are added in the class definition. The static keyword marks any class attributes; everything that isn't marked with static is an instance attribute:

```cpp
class Vector
{
protected:

    float m_x;
    float m_y;
```

```
    float m_z;
    float m_length;

    static int s_vectorCount;
};
```

Function Overloading

There are some features in C++ that don't have direct analogs in Python. The converse is true, as well, of course—there are lots of Python features that C++ doesn't have—but that's unimportant here, since we're focused on *reading* C++ code.

One thing that can be confusing to Python programmers is seeing two functions with the same name. Here's an example in C++:

```
int min(int a, int b)
{
    return (a <= b) ? a : b;
}

int min(int a, int b, int c)
{
    return min(a, min(b, c));
}

void example()
{
    printf("%d %d\n", min(5, 8), min(13, 21, 34));
}
```

It's not clear how this works—if you try to call the min function, which version is called? The C++ compiler makes this decision based on the arguments. If two integers are passed, it calls the first one; if three integers, it calls the second one. The example function prints 5 and 13.

I snuck a useful bit of C++ syntax into the functions—the question mark operator, which lets you choose between two values based on an expression:

```
return (a <= b) ? a : b;
```

The Python equivalent to this is similarly funky:

```
return a if a <= b else b
```

For what it's worth, this Python syntax confuses me every time I see it. So if you want to make a C++ programmer feel just a little bit clueless, make sure you add lots of ternary expressions to your code.

Templates

Another concept from C++ that has no Python analog is *templates*. To simplify things a bit: C++ templates are a way to write one chunk of code that handles multiple types. The compiler generates new code for each set of types used with the template.

The first example in this appendix summed an array of integer values. If you wanted to sum an array of floating-point values, you might write new code:

```
float calculateSum(const vector<float> & numbers)
{
    float sum = 0;

    for (float number : numbers)
        sum += number;

    return sum;
}
```

Or you might write a single version of `calculateSum` using templates and let the compiler do the work for you:

```
template <class T>
T calculateSum(const vector<T> & numbers)
{
    T sum = T(0);

    for (T number : numbers)
        sum += number;

    return sum;
}
```

The templated version of `calculateSum` will work for any type that implements the += operator and supports 0 as a value. That's true for integers and floating-point values, but could also easily be arranged for other types. You could implement += and 0 for the `Vector` class from a few sections ago, for instance, and gain the ability to sum an array of `Vectors`.

In Python, there's no need for any of this. The Python code I wrote to sum a list of values works perfectly well for any type that supports addition and initialization to 0:

```python
def calculateSum (numbers):

    sum = 0

    for number in numbers:
        sum = sum + number

    return sum
```

When you see the C++ template syntax in the examples, it usually marks some bit of code that would work fine in Python without any templating at all.

Pointers and References

There's one final thing that Python mostly hides from view but that C++ makes programmers worry about, and that's passing arguments *by value* versus passing them *by reference*. In Python, simple types like numbers or strings are *passed by value*—a new copy is made whenever they're assigned to a variable or passed as an argument to a function. It's more complicated for types like lists or objects. Here's an example:

```python
def makeChanges (number, numbers):

    number = 3
    numbers.append(21)
    print(number, numbers)

globalNumber = 0
globalNumbers = [3, 5, 8, 13]

print(globalNumber, globalNumbers)
makeChanges(globalNumber, globalNumbers)
print(globalNumber, globalNumbers)
```

When this code is run it prints out:

```
0 [3, 5, 8, 13]
3 [3, 5, 8, 13, 21]
0 [3, 5, 8, 13, 21]
```

Notice how the simple value changes inside makeChanges to 3, then changes back to 0 when makeChanges returns, but the list changes without changing back.

That's because o was passed by value. A new copy was made when makeChanges was called. When makeChanges sets number to 3, it's only changing the copy.

Python didn't make a copy of the globalNumbers list—it just passed the original list. Both numbers and globalNumbers are holding onto the same list. When 21 is appended, it's appended to that list. When you print numbers before returning or globalNumbers after, 21 shows up, because you're printing the same list in both cases.

C++, by contrast, makes all of this more explicit. All variables and arguments are *explicitly* passed by value or passed by reference. The C++ equivalent to the preceding Python code looks like this:

```
void makeChanges(int number, vector<int> & numbers)
{
    number = 3;
    numbers.push_back(21);
    cout << number << " " << numbers << "\n";
}
```

The ampersand in front of numbers is important—it tells the compiler that this argument is passed by reference, not by value, so the compiler won't make a copy of it when makeChanges is called. There's no ampersand for number, so the compiler *does* make a copy of number.

If the ampersands are flipped, then the compiler makes a copy of numbers but not of number:

```
void makeChanges(int & number, vector<int> numbers)
{
    number = 3;
    numbers.push_back(21);
    cout << number << " " << numbers << "\n";
}
```

This version produces different output. Now it's the simple value that is permanently changed, while the list pops back to its original value:

```
0 [3 5 8 13]
3 [3 5 8 13 21]
3 [3 5 8 13]
```

The examples in this book will often use references to avoid making expensive copies of bulky values. In most cases, the references will be marked with the const keyword to mark something that shouldn't be altered, despite being passed by reference. That showed up (and was never explained) in the first C++ example in this appendix:

```
int calculateSum(const vector<int> & numbers)
```

With this usage, no copy is made of numbers, but the compiler won't allow any changes to numbers either. In practice this is really similar to passing it by value, but at much lower cost.

As a final note, in a few cases the examples use the *other* (sigh) C++ syntax for passing things by reference—*pointers*. Pointers and references are almost exactly the same thing, and the differences aren't really important if you're just trying to figure out what the code is doing. The key syntactic differences are:

- Pointers are defined with * instead of &.

- Pointers use -> instead of . to get at members.

- To convert a pointer to a reference, you use *; to convert a reference to a pointer, you use &.

Here's the example code written with pointers:

```
void example(int number, vector<int> * numbers)
{
    number = 3;
    numbers->push_back(21);
    cout << number << " " << *numbers << "\n";
}

void callExample()
{
    int number = 0;
    vector<int> numbers = { 3, 5, 8, 13 };
    cout << number << " " << numbers << "\n";
    example(3, &numbers);
    cout << number << " " << numbers << "\n";
}
```

This book's examples use constant references whenever an argument is conceptually being passed by value, but actually passing the argument by value would be expensive. In all other cases, pointers are used.

Reading C++ for JavaScript Programmers

The examples in this book are all presented in C++. That's the language I do most of my programming in, and it's the language I'm most proficient in.

If you're a JavaScript programmer, don't despair—the Rules are still useful! You don't need to learn how to program in C++ in order to read the examples in this book. Code is code, basically—a loop is a loop, variables are variables, and functions are functions. There are some cosmetic differences, but the basic ideas in this book's C++ examples translate pretty directly to JavaScript, even when that translation isn't immediately obvious!

This appendix explains how to do that translation—how to read C++ and convert it in your head to the JavaScript equivalent. You won't be able to write C++ code after working your way through this appendix—that would take a whole book—but you should be much more capable of reading it.

Types

Time for an example! Here's a simple function that calculates the sum of an array of numbers, first in JavaScript:[1]

```
function calculateSum(numbers) {

    let sum = 0;
```

---

[1] I had to choose a JavaScript version for these examples. For better or worse, I chose ES6. If you're stuck on a version earlier than that, my apologies.

```
    for (let number of numbers)
        sum += value

    return sum;
}
```

And then in C++:

```
int calculateSum(const vector<int> & numbers)
{
    int sum = 0;

    for (int number : numbers)
        sum += number;

    return sum;
}
```

Um...it's the same code. Maybe we don't need an appendix after all.

Or maybe we do. JavaScript syntax was heavily influenced by C syntax, and I won't have to explain what curly braces and semicolons mean like I did in the Python appendix, but there are plenty of quirky differences.

First, everything in C++ is scoped. Imagine a let or const before every variable defined in the examples, because that's implicitly true for all variables in C++.

If you haven't dabbled in TypeScript yet—if you've stuck to straight Java-Script so far in your programming career—then the explicit types in the example might be confusing. The int and const vector<int>& type annotations tell the C++ compiler what kinds of values to expect—in this case, an integer and a list of integers. The compiler needs to know the types before it can actually compile the code.

There are types in JavaScript, too, of course, even if the language doesn't force you to worry about them. If you do care about the type of an expression, you can call typeof(), but typically you don't care. In JavaScript the type details are usually sorted out when the code runs, not when it's compiled. Not always, though—your web browser tries pretty hard to infer types for everything, because if it can then the JavaScript can be compiled to a more efficient form and run a lot faster.

C++ skips right to the "run a lot faster" part, even if that adds some extra steps to writing code. Knowing about types also lets the compiler detect a whole class of bugs earlier, which is a huge advantage.

Here's how you can tell that both of these approaches are appealing: new versions of C++ let you skip the type annotations in lots of cases, and the increasingly popular TypeScript extension of JavaScript lets you type annotations. Now you can write JavaScript/TypeScript that looks more like C++:

```
function calculateSum(numbers: int[]): int {

    let sum: int = 0;

    for (let number of numbers)
        sum += number;

    return sum;
}
```

And C++ that looks more like JavaScript:

```
auto calculateSum(const vector<int> & numbers)
{
    auto sum = 0;

    for (auto number : numbers)
        sum += number;

    return sum;
}
```

The examples in this book stick to "old-school" C++ and use explicit types. That's our policy at Sucker Punch—we think it makes the code easier to read—so I've continued the practice here.

Arrays

Despite the surface similarity between C++ and JavaScript, there's an endless list of quirky differences. Here's a simple example that reverses the values in an array, first in JavaScript:

```
function reverseList(values) {

    let reversedValues = []

    for (let index = values.length; --index >= 0; ) {
        reversedValues.push(values[index]);
    }

    return reversedValues;
}
```

And then in C++:

```
vector<int> reverseList(const vector<int> values)
{
    vector<int> reversedValues;

    for (int index = values.size(); --index >= 0; )
        reversedValues.push_back(values[index]);

    return reversedValues;
}
```

Again, the code looks very similar. The closest analog to a JavaScript array in C++ is the `vector` type. The concepts are the same, but the details are different. In JavaScript, the `length` property tells you how many elements are in the array. C++ doesn't have properties, just data members and methods; you get the count of elements in the vector by calling a `size()` method.

Similarly, both JavaScript arrays and C++ vectors allow new elements to be appended. In C++, it's the `push_back()` method, whereas in JavaScript it's `push()`. That's a pretty easy translation.

It's worth noting that there are big differences lurking beneath the shared syntax. For instance, the JavaScript array `values` could be a list array of *anything* —maybe even a jumble of entirely different types, like [1, "hello", true]. The C++ vector is always a list of integers, no more and no less.

But that won't be a problem when you read the C++ examples. JavaScript allows more type flexibility than the C++ examples use, but JavaScript is completely happy to deal with simply typed lists.

Classes

Both C++ and JavaScript support classes, and the syntax for doing so isn't all that different. The ways the two languages actually *implement* classes are very different, but that's not important for the examples in this book. If you think of a C++ class as being like a JavaScript class where all the fields are defined with public or private field declarations, you'll find the examples easy to follow.

Here's a JavaScript class implementing a 3D vector concept:

```
class Vector {

    constructor () {
        ++Vector.#vectorCount;
    }
```

```
    set (x, y, z) {
        this.#x = x;
        this.#y = y;
        this.#z = z;
        this.#calculateLength();
    }

    getLength () {
        return this.#length;
    }

    static getVectorCount() {
        return Vector.#vectorCount;
    }

    #calculateLength () {
        this.#length = Math.sqrt(
                            this.#x ** 2 +
                            this.#y ** 2 +
                            this.#z ** 2);
    }

    #x = 0
    #y = 0
    #z = 0
    #length = 0

    static #vectorCount = 0
};
```

And here is an equivalent C++ class:

```
class Vector
{
public:

    Vector() :
        m_x(0.0f),
        m_y(0.0f),
        m_z(0.0f),
        m_length(0.0f)
        { ++s_vectorCount; }
    ~Vector()
        { --s_vectorCount; }

    void set(float x, float y, float z);

    float getLength() const
    {
        return m_length;
```

```
    }

    static int getVectorCount()
    {
        return s_vectorCount;
    }

protected:

    void calculateLength();

    float m_x;
    float m_y;
    float m_z;
    float m_length;

    static int s_vectorCount;
};

void Vector::set(float x, float y, float z)
{
    m_x = x;
    m_y = y;
    m_z = z;
    calculateLength();
}

void Vector::calculateLength()
{
    m_length = sqrtf(m_x * m_x + m_y * m_y + m_z * m_z);
}
```

The two versions of the Vector class have the same pieces, but those pieces are rearranged. The translations are straightforward, for the most part. In Java-Script you need to be explicit with your access to fields with the this keyword, or the class name for class fields:

```
class Vector {

    getLength () {
        return this.#length;
    }

    static getVectorCount() {
        return Vector.#vectorCount;
    }

    #length = 0
```

```
    static #vectorCount = 0
};
```

C++ allows explicit specification in these cases—you're allowed to specify this-> and Vector:: to disambiguate normal and static member references, respectively—but it also allows implicit use of members, and that's what the examples all use:

```
class Vector
{
public:

    float getLength() const
    {
        return m_length;
    }

    static int getVectorCount()
    {
        return s_vectorCount;
    }

protected:

    float m_length;

    static int s_vectorCount;
};
```

These two examples also show how member visibility is handled in both languages. Private fields have names with a hashtag (#) prefix in JavaScript. In C++ the private keyword is used for this—it marks the start of a section where all methods and members being declared are considered private. All of the examples in this book use the similar keyword protected.

Moving on to constructors! In JavaScript, a special constructor function is called when a new Vector is created:

```
class Vector {

    constructor () {
        ++Vector.#vectorCount;
    }
};
```

In C++, the class name itself is used for this method. It is nevertheless (and somewhat confusingly) called the *constructor*:

```
class Vector
{
public:

    Vector() :
        m_x(0.0f),
        m_y(0.0f),
        m_z(0.0f),
        m_length(0.0f)
        { ++s_vectorCount; }
};
```

C++ classes also have an important concept that doesn't really exist in Java-Script—the *destructor*. An object's constructor is called when an object is created, and the destructor when it is destroyed. The destructor also uses the class name, this time with a tilde (~) prepended:

```
class Vector
{
public:

    ~Vector()
        { --s_vectorCount; }
};
```

There's no real equivalent to this in JavaScript—the closest you can come to this is registering a callback with a FinalizationRegistry object, which is a recent and (arguably) underbaked addition to JavaScript. This mechanism doesn't have quite the same behavior as a C++ destructor. In C++, the destructor is called immediately when an object goes out of scope. Here's an example where a Vector is created as a local variable inside a function:

```
void functionA()
{
    printf("%d, \n", Vector::getVectorCount());
    Vector a;
    printf("%d, \n", Vector::getVectorCount());
};

Vector b;
functionA();
printf("%d\n", Vector::getVectorCount());
```

This code prints "1, 2, 1" when run—the destructor for a is called when functionA returns, so s_vectorCount is decremented immediately. In JavaScript, any finalization callback is triggered by garbage collection, and the timing of garbage collection is implementation-specific. There isn't a reliable way to get the same timing in JavaScript, as in the preceding C++ example.

That's too bad. The lack of a destructor rules out some useful tricks—Sucker Punch code often uses object lifetimes as a robust way to manage things, and you'll see some of this in the C++ examples. Just remember that the destructor gets called immediately and you'll be able to follow along.

Declarations and Definitions

Next, let's look at splitting a function's declaration from its definition. In JavaScript, all of a class's methods are defined in the class itself:

```
class Vector {

    set (x, y, z) {
        this.#x = x;
        this.#y = y;
        this.#z = z;
        this.#calculateLength();
    }

    getLength () {
        return this.#length;
    }
```

Many of the examples in this book will do the same thing in C++:

```
class Vector
{
public:

    float getLength() const
    {
        return m_length;
    }
};
```

In other cases, though, the examples will split the declaration of the method. First the code establishes that a method with a given name and type signature exists:

```
class Vector
{
public:

    void set(float x, float y, float z);
};
```

The function is then defined separately:

```
void Vector::set(float x, float y, float z)
{
    m_x = x;
    m_y = y;
    m_z = z;
    calculateLength();
}
```

These two forms are typically compiled differently in C++, with methods defined inside the class compiled *inline*, meaning that a separate copy of the function is generated and inserted wherever it's called, while a single copy exists for functions with a separate definition. That's not important for the examples in this book, though, so don't worry about the distinction.

Function Overloading

There are other features in C++ that don't have direct analogs in JavaScript. The converse is true, as well, of course—there are lots of JavaScript features that C++ doesn't have—but that's unimportant here, since we're focused on *reading* C++ code.

One thing that can be confusing to JavaScript programmers is seeing two functions with the same name. Here's an example in C++:

```
int min(int a, int b)
{
    return (a <= b) ? a : b;
}

int min(int a, int b, int c)
{
    return min(a, min(b, c));
}

void example()
{
    printf("%d %d\n", min(5, 8), min(13, 21, 34));
}
```

It's not clear how this works—if you try to call the min function, which version is called? The C++ compiler makes this decision based on the arguments. If two integers are passed, it calls the first one; if three integers, it calls the second one. The example function prints 5 and 13.

In JavaScript, you'd instead write a single min function that supports an arbitrary number of arguments. Something like this:

```
function min () {

    if (arguments.length == 0)
        return Infinity;

    let result = arguments[0];
    for (let index = 1; index < arguments.length; ++index) {
        result = Math.min(result, arguments[index])
    }

    return result;
}
```

This is exactly what Math.min does, of course, so no need to write this function yourself!

Templates

Another concept from C++ that has no Python analog is *templates*. To simplify things a bit: C++ templates are a way to write one chunk of code that handles multiple types. The compiler generates new code for each set of types used with the template.

The first example in this appendix summed an array of integer values. If you wanted to sum an array of floating-point values, you might write new code:

```
float calculateSum(const vector<float> & numbers)
{
    float sum = 0;

    for (float number : numbers)
        sum += number;

    return sum;
}
```

Or you might write a single version of calculateSum using templates and let the compiler do the work for you:

```
template <class T>
T calculateSum(const vector<T> & numbers)
{
    T sum = T(0);
```

```
    for (T number : numbers)
        sum += number;

    return sum;
}
```

The templated version of `calculateSum` will work for any type that implements the += operator and supports o as a value. That's true for integers and floating-point values, but could also easily be arranged for other types. You could implement += and o for the `Vector` class from the last section, for instance, and gain the ability to sum an array of `Vector`s.

In JavaScript, there's no need for any of this. The JavaScript code I wrote to sum a list of values works perfectly well for any type that supports addition and initialization to o:

```
function calculateSum(number) {

    let sum = 0;

    for (let number of numbers)
        sum += number

    return sum;
}
```

When you see the C++ template syntax in the examples, it usually marks some bit of code that would work fine in JavaScript without any templating at all.

Pointers and References

There's one final thing that JavaScript mostly hides from view but that C++ makes programmers worry about, and that's passing arguments *by value* versus passing them *by reference*. In JavaScript, simple types like numbers or strings are passed by value—a new copy is made whenever they're assigned to a variable or passed as an argument to a function. It's more complicated for types like lists or objects. Here's an example:

```
function makeChanges (number, numbers) {
    number = 3;
    numbers.push(21);
    console.log(number, numbers);
}

let number = 0;
let numbers = [3, 5, 8, 13];
```

```
console.log(number, numbers);
makeChanges(number, numbers);
console.log(number, numbers);
```

When this code is run it prints out:

```
0 (4) [3, 5, 8, 13]
3 (5) [3, 5, 8, 13, 21]
0 (5) [3, 5, 8, 13, 21]
```

Notice how the simple value changes inside makeChanges to 3, then changes back to 0 when makeChanges returns, but the list changes without changing back. That's because 0 was passed by value. A new copy was made when makeChanges was called. When makeChanges sets number to 3, it's only changing the copy.

JavaScript didn't make a copy of the globalNumbers list—it just passed the original list. Both numbers and globalNumbers are holding onto the same list. When 21 is appended, it's appended to that list. When numbers is logged before returning or globalNumbers after, 21 shows up, because you're printing the same list in both cases.

C++, by contrast, makes all of this more explicit. All variables and arguments are *explicitly* passed by value or passed by reference. The C++ equivalent to the preceding JavaScript code looks like this:

```
void makeChanges(int number, vector<int> & numbers)
{
    number = 3;
    numbers.push_back(21);
    cout << number << " " << numbers << "\n";
}
```

The ampersand in front of numbers is important—it tells the compiler that this argument is passed by reference, not by value, so the compiler won't make a copy of it when makeChanges is called. There's no ampersand for number, so the compiler *does* make a copy of number.

If the ampersands are flipped, then the compiler makes a copy of numbers but not of number:

```
void makeChanges(int & number, vector<int> numbers)
{
    number = 3;
    numbers.push_back(21);
```

```
        cout << number << " " << numbers << "\n";
}
```

This version produces different output. Now it's the simple value that is permanently changed, while the list pops back to its original value:

```
0 [3 5 8 13]
3 [3 5 8 13 21]
3 [3 5 8 13]
```

The examples in this book will often use references to avoid making expensive copies of bulky values. In most cases, the references will be marked with the const keyword to mark something that shouldn't be altered, despite being passed by reference. That showed up (and was never explained) in the first C++ example in this appendix:

```
int calculateSum(const vector<int> & numbers);
```

With this usage, no copy is made of numbers, but the compiler won't allow any changes to numbers either. In practice this is really similar to passing it by value, but at much lower cost.

As a final note, in a few cases the examples use the *other* (sigh) C++ syntax for passing things by reference—*pointers*. Pointers and references are almost exactly the same thing, and the differences aren't really important if you're just trying to figure out what the code is doing. The key syntactic differences are:

- Pointers are defined with * instead of &.

- Pointers use -> instead of . to get at members.

- To convert a pointer to a reference, you use *; to convert a reference to a pointer, you use &.

Here's the example code written with pointers:

```
void example(int number, vector<int> * numbers)
{
    number = 3;
    numbers->push_back(21);
    cout << number << " " << *numbers << "\n";
}

void callExample()
{
    int number = 0;
```

```
    vector<int> numbers = { 3, 5, 8, 13 };
    cout << number << " " << numbers << "\n";
    example(3, &numbers);
    cout << number << " " << numbers << "\n";
}
```

This book's examples use constant references whenever an argument is conceptually being passed by value, but actually passing the argument by value would be expensive. In all other cases, pointers are used.

Index

About the Author

Chris Zimmerman cofounded the video game studio Sucker Punch Productions in 1997 and led the coding team through 20-plus years of successful video games, including three *Sly Cooper* games and five *inFamous* games, culminating in 2020's Game of the Year candidate *Ghost of Tsushima*. He split his time between designing and writing code, like the melee combat in *Ghost*, and the day-to-day work of building and managing a 20-something-person coding team. Prior to Sucker Punch, Chris spent roughly a decade at Microsoft, but the things he worked on there were much less interesting. He graduated from Princeton in 1988, and as a result owns more orange clothing than you do.

Colophon

The cover design and original cover art are by Susan Thompson. The cover fonts are Guardian Sans and Gilroy Semibold. The text fonts are Scala Pro, Benton Sans, and Minion Pro; the heading font is Benton Sans; and the code font is Ubuntu Mono.

CPSIA information can be obtained
at www.ICGtesting.com
Printed in the USA
JSHW041634271222
35427JS00001B/1

9 781098 133115